Dictionaries of Civilization

Greece

Stefania Ratto

Translated by Rosanna M. Giammanco Frongia

University of California Press
Berkeley   Los Angeles   London

Dictionaries of Civilization
Series edited by Ada Gabucci

University of California Press, one of the most distinguished university presses in the United States, enriches lives around the world by advancing scholarship in the humanities, social sciences, and natural sciences. Its activities are supported by the UC Press Foundation and by philanthropic contributions from individuals and institutions. For more information, visit www.ucpress.edu.

University of California Press
Berkeley and Los Angeles, California

University of California Press, Ltd.
London, England

© 2006 by Mondadori Electa S.p.A., Milan
English translation © 2008 Mondadori Electa S.p.A.

Cataloging-in-Publication Data for this title is on file with the Library of Congress.

ISBN-13: 978-0-520-25647-7 (pbk.: alk. paper)

Manufactured in Spain

16   15   14   13   12   11   10   09   08
10   9   8   7   6   5   4   3   2   1

Art direction
Dario Tagliabue

Graphic design
Anna Piccarreta

Layouts
Elena Brandolini

Editorial direction
Virginia Ponciroli

Editing
Carla Ferrucci

Picture research
Elena Demartini
Chiara Franchini
Matteo Penati

Technical coordination
Andrea Panozzo

Quality control
Giancarlo Berti

English-language translation
Rosanna M. Giammanco Frongia

English-language typesetting
Michael Shaw

Cover
Riace Bronzes, Bronze A, ca. 455 BC. Reggio Calabria, Museo Nazionale.
Page 2
Erechtheum caryatids, 420–406 BC, Athens.

Contents

Introduction

This attractive book opens the door on a vast world and a society that bequeathed us an enormous heritage in literature, monuments, and art, so much of which is already known, and so much still unexplored. Because the material is so vast, we had to draw chronological and geographical boundaries. The need to define contours as homogeneous as possible for the social and cultural phenomena analyzed, led us to focus our narrative around the polis, understood as the most typical, original form of political state organization bequeathed us by the ancient Greek world.

For this reason, the time period covered in this book begins in the eighth century BC (after the Mycenaean civilization and the dark centuries known as the "Hellenic Middle Ages") when the Greek polis began its ascent, and covers about five centuries, up to the transition to Hellenism, symbolically represented by the rise to the throne of Alexander the Great. In fact, while it is true that Alexander's reign did not bring about an extinction of the urban model of the polis (which, in fact, was exported far beyond the shores of the Aegean Sea), it did mark the end of an urban-centered civilization based on politically independent city-states and ushered in such momentous ideological and cultural changes as to constitute an epochal turning point, in fact, the start of a new civilization.

Still, chronological boundaries should be flexible, and in fact we often expanded them to follow the evolution of certain cultural phenomena or architectural types. As to geographic boundaries, our somewhat "artificial" decision to confine this work to Greece "proper" leaving out the Greek colonies, Magna Grecia in particular, was dictated by the existence there of artistic and cultural specificities that properly ought to be the subject matter of separate studies.

Within the time span and the geographic space we set, then, the narrative unfolds in chapters centered around a few key themes that are particularly suited to the illustrative approach used in this series. We gave priority to material sources, iconographic ones in particular. True to the archeological research method, we tried to highlight their relationship to historical sources, so as to provide a well-rounded body of information.

Among the iconographic sources, we paid special attention to vase art, which is unique to the Greek experience and an exceptional source of information. Indeed, the high artistic level of these vases notwithstanding (they afford us a glimpse into the great paintings that have been lost), in them an artisanal quality has survived that explored themes from daily life, something that is usually left out of official art, yielding important, first-hand testimony on how the lower classes saw themselves, including pottery shop workers and some of their customers.

In choosing this approach, dictated as it was by needs of simplicity and synthesis, we ran the risk of generalization. Although we tried to suggest, at least broadly, the complexity of the topics covered and their evolution over time, the treatment may at times seem circumscribed, narrowed to the better documented periods and areas. To give an example, the chapters on political institutions and urban planning are conditioned by the prevalence of data from the Classical Athenian age, a period we know well because we rounded out the data gathered from the excavation of hugely important complexes with vast amounts of knowledge contained in historical and literary sources. Nevertheless, current archaeological research tends to look critically at

the "Athenian democratic paradigm" by showing more clearly how the Greek cities were inspired by a plurality of models and concepts about the organization of urban space and the structure of society, of institutions, of the economy, and of religious and funeral rituals.

Because we had to be selective, we focused on urban reality narrowly understood, and expanded our coverage to the organization of the territory only for large monumental complexes such as sanctuaries. As a result, except for some incidental information, we did not cover what many consider today a primary area of archaeological research, the relationship between the city and its surroundings dotted with villages, factories, mines, and workshops that were the seat of primary production activities that left archaeological traces perhaps less relevant, but still important for reconstructing the life of the lower classes.

We also included a basic chronology of events joining together the many historical tiles constituted by each entry; a glossary of technical terms used in architecture and in the study of vase art; and a brief bibliography for further reading on specific topics.

Historical Figures

Daedalus
Lycurgus
Solon
Exekias
Euphronius
Cleisthenes
Themistocles
Hageladas of Argos and Alcamenes
Pericles
Phidias
Polyclitus
Socrates
Alcibiades
Plato
Aeschines and Demosthenes
Aristotle
Praxiteles
Scopas

◀Double herm with Herodotus and
Thucydides, Roman copy of a Greek
original from 380–360 BC. Naples,
Museo Archeologico Nazionale.

"In fashioning the statues he surpassed all other men by such distance, that later generations would say that his statues were like living beings" (Diodorus Siculus)

Daedalus

Artist

Chronology
8th century BC?

Principal events
Athenian period:
Out of jealousy he kills his apprentice nephew Talos who had invented the saw by taking inspiration from shark's teeth; sentenced by the Areopagus, he is banished into exile.
Cretan period:
He becomes architect to King Minos, but because he helped Ariadne save Theseus, he is thrown into the labyrinth with his son Icarus, from where he escapes by fashioning wings with feathers and wax.
Sicilian period:
Having found shelter with King Cocalus, he built many buildings for him.

▶ *Lady of Auxerre*, 650–625 BC. Paris, Musée du Louvre.

The name of Daedalus, the earliest artistic figure known to the Greeks, is a cognate of the adjective *daidaleos* ("cunningly wrought") that was already used in Homeric poems to denote complex, intricate work. Indeed, Daedalus is a complex figure, a symbol of infinite technical skill that is more akin to magic than to art. Tradition attributed all sorts of inventions to him, from the axe to fish glue. He spent the most significant period of his active years on the island of Crete, where he was said to have created a *choros* (choir or dance) for Cnossus, the wooden cow that made it possible for Pasiphaë to couple with the bull that she had come to covet, and the labyrinth that confined the Minotaur—the monster child born from that union. Daedalus was also said to be the founder of a new type of statuary that rendered the human body naturalistically, and his Cretan pupils Dipoinos and Skyllis are credited with introducing the use of stone in sculpture and its diffusion in the Peloponnesus and the islands.

Today, archaeological sources support some of the suggestions found in ancient literature, for the earliest examples of large-scale statues are indeed from Crete: there, in the seventh century BC, a uniform style derived from the East had developed, characterized by a frontal figure, stiff limbs and a geometrically-shaped head, a style that has been called "Daedalic."

Typical features of Daedalic art include the rigid vertical posture with the arms aligned with the body, derived from earlier wood statues, and the triangular face with a low forehead, framed by a heavy, Egyptian-style hairdo.

This statue which stood in the temple to Artemis in Delos, is made of white marble typical of Naxos. 175 cm high, it is the earliest Greek sculpture of a human figure that has survived.

Under her right hand, which was perforated for holding a metal object, is a bustrophedic (written from right to left and vice versa) inscription informing the viewer that the statue was dedicated to the goddess by Nikandre, a maiden, on the occasion of her marriage to Phraxos.

▶ *Nikandre of Naxos, from Delos, ca. 650 BC. Athens, National Archaeological Museum.*

"Instead of imitating other cities, he conceived ideas that were even the opposite of most of them: thus his city became unusually fortunate" (Xenophon)

Lycurgus

Political leader

Chronology
9th–8th century BC

Principal events
Ca. 900 BC: Sparta is born from the union of five villages.
825–800 BC: Promulgation of the *rhetra*, the laws of Sparta, traditionally attributed to Lycurgus.
754–753 BC: Beginning of the List of Ephors, the highest Spartan magistrates.

Related entries
Political institutions, School and education, Music and dance, Sports, Sparta

▶ Bust known as "Lycurgus," Roman copy of a probably Greek original. Naples, Museo Archeologico Nazionale.

Greek tradition attributes to the legendary figure of the lawgiver Lycurgus the foundation of Sparta: legend has it that he was inspired by no less than the oracle of Delphi. In reality, the city developed gradually out of the need of the few Spartan citizens to control a large number of subjected peoples. Sparta's political system rested on monarchical power, embodied by two kings who sat on the throne by divine right and were commanders-in-chief. Their power was checked and mitigated by the *gerousia*, a council of elders elected by the *apella*, the assembly of all citizens that also had the power to vote on the resolutions submitted by the council.

The citizens who enjoyed full rights, the Spartiates, were a small minority, however, the mass of Spartans being Perioeci, freemen who inhabited the subjected cities of Laconia and Messenia and who were required to serve in the army but could not participate in the assemblies. On the lowest rung of the social ladder were the Helots, of non-Dorian stock, effectively state-owned slaves bound to the land; their labor allowed the Spartiates to devote their time to war, for the entire system was geared to increase the army's strength. This was also the goal of the harsh physical training to which women were subjected as well, the custom of exposing weak children to the elements, the obligation to have the state educate the children (*agoge*), and the imposition of a communitarian life that banished the private sphere.

This warrior is wearing a Corinthian-type helmet that totally covers the face and is topped by a tall crest placed in an unusual crosswise position, possibly to differentiate the officers from the rank-and-file.

The tresses falling on the chest were typical of Spartan soldiers. Tradition has it that Lycurgus forbade adult Lacedaemonian men to cut their hair, since he believed that long tresses struck fear and respect.

The cloak that totally envelops the body is perhaps the phoinikis, *introduced by Lycurgus, a crimson garment said to be endowed with the magical power of repelling blows; it also hid the blood stains caused by wounds.*

▲ Bronze statuette of cloaked Spartan warrior, end of 6th–early 5th century BC. Hartford, Conn., Wadsworth Athenaeum.

"I wrote laws that apply to the humble as well as the powerful, adapting fair justice to each" (Solon)

Solon

Political leader

Chronology
Ca. 640–561 BC

Principal events
Ca. 594 BC: Elected archon with extraordinary powers, he achieves an agrarian reform, a constitutional reform, the setting of weight and measure standards, and a revision of testamentary and family law.
593 BC: He leaves Athens for ten years, traveling to Asia Minor, Egypt and Cyprus.
562 BC: Back in Athens, he sees his reforms fail and tries to warn his fellow citizens against the risk of tyranny.
561 BC: Pisistratus becomes tyrant; probable year of Solon's death.

Related entries
Political institutions

▶ Bust of Solon, Roman copy from a probably Greek original. Naples, Museo Archeologico Nazionale.

In the early sixth century BC, at a time of harsh social conflict and economic crisis that reduced many freemen into servitude, the Athenian aristocrats, sole holders of political power, elected Solon archon (annual chief ruler), entrusting him with the task of arbitrator and peacemaker (*diallaktes*) among the clashing social groups. The descendant of an ancient noble family, Solon opposed the people's demands for a redistribution of lands but also tried to restrict the power of the aristocracy with decrees that abolished mortgages on the peasants' lands and enslavement for nonpayment of debts. Extending his reforms to constitutional law, he promulgated a code of laws to replace Draco's, dividing the citizens into four census classes that became the basis for taxation and military service, and for qualification to public office. Thus all the citizens received the right to vote, and political power stopped being the prerogative of the blood nobility, becoming accessible to anyone having a minimum annual income.

Having achieved his task, Solon left Athens for ten years, in which time his laws could not be modified; he wanted to remove himself from the pressure of the clashing parties, and entrusted the defense of his laws to poems of his own creation that were meant to be recited at symposia.

Solon believed that his laws should be directly accessible to all citizens, for which reason he "published" them in the prytaneum, *the city's town hall, using an original device called* axones.

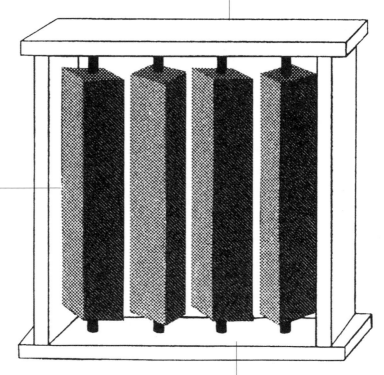

The axones *were wooden tablets that revolved around a pin attached to a frame: by rotating the tablets, one could read the entire text of the laws carved on them.*

According to some scholars, a second set of the laws was carved on rolling marble supports, the kyrbeis, *and displayed in the Stoa of the Agora Kings.*

▲ Drawing reconstructing Solon's *axones* (from Settis, *Atlante*, 2002).

"My hangman. Stable and ramrod-straight ... Now he is one with the Trojan sod ... I am the one who drowned him ... Now let him show his affection for this man: and may death be swift!" (Sophocles, Ajax)

Exekias

Artist

Chronology
Second half of the sixth century BC.

Important events
Ca. 550–525 BC:
Exekias is active as a painter. Perhaps his years as a potter were longer.

Related entries
Pottery art

▼ Belly amphora by Exekias (detail), *The Death of Ajax*, ca. 530 BC. Boulogne-sur-Mer, Musée Communal.

Active from about 550 to 525 BC, Exekias is the greatest painter of black-figure Attic vases. He probably owned a workshop that he personally supervised and was both a potter and a painter, marking both fields deeply and creating new ceramic forms and a pictorial language that treated traditional mythological subjects with originality.

Although he preferred large-size vases, Exekias did not create monumental compositions crowded with figures. He favored single scenes from well-known mythological episodes, fixed as if in a film frame and imbued with an atmosphere of concentration weighted with restlessness: Achilles and Ajax playing a game of dice during a respite from the battle, Ajax engrossed in preparing his suicide, or Achilles about to strike the fatal blow to Penthesilea. Although still drawn without facial expression in the Archaic style, his figures project a great sense of drama and are characterized by a statuesque dignity that approaches sculpture, allowing us a glimpse into the great, lost art of Greek painting.

We also find these traits in the other genre that Exekias was active in, small, painted terracotta tablets (*pinakes*) used to decorate the inside walls of tombs, which depicted mourning Athenians with the solemnity and dignity of gods.

Penthesilea, the mythical queen of the Asiatic Amazons, led her women warriors to the aid of the besieged Trojans.

The scene depicts the duel's supreme moment: as Penthesilea's spear brushes against Achilles' armor without striking him, the hero pierces the Amazon's throat with his spear.

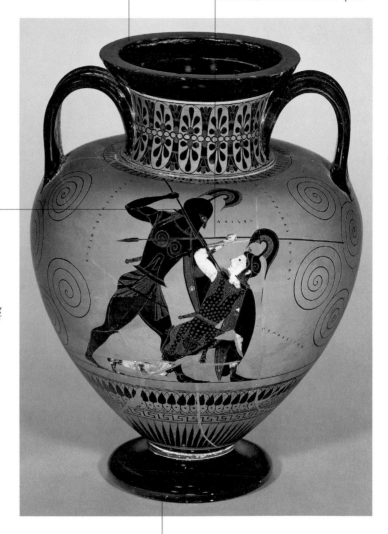

Achilles' helmet is pulled down to shield his face, while Penthesilea's face is bare, thus heightening her vulnerability and allowing their eyes to meet. According to a late version of the myth, the love between the two warriors sprang from this glance, but it was, alas, too late.

▲ Neck amphora by Exekias, *The Duel of Achilles and Penthesilea*, from Vulci, 540–530 BC. London, British Museum

Exekias signed this amphora as the potter ("Exekias epoiese"—"Exekias made me"), though the stylistic details lead us to believe that he also painted it.

"People forced to sit in the shadow, some even spending their day next to the fire: when the body weakens, the spirit also grows weary" (Xenophon)

Euphronius

The painter and ceramist Euphronius was active in Athens from the end of the sixth to the beginning of the fifth century BC, a time of great artistic flourishing that coincided with the tyranny of Pisistratus and the subsequent return to a democratic regime. His career may be reconstructed through the signature he painted on his vases. For twenty-five years Euphronius worked for several workshops. Starting in about 500 BC, he stopped signing his name as painter ("Euphronius painted me") and began to sign as potter ("Euphronius made me"), which was a greater honor since the potter was usually also the owner of the business.

At this time, he also offered a votive base, found on the Acropolis, to Athena who was the patron goddess of potters, perhaps in thanksgiving for the position he had reached. In those years, the "black-figure" technique had been replaced by "red-figure" painting that used black paint on the background, leaving the figures with the original red clay color and filling in the details with black brush lines. This new technique allowed the painter to add details and even foreshortening and movement techniques never tried before. Euphronius exploited the new technique to the fullest, attempting daring experiments and building grandiose scenes. His fame and the emulation he stirred in contemporary artists are aptly expressed by his somewhat younger fellow artist Euthymides who wrote, on one of his best vases, the famous challenge, "like Euphronius never made."

▶ *Kylix* by
Euphronius, signed
on the foot by the
potter Chachrylion,
*Heracles and
Geryon*, from Vulci,
ca. 515 BC. Munich,
Antikensammlung.

This krater, now at the Metropolitan Museum, was probably found while excavating an Etruscan tomb; it was broken into pieces in order to carry it more easily out of Italy. Its sudden appearance in New York in perfectly restored shape caused a sensation in the art world.

Sarpedon, a son of Zeus and Laodamia, is mentioned in the Iliad *as the leader of the Lycian troops who were allied with the Trojans; he was killed in battle by Patroclus.*

▲ Krater by Euphronius, *The Slaying of Sarpedon*, 515–510 BC. New York, Metropolitan Museum of Art.

After the death of Sarpedon, Zeus sent Hermes onto the battlefield escorted by Sleep and Death (Hypnos and Thanatos) to remove his son's body and return it to Lycia where he would be given a state funeral.

Euphronius painted the vase but did not make it, since the signed potter is Euxitheus.

This vase is known as the "cup of Leagros" on account of the inscription that reads "Leagros kalos" (Leagros is handsome). The name of this youth recurs frequently in the work of Euphronius; indeed, the painter Smikros depicted on one of his own vases a tryst between Euphronius and Leagros.

Often Athenian ceramists inscribed on their vases the names of the city's best-known youths, followed by the adjective kalos, handsome, perhaps a reflection of the artist's taste, or perhaps done on commission.

▲ *Kylix* by Euphronius known as "Cup of Leagros" (detail), from Vulci, ca. 510 BC. Munich, Antikensammlung.

This young man is parading on his horse at the dokimasia, *the annual review of Athenian knights. He wears short fur boots, a richly embroidered mantle, and a typical traveler's hat, the petasos, secured by a ribbon.*

"He divided into ten tribes the Athenians ... previously divided into four and changed the names taken from the children of Ion ... with those of other heroes, all from the state except for Ajax" (Herodotus)

Cleisthenes

The literary tradition looks upon Cleisthenes as the father of Athenian democracy. Although a member of the noble Alcmaeonidae, the family that drove out the Pisistratidae, he became the advocate of the middle classes who feared a return to an aristocratic rule. Appointed archon in 508 BC, he began a vast reform directed to eliminate class conflict and ward off forever the return of tyranny. To this end, he subdivided Attica into three regions: city, inland, and coast, each in turn divided into ten districts, the *trittyes* ("thirds"); in groups of three (one from each region), the thirty *trittyes* formed ten territorial tribes. Each tribe represented all social groups and the needs of the different Attican regions, so that the coastal merchants or the landowners of the hinterland could no longer bind into homogenous interest groups. Furthermore, each *trittys* had to supply a cavalry squadron and a hoplite regiment led by a *strategos*, elect an archon every year and choose by lots fifty members of the governing council (the *boule*) that acted as a prytany and took over the presidency of the council in turn for the tenth part of each year. The legislation submitted by the *boule* was approved or rejected by the full assembly (the *ekklesia*) of citizens, composed of all males at least twenty years of age and with Athenian parents.

Political leader

Chronology
Ca. 565–490 BC

Principal events
525 BC: First archonship.
Ca. 512 BC: Probably in exile.
510 BC: Hippias is banished and Cleisthenes and the other Alcmaeonidae return from exile.
508 BC: Second election to archon and constitutional reform.

◄ Basement ruins of the monument to the Eponymous Heroes, in the Athens Agora, second half of the 4th century BC.

This monument, built around the middle of the fourth century BC near the bouleuterion, memorialized the heroes who gave their names to the ten tribes founded by Cleisthenes and symbolized the unity of the Athenian state.

The bronze statues of the heroes stood on a long, rectangular base. On each side were two tripods, typical presents offered to winning athletes and to heroes.

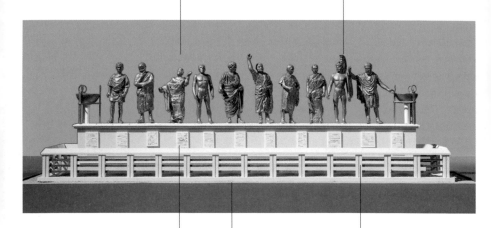

Directly below each statue was a tablet with notices that concerned each corresponding tribe.

The ten eponymous soldiers had been chosen by the oracle of Delphi from a list of one hundred names forwarded by Cleisthenes.

On the monument balustrade, wooden tablets painted white were displayed on which were written the bills, the dates, and agendas of the assemblies, the calls to arms, and other public notices.

▲ Model reconstructing the monument to the Eponymous Heroes. Athens, Agora Museum.

▶ View of part of the walls of Themistocles, near the Ceramicus, Athens.

"He ordered them ... to collect anything that might be used for fortification. For this reason, the walls of the Athenians are made of chapels and tombs" (Nepos)

Themistocles

Until the fifth century BC, Athens lacked a large fleet: its rivals Corinth and Aegina had the mightiest navies. The few ships they had were docked in Phaleros bay nearby, since the Piraeus peninsula was not yet used as a port. It was only after Persia conquered the Ionian cities that the Athenians realized the need for a fleet. The driving force behind this project was Themistocles: elected archon in 493 BC, he immediately set out to plan a military port at the Piraeus, building dockyards, dry docks, and a reinforced wall to protect the three natural bays of Khantaros, Zea, and Munichia.

His political opponents thwarted the construction of the fleet, fearful that the need to use the thetes—the lowest census class that until then had been exempted from military duty—would increase their political weight. The naval plan was resurrected ten years later, in 482 BC, driven by the resurgence of conflict with Aegina and by news of massive Persian preparations for an impending attack. Financing for the navy came from the discovery of new silver seams in the Laurion state mines, and the wealthier citizens paid for fitting out the ships. Within a few years, the fleet grew from one hundred to almost two hundred units and Athens became the leading naval power in Greece.

Political leader

Chronology
Ca. 528–462 BC

Principal events
493 BC: Elected archon, he orders the building of the military port of Piraeus.
483 BC: A maritime law sets aside the profits from the Laurion mines to build one hundred triremes.
480 BC: The Greek fleet defeats the Persians at Salamis.
478 BC: Construction of the new Athenian walls and the Piraeus.
477 BC: The anti-Persian Delian-Attic league is born.
471 BC: Themistocles is ostracized and flees to Argos.
Ca. 468 BC: Accused of secret arrangements with Persia, he is sentenced to death *in absentia*.
465 BC: He flees to the Persian king Artaxerxes I who grants him in fee the city of Magnesia on the Meander, where he lives out his last days

Related entries
Political institutions, fleet

23

The chronology of this bust's original is uncertain: some believe it was made when Themistocles was still alive, while for others it is a reconstruction made long after his death.

This bust seems a realistic reproduction of Themistocles' features; usually in the fifth century BC Greek portraits were idealized and only a few well-known features identified the subject, such as the shape of the skull or the beard style.

▲ Herm with portrait of Themistocles, Roman copy, from Ostia. Ostia, Museo Archeologico.

If it was indeed made when he was alive, this bust would be the earliest example of a physiognomic portrait in Greek art.

▶ Attic volute krater by the Bologna Painter 279 (detail), *Battle of the Seven Against Thebes*, from the Spina necropolis, 440 BC. Ferrara, Museo Archeologico Nazionale.

"Thus the soothsayer [Amphiaraus] … mixing against his will / with impious-mouthed men / who march to an enterprise with no return / with Zeus' will, will be swept away with them" (Aeschylus)

Hageladas of Argos and Alcamenes

In 1972 near Riace in Calabria, a scuba diver spotted two large bronze statues lying at the bottom of the sea. After five years' restoration, the statues were displayed in public in 1980 causing a sensation and leaving the scholars with the difficult task of dating them (very few original bronze statues from antiquity survive) and identifying the authors, the characters represented and the time and context of their original location. "Bronze B" was quickly identified as the work of Alcamenes, a contemporary and rival of Phidias, whom Pausanias had indicated as the author of the western pediment of the temple of Zeus at Olympia, based on stylistic analogies with the centaur heads of the pediment and the Heracles of some metopes.

In 1995, geological testing of the casting clay found in the statues confirmed that "Bronze B" had been made in Athens and "Bronze A" in Argos. In 1999, Paolo Moreno identified Hageladas of Argos, a sculptor who had worked with Alcamenes on the eastern pediment at Olympia, as the artist of "Bronze A." He also suggested that the two statues might represent Tydeus and Amphiaraus, part of the *Seven Against Thebes* monumental complex in the Argos Agora, a monument built jointly by the citizens of Athens and Argos to commemorate their allied victory against Sparta at Oinoe in 456 BC.

Artists

Chronology
5th century BC

Principal events
Ca. 473: Hageladas builds in Delphi the *thesauros* (treasury) dedicated by the Tarentines after a victory over the Messapians.
460–455 BC: Hageladas builds a statue to Zeus in Naupactos for the Messenian refugees.
456 BC: Alcamenes and Hageladas work on the decorations to the temple of Zeus in Olympia.
448 BC: Alcamenes secures his fame in Athens with his statue of *Hermes Propylaios*.
Ca. 430 BC: Hageladas creates his last work, *Heracles Alexikakos*, for the shrine of the same name in the Attic *deme* of Melitene.
420–415 BC: In Athens, Alcamenes fabricates the cult statues for the temple of Hephaestus.

Related entries:
Olympia

The mythical expedition of the Seven against Thebes was organized by Adrastus, king of Argos, to bring back Polynices, the brother of King Eteocles, who had been unjustly exiled.

Tydeus's red lips and silver teeth perhaps hint at the hero's ferociousness: having been dealt a mortal blow by Melanippus, he ate his brain. For this reason, Athena refused to grant him the immortal status that Zeus had requested.

The statue originally had a shield in the left hand and a tilted spear in the right.

The unique weight distribution of the body, with the weight resting on the stretched leg and the other leg bent, and the position of the arms would be copied by Polyclitus in his Doryphorus.

Bronze A is believed to represent Tydeus, an Aetolian hero who took part in the expedition as ambassador to the court of Eteocles. When the king refused to receive him, he challenged the Theban champions to a duel and defeated all of them.

▶ *Bronzi di Riace*, Bronze A, ca. 455 BC. Reggio Calabria, Museo Nazionale.

Bronze B is said to represent Amphiaraus, cousin to the King of Argos. Endowed with the power of divination, Amphiaraus tried to prevent the expedition against Thebes for he predicted it would end disastrously, but was forced to join nevertheless.

The unusual indentation under the hero's skull was perhaps meant to support a laurel wreath that identified him as an Apollo-inspired prophet.

Amphiaraus's sorrowful look perhaps alludes to his prophecy about the grievous outcome of the expedition in which all the Argive heroes would perish. Tydeus looks at him scornfully, establishing a connection between the two statues in the group monument.

The statue was completed by a spear held in the right hand, a sword suspended from the left side and a helmet of which only a piece survives.

▶ *Bronzi di Riace*, Bronze B, ca. 455 BC. Reggio Calabria, Museo Nazionale.

"Powerful for dignity and judgment, clearly incorruptible by money, he ruled the people without restricting their freedom, nor was he swayed by them any more than he swayed them" (Thucydides)

Pericles

▶ Portrait of Pericles, Roman copy of an original by Cresilas from 440–430 BC. London, British Museum.

After the Persians destroyed Athens, Pericles became the leading advocate of the city's thirst for revenge: for thirty years he ruled the political scene uncontested, giving birth to a unique period of creative frenzy. While on the domestic front he promoted several important democratic reforms such as compensating public officers and admitting the two lowest census classes to high magistrate positions, abroad he pursued a hard imperial policy directed to achieve Athens's hegemony over all of Greece.

To further this ambitious design, Pericles surrounded himself with architects and artists who were charged with an extraordinary urban renewal plan. Foremost was the reconstruction of the Acropolis as the religious center of all of Greece, but in a few years the Odeion, the temple to Hephaestus on the Agora and that to Poseidon on Cape Sunium were also completed. In those same years, the urban planner Hippodamus of Miletus designed new residential districts in the Piraeus, now linked to Athens by the Long Wall. This exceptional construction and artistic activity was hugely expensive and Pericles had to often defend himself from scandals and charges of wasting the money of citizens and allies. His prestige was tarnished only after the Peloponnesian war broke out, when Athens was traumatized by the Spartan invasion. He died of the plague in 429 BC.

"Phidias oversaw all these works on behalf of Pericles, though more than one had great architects and artists of their own"
(Plutarch)

Phidias

When Pericles appointed him to supervise reconstruction of the Acropolis, Phidias was already established as the official Athens artist, having debuted in the city with the bronze statue of Apollo "who rescues from the grasshoppers," and later with the group monument at Delphi dedicated to the Marathon victory, and the bronze statue of Athena Promachos (combatant) that towered above the Acropolis from its height of twenty-three feet and had required about three tons of bronze and no less than one hundred and eighty workers to build.

The project to rebuild the Acropolis included as religious focal point another colossal statue, this one dedicated to Athena Parthenos, which, together with the temple that housed it, the Parthenon, had been conceived as a grandiose ex-voto to commemorate the victory of civilization over Persian barbarism, in which Athens had played such a major role. The entire artistic plan of the Acropolis revolved around this theme, and even the material used—marble from the marble quarries of Mount Pentelicon, near Athens— contributed to exalt the city's greatness, thus spreading the idea that it had a natural right to a position of supremacy over all of Greece.

After the Parthenon was inaugurated, Phidias moved to Olympia where he created another masterpiece, the colossal gold-and-ivory statue of Zeus, acclaimed as one of the seven wonders of the world. Only Pericles' decline would tarnish his star, dragging him into the mud with vile accusations of theft and impiety.

Artist

Chronology
Ca. 490–430 BC

Principal events
Ca. 460–455 BC:
Bronze statue of Apollo
"the rescuer from the grasshoppers."
Ca. 450 BC: Bronze
statue of Athena
Promachos.
447 BC: He becomes
director of the
Acropolis works.
438 BC: The Parthenon
is inaugurated;
dedication of the statue
of Athena Parthenos.
437 BC: Colossal gold-
and-ivory statue for
the temple of Zeus
at Olympia.
432 BC: Return to
Athens and trial for
theft and ungodliness;
he either flees to Elis or
dies in an Athenian jail.

Related entries
Pericles, Zeus, Athena,
Athenian Acropolis,
Olympia

◀ *Kassel Apollo*,
Roman copy of *Apollo Parnopios* by Phidias
from 460–450 BC.
Kassel, Staatliche
Kunstsammlungen.

Of all the ancient copies, the Varvakeion statuette is the most faithful reproduction of Phidias's colossal statue covered in gold and ivory that took thirteen years of work and a ton of gold.

The cost of the statue was equal to the cost of building 230 triremes. The goddess's gold gown was considered part of the state treasury.

Athena in arms wears a Doric peplum and a large aegis covers her breasts; she holds a Nike (victory) in her right hand. Ivory was used for the loose parts and gold for the clothes and for accents.

The shield had a 12-foot diameter; the sandals were decorated with scenes of battles with the Amazons, the Giants, and the Centaurs, subjects that had become popular after the Persian wars because they symbolized the victory of civilization over the barbarians.

In the original statue, the goddess stood on a dark stone pedestal on which the scene of Pandora's birth was carved in white marble.

To construct the statue of Zeus, Phidias had a workshop built that reproduced the dimensions of the temple cell where the statue would stand. The workshop still exists in Olympia, having become a Byzantine church.

Some ancient commentators wrote that the colossus seemed out of proportion with the temple cell, and that if it were to stand, its head would crash through the ceiling.

The god wore an olive wreath like the winning Olympian athletes; in his left hand he held a scepter topped by an eagle, and in his right, a gold-and-ivory statue of Nike.

The colossal statue of Zeus Olympic was totally covered in gold and ivory and represents the god seated on a throne enriched with precious stones, the feet decorated by four dancing Nikai.

◀ *Athena Parthenos of the Varvakeion*, Roman copy of the gold-and-ivory original by Phidias from 438 BC. Athens, National Archaeological Museum.

▲ Reconstructed vertical section of the temple of Zeus in Olympia (18th-century engraving by Fischer von Erlach).

The Centaurs, guests at the wedding of Pirithous, became drunk and tried to rape Hippodamia the bride, unleashing a great battle that ended with the victory of the Lapiths.

In Greek mythology, it was the Lapiths, a people from Thessaly, who waged battle against the Centaurs who were half-man and half-horse creatures who lived in the surrounding forests.

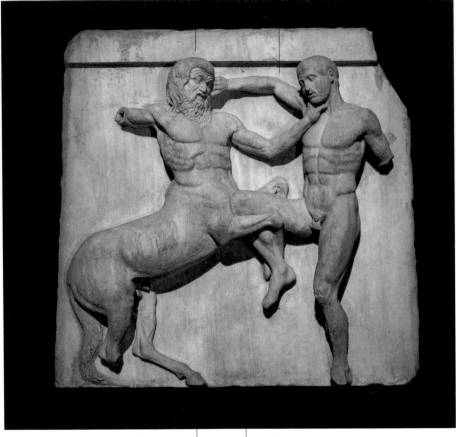

The trabeation of the Parthenon was decorated with ninety-two metopes, of which only nineteen from the southern side are in a good state of conservation. In 1910 Lord Elgin brought back fifteen of them and sold them to the British Museum.

The metopes depicted the battle of the Giants (east), of the Amazons (west), the Trojan war (north), and the battle of the Centaurs (south).

▲ Metope XXXI south from the Parthenon, *Centaur and Lapith*, 447–432 BC. London, British Museum.

The water bearers, together with the sacrificial animals, the bearers of offerings and sacred vestments, the musicians, and the city notables, marched in the first part of the procession, the "sacrificial pomp."

The water was carried in large hydriai, typical three-handled jugs that took the name of their contents. It was used for the ritual ablutions of the priests that preceded the sacrifice of the victims.

This frieze is 160 meters long: it ran along the four sides of the temple cell, crowning the exterior walls. It depicts the Pan-Athenaean procession, the feast of all Athenians. Celebrated every year on the birthday of Athena, it reached the Acropolis from the Pompeion located in the Ceramicus.

▲ Northern frieze of the Parthenon, *Water Bearers*, 447–432 BC. Athens, Acropolis Museum.

The presence of the metope, typical of the Doric order, and the frieze, typical of the Ionic order and usually placed on the temple architraves, is one of the novelties of the Parthenon.

The horse races were part of the games that lasted an entire week, culminating in the chariot races, as depicted in other parts of the frieze.

The procession did not end at the Parthenon; even after it was built, the sacrifice and the delivery of the peplum to the goddess continued to be celebrated at the altar west of the temple, before an ancient wooden statue of Athena Polias.

▶ Northern frieze of the Parthenon, *Parade of Knights*, 447-432 BC. Athens, Acropolis Museum.

The parade of knights was the concluding moment of the parade honoring Athena. Thus the frieze does not depict the actual unfolding of the procession, but rather a compendium of different events that succeeded each other.

The archon king who, as priest, supervised the
sacrifice to Athena, is here folding the peplum
with the assistance of a young attendant.
Behind him, a priestess welcomes women
bearing small cushioned seats on their heads.

The two processions started from
the south-western corner of the cell
and met at the eastern side where,
in the center, the delivery of the
peplum to Athena in the presence
of the other deities was depicted.

Athena's peplum was woven and
embroidered by ergastinai, young
women from the best Athenian
families who toiled at it for nine
months before the procession.

▲ Eastern frieze of the
Parthenon, *Delivery of the
Peplum*, 447–432 BC.
Athens, Acropolis Museum.

The gods who are witnessing the birth of Athena are seated symmetrically at each side of the main scene which has not survived.

The eastern and western pediments of the Parthenon portrayed, respectively, the birth of Athena from the head of Zeus and the contest between the goddess and Poseidon for dominance over Attica.

The posture of the various figures creates a rising movement toward the center, purposely studied to adapt them to the triangular shape of the pediment without injecting stiffness into the composition.

▲ Eastern pediment of the Parthenon, *Group of Gods*, 447–432 BC. London, British Museum.

In other copies of this statue, the Amazon has a deep bleeding wound on her right thigh. Here she is shown reaching for the bow with her right hand.

The head was incorrectly assembled to the body: in reality, it is a copy of the Wounded Amazon attributed to Polyclitus.

According to Pliny, Phidias, Polyclitus, Cresilas, and Phradmon took part in a contest called by the city of Ephesus for sculpting an Amazon statue to be dedicated to the shrine of Artemis. The same artists were called to be the judges, and they awarded first prize to the statue of Polyclitus and second prize to Phidias.

The identification, through Roman copies, of the stylistic types used in identifying the various sculptors is problematic. Most scholars concur that the Mattei Amazon is a copy of a Phidias original because of the analogies with some images of amazons depicted in the metopes of the Parthenon.

▶ Mattei Amazon, Roman copy of an original by Phidias from 440–430 BC, from Villa d'Este. Rome, Musei Capitolini.

"Polyclitus of Sicyon made the Diadoumenos, an effeminate boy statue … as well as the Doryphorus, the figure of an already virile youth" (Pliny)

Polyclitus

Born in Argos around 480 BC, Polyclitus reached the apex of his career around 420 BC. At first, he worked mainly in Olympia where he specialized in bronze statues of athletes, some of whose original bases have survived, such as the *Cyniscus* of Mantinea, along with some Roman marble copies. He then moved to Attica where, in 435 BC, he took part with Phidias, Phradmon, and Cresilas in the famous competition held by the city of Ephesus, and won first prize. In his final years he produced his greatest masterpieces such as the *Diadoumenos* and the gold-and-ivory enthroned *Hera* for her temple at Argos: this was the only cult statue he ever made; it has been reconstructed from reproductions on coins.

In addition to practicing his art, Polyclitus was also a theoretician: starting from a study of the bodies of athletes, in which he always showed an interest, he developed a set of rules on how to give symmetric proportions and a harmonious rhythm to statues, inventing a new way of representing the standing male figure in an attitude midway between rest and movement. He collected his theories in a treatise, the *Canon*, which was appreciated by Aristotle who considered him the greatest of sculptors. However, not every one approved of the constant application of the same rules of symmetry and balance and some contemporaries, as well as later critics, accused him of being repetitive.

Artist

Chronology
Ca. 480–420 BC

Principal events
Ca. 460–450 BC: Early works, especially those of the Olympia sanctuary (*Discophorus, Wesmacott Ephebus, Cyniscus*).
Ca. 440 BC: Sculpts the *Doryphorus*.
Ca. 435 BC: Contest with Phidias, Cresilas, and Phradmon to create an Amazon statue, commissioned by the city of Ephesus.
Ca. 430 BC: Sculpts the *Diadoumenos*.
Ca. 420 BC: Sculpts the gold and ivory statue of Hera for the sanctuary at Argos.

Related entries
Olympia

◄ Polyclitus, head of the *Doryphorus* (The Spear Bearer), Roman copy of an original from ca. 440 BC, from Herculaneum. Naples, Museo Archeologico Nazionale.

39

Traces of oxidation recently found on the forearm have been interpreted as the marks left by the loop of a bronze shield. Furthermore, the smoothing on the outside of the forearm would hint that it was smoothed out to accommodate the loop.

The Doryphorus *is the most famous and copied of Polyclitus's work. Some have identified it with the* Canon, *the statue where the artist applied the theories of his treatise.*

According to the new reconstruction theory, the fingers of the right hand are curved to hold the hilt of a sword that pointed backwards.

The reconstruction of the Doryphorus *armed with spear, shield, and sword gives the statue a realistic military look, which does not easily reconcile with the theory that it was meant to be an abstract representation of the* Canan.

▲ *Doryphorus*, Roman copy of an original by Polyclitus from ca. 440 BC, from Pompeii. Naples, Museo Archeologico Nazionale.

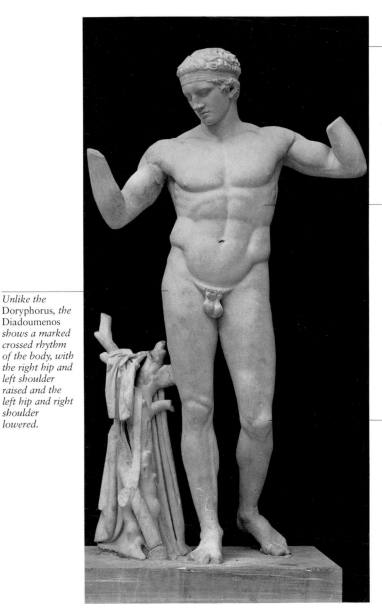

This statue, the Diadoumenos, portrays a winning athlete tying a fillet around his head, the diadema that was awarded to the winners of competitions.

The greater flexing of the torso and a slight bending to the right give this statue a more marked tridimensionality that goes beyond a rigid frontal view.

Unlike the Doryphorus, the Diadoumenos shows a marked crossed rhythm of the body, with the right hip and left shoulder raised and the left hip and right shoulder lowered.

According to the typical counterbalance of Polyclitus, all the weight rests on the straight leg, while the left leg is flexed and moved backwards.

▲ *Diadoumenos* (Man Tying a Fillet), Roman copy of an original by Polyclitus from ca. 430 BC. Athens, National Archaeological Museum.

While Phidias's Amazon has a wound on the leg, Polyclitus's discovers the chest wound as she removes the chiton with her left hand.

This type has been generally identified as a copy of the statue with which Polyclitus won the contest with Phidias, Cresilas, and Phradmon for the creation of the Amazon of Ephesus.

The statue's weight distribution is consistent with the counterbalancing rhythm typical of Polyclitus, with a correspondence between raised hip and lowered shoulder, and vice versa.

Pliny's anecdote seems to be confirmed by the existence of four different statue types from the same period that portray wounded Amazons.

▲ *Amazon*, Roman copy of an original by Polyclitus from 440–430 BC. Athens, National Archaeological Museum.

▶ Portrait of Socrates of the first type, Roman copy of an original from the early 4th century BC. Naples, Museo Nazionale.

"The hour of departure has arrived, and we go our ways—I to die, and you to live: which is better, God only knows"
(Plato, Apology)

Socrates

His vast fame notwithstanding, Socrates is not a well-known figure, having left no writings, and we must reconstruct his personality and his thought from the descriptions handed down by disciples and contemporaries. Socrates' philosophical doctrine centered around ethics and the knowledge of man. He used dialectics much like a midwife, to drive his interlocutors to realize that true wisdom consists in knowing that one does not know. The originality of his thought made him highly popular, though many mistook it for a contempt of traditional values. This, and his close relationship with leaders who later fell into disgrace, such as Alcibiades and Critias, led to his indictment on charges of impiety and corruption of the young; after a trial at which he was found guilty and sentenced to death, Socrates chose suicide.

After his death, two portraits were made that experts have reconstructed from Roman copies. The earliest one dates to the first half of the fourth century BC and was commissioned privately, perhaps by members of Plato's Academy: its features recall the physiognomy that many, including Plato, had described: bulging eyes, a pug nose, and fleshy lips that gave him the look of a satyr. The second portrait, attributed to Lysippus, was commissioned by Athens following the philosopher's official rehabilitation, and in accordance with the probably honorific use, his Silenus-like features were toned down.

Philosopher

Chronology
470–399 BC

Principal events
431–404 BC: He is a hoplite in the Peloponnesian war.
411 BC: The oligarchic government of the Four Hundred promoted by Alcibiades takes over in Athens.
410 BC: Democracy is temporarily restored.
406 BC: As a member of the *boule*, Socrates is against the death sentence imposed on the conquering generals of Arginusae.
404 BC: The Thirty Tyrants regime takes over in Athens, led by Critias and Theramenes; though he had been Critias's friend, Socrates opposes a political purge.
403 BC: Democracy is restored and there is a general amnesty.
399 BC: Socrates is tried and sentenced to death.

Related entries:
Alcibiades, Plato

"The enormous donations ... the glory of his ancestors, the power of his eloquence, his beauty and physical strength ... led the Athenians to be lenient over the rest" (Plutarch)

Alcibiades

Political leader

Chronology
450–404 BC

Principal events
420–419 BC: Elected *strategos*, he leads the political faction that wants to continue the conflict with Sparta.
415 BC: Chosen as one of the commanders of the Athenian expedition to Sicily; scandal of the herms and flight to Sparta.
411 BC: Protected by the satrap Tissaphernes, he supports the oligarchic regime of the Four Hundred; he supports the revolt of the Athenian fleet anchored at Samos against the oligarchs and is elected fleet *strategos*.
408 BC: Triumphal return to Athens.
407 BC: After Athens is defeated at Notion, he is deposed and retires to Thrace.
404 BC: Athens is defeated by Sparta. Alcibiades flees to Phrygia where he is murdered.

Related entries:
Socrates, Hermes

The name of Alcibiades, scion of a noble Athenian family and a disciple of Socrates, is linked to one of the darkest episodes in the history of Athens that coincided with the end of the city's rise and the beginning of her political and military decline. In 415 BC, while the government was debating the suitability of a Sicilian expedition to aid the allied cities that had requested protection against Syracuse's expansionistic aims, at the dawn of a moonless night, the herms (the columns topped by busts of heroes or divinities that protected the crossroads) were found mutilated. The opponents of the expedition read a bad omen in this vandalism and Alcibiades, the most prominent supporter of the expedition and one of its *strategoi*, was accused of having a hand in the crime and of having profaned with a sacrilegious parody the Eleusinian mysteries.

Still, the party that supported the expedition prevailed momentarily and the triremes were allowed to leave, but after the first military operations Alcibiades was recalled and ordered to stand trial. He fled instead and took refuge in the Spartan territory, becoming a soldier of fortune. In the ensuing years, he tried with all his might to recapture a role in Athenian political life. He was killed in Phrygia in 404 BC by Persians, whose ally he had been in the past.

Many magistrates and private citizens dedicated herms in the Athens Agora. Several herm fragments were found near the northwestern access to the square.

This head was dated to 480–470 BC and could be one of the herms that were vandalized on the eve of the Athenian expedition to Sicily.

This head of Hermes has traces of repairs to the nose: the breakpoint was smoothed out and perforated for the stucco to take hold, or to hold a pin that supported the missing piece.

◄ Statue known as "Alcibiades," Roman copy of an original from the 4th century BC. Vatican City, Musei Vaticani.

▲ Herm fragment from the Athens Agora, ca. 480–470 BC. Athens, Agora Museum.

Two equal heads are joined in the back and crowned by a metal band, a symbol of royalty. After the herm scandal of 415 BC, this herm, incorrectly known as "Andocides'," became famous and many copies of it were made.

The original, of which this is a double copy, represented Aegeus, one of the heroes who gave their names to the Attic tribes.

▲ Double herm of Aegeus, Roman copy of an original from ca. 440 BC, from Marina di San Nicola. Rome, Museo Nazionale Etrusco di Villa Giulia.

The scholar Paolo Moreno believes that the herm of Aegeus is the work of Phidias who used as model the head of Tydeus (Riace Bronze A) sculpted by his teacher Hageladas of Argos.

During the "night of the herms" this herm of Aegeus was the only one that was spared; because it was located near the residence of Andocides, he became a prime suspect and was incarcerated.

"Calamities would never cease ... unless men who were truly ... philosophers came to power ... or unless the city's political leaders ... became philosophers" (Plato)

Plato

Plato, the scion of an aristocratic family, was a disciple of Socrates; after his teacher's tragic death, he left Athens for long travels that kept him away from public life. Returning home in 385 BC, he took up philosophy again and, unlike Socrates, founded a true school of philosophy. The Academy took its name from the hero Academos, to whom the land where the school rose was consecrated. It was in a secluded area not far from Athens where a gymnasium had been active since the time of Solon, enclosed by a fence and supplied with water by the Pisistratidae.

Here Plato spent a good part of his life, teaching and writing; he only left Athens for a stay in Syracuse as the guest of Dionysius II, a tyrant who, Plato had hoped for a time, might translate his political theories into practice. His written dialogues became the first core of the Academy's library. Like the other gymnasia, at first the library was open only to its disciples for payment of a fee; still, it contributed to spread the idea of conserving and continuing thought by preserving it in written form. The Academy survived Plato's death and became an active center of political and philosophical studies that survived until the sixth century AD.

Philosopher

Chronology
427–347 BC

Principal events
407 BC: Meets Socrates and begins to be interested in philosophy.
399 BC: Travels to Megara, Cyrene, Tarentum, and Syracuse.
396–388 BC: Writes the early "Socratic" dialogues.
387 BC: Returns to Athens and founds the Academy; begins to write the "academic" dialogues.
367–365 BC: Resides in Syracuse as guest of Dionysius II.
367–361 BC: Writes his "late" dialogues.
361–360 BC: Second stay in Syracuse.

Related entries
Socrates

◄ Inscribed herm of Plato, Roman copy of an original by Silanion from ca. 350 BC. Berlin, Antikensammlung.

"And yet he is not Greek: he has nothing in common with Greeks … he is a Macedonian ragamuffin, from that region where once not even a slave could be bought" (Demosthenes)

Aeschines and Demosthenes

▶ *Aeschines*, Roman
copy of an original
from the end of the 4th
century BC, from the
Villa dei Papiri,
Herculaneum. Naples,
Museo Archeologico
Nazionale.

In the years of Macedonia's rise to power, Aeschines and Demosthenes were the advocates of opposite factions in Athens. The former supported Philip as a peacemaker who could settle internal conflicts in Greece; the latter proudly opposed the "barbarian" and defended democratic ideals. After a long career as a scribe, Aeschines had become *boule* secretary. Demosthenes was a legal logographer who wrote speeches for a fee. Their political roles were such that both were sent often as envoys to the court of the Macedonian king, from which they came away with opposite impressions.

The clash between the two orators was dramatic at times, and became personal. On several occasions, Demosthenes accused Aeschines of having been corrupted by Philip; Aeschines saved himself by only a handful of votes. In 337 BC, Aeschines criticized the city's proposal to award a gold crown to Demosthenes for the services he had rendered and violently attacked his politics. Soundly defeated, Aeschines was unable to pay the fine imposed for his reckless accusations and was exiled to Rhodes. For his part, Demosthenes continued his relentless campaign against Macedonia until 322 BC when the uprising of the Greek city-states failed, driving him to suicide.

In the pro-Macedonian era that followed, the figure of Aeschines was rehabilitated and a bronze statue dedicated to him, probably in the Agora.

This statue stood in the Agora between the temple of Ares and the Altar of the Twelve Gods, promoting the image of Demosthenes as the advocate of democracy.

The bronze statue of Demosthenes, of which this is the most famous copy, was commissioned by Demochares, the head of the democratic faction and the orator's nephew, to rehabilitate his name.

The austere, collected expression of the statue, with the hands clasped and the pensive face, corresponds to the description of Demosthenes from the written sources; it would be heavily imitated in later years.

► Demosthenes, Roman copy of an original by Polyeuktos from ca. 280 BC. Vatican City, Musei Vaticani.

"It is clear that the city is a natural product and that man is by nature a social animal ... much more so than any bee or head of cattle" (Aristotle)

Aristotle

Philosopher

Chronology
384–322 BC

Principal events
367 BC: Moves to Athens from Macedonia, where his father was a physician at the court of King Amyntas II.
367–347 BC: Attends Plato's Academy.
347–345 BC: He lives in Axos and later in Mitylene where he teaches and researches the natural sciences.
343 BC: Moves to Pella, Macedonia, and is hired by Philip to tutor his son Alexander.
336 BC: Returns to Athens and founds the Lyceum.
323 BC: The anti-Macedon party prevails in Athens; Aristotle leaves the city and retires to Chalcidice.

Related entries
Plato

▶ Portrait of Aristotle, Roman copy of an original probably from the early 2nd century BC. Vienna, Kunsthistorisches Museum.

A native of the Chalcidice peninsula, Aristotle attended Plato's Academy for twenty years. Later he became teacher to Alexander the Great, whose personality and politics he vainly tried to influence. Returning to Athens, he founded his own philosophy school, the Lyceum, so called because it was set in a green area consecrated to Apollo Lyceus.

Most of Aristotle's surviving works are classroom notes, either penned by him or jotted down by his students during his lessons, and range over all the known fields of knowledge at the time. The *Physics* books dealt with the disciplines that today we call "scientific" (from astronomy to zoology); the later ones with so-called "first philosophy" which from Aristotle came to be called, appropriately, "metaphysics" (*meta ta physika* or "after the physics books"). Many of his works also touched on logic, aesthetics, rhetoric, and politics.

Because of his all-inclusive, analytical, and systematic qualities, the thought of Aristotle had an enormous influence in Western culture. Thanks to Arab philosophers such as Avicenna and Averroes, his thought became once more the subject of debate around the year 1000 and penetrated European culture from the mid-thirteenth century onwards, when Scholastic doctors of the Church such as Thomas Aquinas cemented the Church's official dogma upon it. From that time on, Aristotle's authority in the sciences and in philosophy was unquestioned and every subsequent intellectual development had to be justified within its terms.

"When fashioning the statue of Cnidian Aphrodite, he gave it the form ... of his mistress Cratina, that the wretched people might have Praxiteles' mistress to worship" (Clement of Alexandria)

Praxiteles

Praxiteles was the greatest exponent of Attic sculpture in the fifth century BC. His workshop, which he rarely left, was in Athens though he received commissions from cities all over Greece and his oeuvre—more than forty statues, some of which even reached Asia Minor—made him extremely wealthy. Unlike other great sculptors, Praxiteles preferred to use marble. His bodies are supple, very unlike the clearly marked musculature typical of Classical sculpture; for this reason, he came to be known as the painter of *charis*, of grace.

Once he had completed a statue, Praxiteles had great artists such as Nicias paint it using an almost transparent glaze over the bare flesh and thin coatings of color over eyes, lips, and clothing: the effect was surely very different from the Roman copies that have survived. Praxiteles preferred to create lithe figures in sinuous poses that often required a support. His divinities, inspired by an ideal of perfect, youthful beauty, projected a human look, more than an austere divine one, and this earned him the criticism of some of his contemporaries. He was also the first artist to represent Aphrodite totally naked. The statue, refused by the people of Kos who found it too daring, was placed in the shrine of the goddess at Cnidus. It became his most famous work, making him one of the most reproduced sculptors in antiquity.

Artist

Chronology
Ca. 390–328 BC

Principal events
Ca. 375–330 BC:
Flourished as a sculptor
in these years.
Early works: *Pouring Satyr, Satyr at Rest, Eros of Thespiae.*
364–361 BC: According to Pliny the Elder, his best work was done in this period, perhaps when he made *Aphrodite of Cnidus.*
Mature works: *Apollo Sauroktonos, Apollo Lyceus, Hermes and the Infant Dionysus, Artemis Brauronia.*

Related entries:
Aphrodite, Hermes, Dionysus, sacred buildings and temples, Olympia

◀ *Satyr at Rest,* Roman copy of a Praxiteles original from ca. 370 BC. Rome, Musei Capitolini.

The Aphrodite of Cnidus *was one of the most famous statues in antiquity, a type recognized already in 1728 from effigies on coins from Cnidus. Over fifty copies are extant, with the one conserved in the Vatican Museums considered the best.*

The statue stood in the center of a small temple in Cnidus that had two doors, thus allowing the visitors to circle it and admire it from all sides before leaving from the back door.

Ancient sources reported several instances of men who fell hopelessly in love with the statue, whose beauty was considered perfect. The profane character of this statue of a deity was criticized by Christian authors.

The goddess is depicted as she drops her robe on a water jug (a hydria) before taking a bath.

▲ *Aphrodite of Cnidus*, Roman copy of an original by Praxiteles from ca. 360 BC. Vatican City, Musei Vaticani.

This statue, Hermes Carrying the Infant Dionysus, *was found in 1877 in excavating the temple of Hera at Olympia, in the same spot where Pausanias, the second-century* AD *author who wrote* A Guide to Greece, *recounted having seen it.*

Some experts believe that this is the only original work of Praxiteles that has survived to our day; others think it is a copy or the work of a later sculptor by the same name. If Hermes Carrying the Infant Dionysus *is indeed an original, it is difficult to understand why it was never copied in Roman times.*

According to Praxiteles' style, the two divinities form a "graceful scene" very far from the myth that surrounded them: Hermes holds little Dionysus on his arm and offers him a bunch of grapes.

The suppleness of Hermes' body is made possible by the fact that he is leaning on a support with his left hand.

▲ Praxiteles, *Hermes Carrying the Infant Dionysus*, from Olympia, ca. 340 BC. Olympia, Archaeological Museum.

The identification of this statue with an ecstatic Satyr dancing frenetically is suggested by the shape of the ears and the fixed gaze, and by its resemblance to several reproductions on precious stones, reliefs, and sarcophagi from the Late Hellenistic and Roman era.

This statue, six-and-a-half feet high, was found by a fishing boat in the sea between Mazara del Vallo (Sicily) and the African coast in the spring of 1998.

The missing hands probably held Dionysiac symbols such as the thyrsus (a cane wound with ribbons and crowned with a pinecone) on the right and a kantharos (wine cup) on the left, with a leopard skin hanging from the left arm.

▲ Dancing Satyr from Mazara del Vallo, ca. 360 BC. Mazara del Vallo, Museo del Satiro.

The historian Paolo Moreno has suggested this is the Satyr Periboetos (screaming in a frenzy) by Praxiteles. There are no copies in the round, perhaps because of the difficulty inherent in rendering into marble the daring suppleness of the body that was supported on one foot only.

It was the statue of a maenad created in Parian marble ...
although made of hard marble, it was easy to see the sweet
outline of a woman" (Callicrates)

Scopas

Scopas was born on the island of Paros, famous for its marble quarries and because it was the birthplace of many sculptors. He was active in Attica, the Peloponnesus, and Asia Minor, and mostly sculpted in stone. Because his activity was linked for the most part to the construction of large shrines, Scopas's subjects are mostly religious, but instead of depicting the Olympic grandiosity of the gods, he preferred their more human and passionate features, favoring highly dramatic scenes rendered with twisted bodies, dramatic chiaro-scuro modeling effects, deeply set eyes and mouths expressively open. For this reason, ancient sources that tended to condense the styles of the leading artists in stereotypical, though effective, formulas, describe Scopas as the artist of *pathos*, that is, of passion, as opposed to Praxiteles who was the artist of grace.

Like Phidias, Scopas must have been an architect as well, because he was appointed to supervise the reconstruction of the temple of Athena Alea at Tegea, destroyed by a fire in 395 BC. Although the sources do not specify whether he was also in charge of coordinating the sculptural decorations, the surviving fragments of the figures adorning the pediments reflect a uniformity of style that blends with the uniqueness of Scopas's art as can be reconstructed from the Roman copies, leading us to believe that they are the only originals for which attribution is certain.

Artist

Chronology
Ca. 395–350 BC

Principal events
Post 371 BC: Directs the works to rebuild the temple of Athena Alea at Tegea.
360–351 BC: With Timotheus, Leochares, and Bryaxis decorates the marble tomb of the satrap Mausolus in Halicarnassus.
Post 356 BC: Takes part in the reconstruction of the Artemision at Ephesus that was destroyed by a fire, sculpting the decorations on the lower part of a column.

Related entries
Dionysus

◀ Scopas, western pediment of the temple of Athena Alea at Tegea, ca. 370 BC. Athens, National Archaeological Museum.

The strongly protruding eyebrow arches project shadows around the deep-set eyes and are a "signature trait" of Scopas's art.

Like the Satyrs, the Maenads (or Bacchantes) were part of Dionysus's retinue and personified the orgiastic spirits of Nature.

The twisted body displays analogies with the Satyr found in Mazara del Vallo.

The semi-naked Maenad is caught in a frenetic dance as she pirouettes around her right leg, the arms stretched by the centrifugal force and the head thrown back, her hair disheveled.

▲ *Dancing Maenad*, Roman copy of an original by Scopas from ca. 350 BC. Dresden, Staatliche Kunstsammlungen.

This Meleager, *generally attributed to Scopas, is one of the few sculptures that is never cited in ancient sources, though its popularity is documented by the more than twenty copies that survive.*

The dog and the chlamys, *a short cape worn by soldiers and hunters, allude to the myth, the great hunt organized by Meleager to kill the wild boar, in which the hunters from all neighboring cities took part.*

Meleager was the son of the king of Calydon, in Aetolia, whose kingdom was threatened by a huge wild boar sent by Artemis because she had not been included in a sacrifice offered to all the gods.

To exact revenge, Artemis stirred up a quarrel in dividing the spoils of the wild boar, in which Meleager killed his mother's brothers. In the war that ensued, Meleager, cursed by his mother, died pierced by Apollo's arrow.

▲ *Meleager,* Roman copy of an original by Scopas from ca. 350 BC. Vatican City, Musei Vaticani.

Power and Public Life

◄ Small bronze of a warrior with crested helmet, early 5th century BC. Paris, Musée du Louvre.

Political Institutions

Related entries
Lycurgus, Solon, Cleisthenes, Pericles, justice and the courts, theaters, assembly buildings, public banquet halls, porticoes, Athenian Agora

As monarchies declined, each *polis* adopted comparable institutions that remained fundamentally unchanged even if modifications were introduced over the years. The kings' absolute power was distributed among the high magistrates, either singly or in boards, who were given administrative, executive, military, and religious powers. The magistrates were assisted by restricted councils such as the Athenian *boule*, the elder councils of Sparta and Elis (with 30 and 60 members respectively), of Tegea (40), and of Argos (80) whose functions included evaluating the magistrates' proposals, reviewing their accounts, drafting bills and dealing with major financial, administrative, and military issues.

The council members were supported at the city's expense and enjoyed immunity. The people expressed their wishes directly in assemblies formed by all the citizens who enjoyed full rights (the Athenian *ekklesia*, Sparta's *apella*, the *heliaia* of the Dorian cities) where they elected magistrates and voted on the *boule's* resolutions. Each citizen had the right to speak, however only those proposals authorized by the council could be debated and voted on. Voting took place by a show of hands or by acclamation. In some cases, secret balloting was used. Judicial power was divided among several courts, each with jurisdiction over different kinds of crime.

▶ Attic red-figure *pelike* by the Harrow Painter, *Oration Scene*, ca. 480 BC. Paris, Musée du Louvre.

This stele depicts the personification of Justice (or Democracy) crowning the People (demos) personified as a bearded, enthroned man, with a wreath.

Eucrates' law, which had the purpose of discouraging pro-Macedonian uprisings, was only in force until 322 BC, when Athenian democracy was swept away by the Macedonian occupation.

The law put forward by Eucrates in 336 BC tried to discourage tyranny by providing, among other things, exemption from punishment for the murder of anyone who tried to overthrow democracy.

▲ Stele with the law against tyrants, 336 BC. Athens, Agora Museum.

This stele was found in 1952 in the northeastern corner of the Athens Agora, in a building that has been identified as the Court of Justice.

The Tyrannicides *is an ideal group portrait of Harmodius and Aristogiton, two friends who killed the tyrant Hippias, son of Pisistratus.*

The bearded head of Aristogiton, which is missing in this copy, is a plaster cast from the copy conserved in the Vatican Museums.

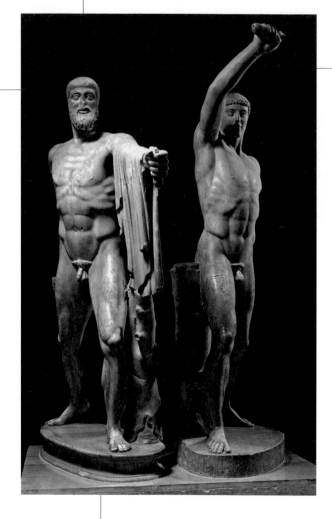

This composition was sculpted by Antenor in 509 BC, after Hippias had been murdered and democracy restored. It was carried to Persia by Xerses when Attica was invaded in 480 BC, and immediately replaced with a sculpture by Kritios and Nesiotes.

▲ *Tyrannicides* group, Roman copies of originals by Kritios and Nesiotes, from 476 BC. Naples, Museo Archeologico Nazionale.

Alexander the Great returned Antenor's sculpture to Athens but, strangely, apparently no copy was ever made. It is possible however, that in the Tyrannicides *created by Kritios and Nesiotes elements of the earlier version survive.*

In Athens, the people's assembly (ekklesia) *met on the Pnyx, a hill located a few minutes' walk from the Agora that had an enclosed, terraced slope and a stepped podium for the speakers.*

To encourage less wealthy citizens to participate, starting under Pericles the payment of an attendance bonus was introduced.

Participation in the assemblies called by the boule *was mandatory. Those who failed to participate were fined such strong penalties that sometimes poor citizens preferred not to register in the books of the citizens with the right to vote.*

▲ Athens, podium on the Pnyx.

"When written laws exist, / equal justice is meted out to poor and rich alike / … then the little man / who is in the right / can defeat the big man" (Euripides)

Justice and the Courts

The sources and documents that shed light on the practical aspects of the administration of justice in the Greek cities refer almost exclusively to Athens. The principal Athenian court was the Heliaea; located in the Agora, it tried all felonies with the exception of murder. The court that heard murder cases was the Areopagus, but there was also a court, the Delphinium, that heard murder cases with "justifying motives" or extenuating circumstances. Furthermore, a sort of religious tribunal that met in the *prytaneum* was charged with cleansing the city from the impurity of homicide when there was no guilty party or when the murder was not caused by a human hand. Public officials on the other hand, were tried by the *boule* and crimes against the state by the entire assembly.

To avoid the possibility of tainted jurors, the juries were very large and drawn by lots using a complex procedure. Because the laws enunciated general principles with no exact correspondence between specific crime and penalty, the outcome of a trial depended heavily on the oratorical skill of the parties. Since both accused and accuser personally took the stand, starting in the fifth century BC the logographers were born, attorney-like speechwriters. The jurors did not take sides during the trial, but as they left the court at the end of the proceeding, they voted for either acquittal or conviction.

▼ Bronze *pinakion* (card) of a justice, from the Athens Agora, first half of the 4th century BC. Athens, Agora Museum.

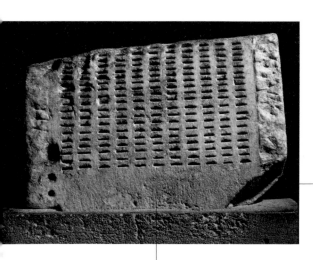

The kleroterion *was a stone tablet used in Athens to draw by lots the citizens who were called to be jurors for one day in the various court sections. Several kinds of* kleroteria *existed, with complex selection mechanisms that also probably varied, depending on the period of the year or the circumstances.*

In the first column were inserted the letters referring to the various court sections; in the other columns, the cards of the prospective jurors from each tribe.

The kleroterion *was used together with small bronze cards that had inscribed the first and family name, the* deme *to which he belonged, and the court section of each prospective juror.*

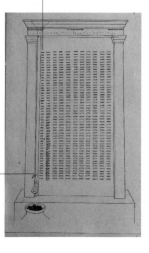

On the left of the kleroterion, *a mechanism consisting of a funnel linked to a bronze pipe pushed down, one by one, small white or black marbles. If the marble was white, the prospective jurors of the corresponding row were selected; if black, they were rejected.*

▲ ► Fragment of *kleroterion*, from the Athens Agora, and drawing reconstructing its use, 5th century BC. Athens, Agora Museum.

To cast their vote, the jurors initially used pebbles or shells that they dropped in one container if they voted to convict, or in another if they chose to acquit.

As the jurors went to the ballot box, they covered the disk so that no one could see whether the pin was full or empty. The discarded disk was collected in another container.

During the fourth century BC, to ensure voting secrecy, small bronze disks with a central pin began to be used: the pin was full for acquittal, pierced for conviction.

The ballot box consisted of two clay tiles set on the ground; it was found in a peristyle building in the northeastern corner of the Agora, where one of the court sections had its seat, and still contained some disks.

▲▶ Juror disk and ballot box, from the Athens Agora, 4th century BC. Athens, Agora Museum.

"Athenians ... were about to decide about an ostracism, a weapon that they like to use to strike at fame and power ... it soothes their envy more than their fear" (Plutarch)

Ostracism

Most likely introduced by Cleisthenes, ostracism became a law in Athens in the early part of the fifth century BC, when it was used for the first time against Hipparchus, a relative of the tyrant Pisistratus.

Ostracism was a ten-year exile imposed on the citizens whom the state reputed dangerous; in the legislators' intention, it was devised to defend democracy from the threat of a return to tyranny. Because it was used improperly by political factions, it was discarded already by the end of the fifth century, after being applied in only about ten cases. Once a year, the *boule* decided whether to proceed to ostracize someone. A citizens' general assembly was called and the name of the people to be ostracized written on clay shards (*ostraka*). If at least six thousand voters attended, the person whose name received the largest number of votes was sentenced to exile; he did not lose his civil rights, however, and his property was reinstated in full upon his return. In addition to Athens, forms of ostracism for limited periods of time also existed in other Greek cities and in colonies such as Argos, Megara, Miletus, and Syracuse.

Related entries
Cleisthenes, political institutions, Athens Agora

▼ *Ostrakon*, a graffito with the name of Themistocles, son of Neokles, from the Athens Agora, 5th century BC. Athens, Agora Museum.

"The Lydians ... were the first people that we have knowledge of, who minted gold and silver coins and first engaged in retail commerce" (Herodotus)

Mint and Coins

Until the seventh century BC, the ancient world had no coins and commerce was based on barter. The first coins appeared toward the end of the seventh century BC in Asia Minor, where Greek coastal colonies traded with the kingdom of Lydia; there, in a votive pit under the foundations of the Archaic temple of Artemis near Ephesus, archeologists uncovered a cache of coins made of electrum (a gold and silver alloy). For the first time in history, a warranty "seal" had been impressed on a piece of precious metal by the authority that minted it, thus informing the user of the office responsible for the weight and quality of the metal.

► Iron *obeloi* (skewers) from the Heraion of Argos, early 7th century BC. Athens, Numismatics Museum.

In Greece, coins came into use in the middle of the sixth century BC; the metal of choice was silver, which was plentiful and easy to use. Weight systems varied from city to city, though the name of the base unit did not: it was the drachma, divided into six obols. To explain the origin of these names, ancient historians theorize that the former is derived from *drax* (handful) and the second from *obelos* (skewer), apparently because before coins were invented, iron skewers used to roast meat served as money. A more likely explanation, however, is that the extension of the meaning was due to their use in religious sacrifices, where offers were quantified in number of skewers.

The small Artemision treasure was found in 1905 during excavations commissioned by the British Museum.

According to an agreement reached with the Turkish authorities, the vase containing the coins was taken to London, while the original coins went to the Istanbul Archaeological Museum.

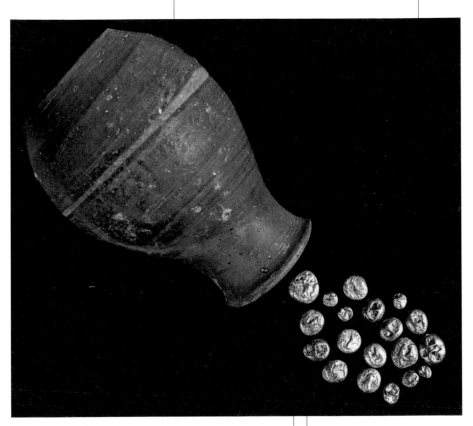

The minted coins were impressed on one side only and mostly stamped with figures of animals, especially the lion, probably a symbol of the king of Lydia.

The cache also included unfinished, unstamped coins with an irregular surface. All the coins however followed the same weight system.

▲ Coin treasure from the Artemision of Ephesus, ca. 600 BC. London, British Museum.

The first Greek coins were probably minted in Aegina toward the middle of the sixth century BC. The Aegina drachma weighed 6.30 grams; the stater, a di-drachma, was worth two drachmas.

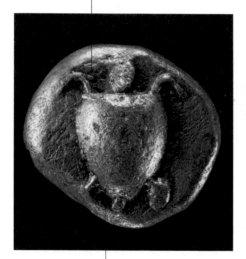

The city chose, as stamp for the right side of the coin, a marine turtle in relief.

The reverse of the coin had no figure, the design consisting in a square with partitions formed by the coining stamp.

▲ Silver stater, from Aegina, late 6th century BC. London, British Museum.

The first Athenian coins were probably introduced by the tyrant Pisistratus; they were stamped with different reliefs such as amphoras, wheels, astragali, shields, or horse figures.

Athenian coins were called "owls" from the stamp on the back. They were popular throughout the Mediterranean and remained substantially unchanged for about three hundred years except for minor variations in style or in the figures.

Coins with the head of Athena stamped on the face and the little owl, sacred to the goddess, on the back, were introduced in about 525–500 BC. In 480 BC, after the Persian defeat, Athena's helmet was decorated with a wreath of olive leaves.

▲ Athenian five-drachma coin, silver, ca. 480 BC. London, British Museum.

The Mint was a large rectangular building identified in the southeastern corner of the Agora, now partially covered by the Church of the Apostle Saints and a nymphaeum erected in the 2nd century AD.

The building, whose plan is not very clear, consisted of several rooms laid out around a central courtyard.

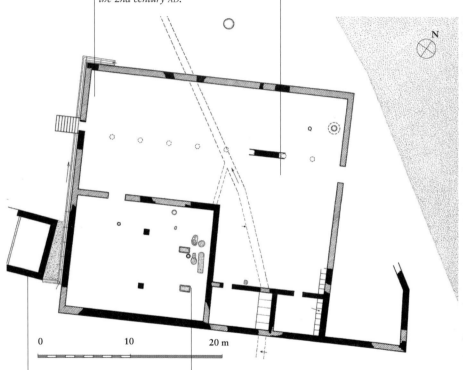

N

Nearby, a fifth-century BC inscription refers to coin issues, and one from the fourth century BC bears the names of the magistrates in charge of overseeing the Mint.

The possible identification of this building with one of the Athenian Mints is linked to the presence of several bronze planchets used to stamp coins. The building also held some furnaces and large water tanks.

▲ Plan of the Mint that stood in the Athenian Agora, ca. 400 BC (From McCamp II, 2003).

"These bold soldiers rush side by side into the thick fray / with spears and swords in the front line / some of them die to save the rest of them that follow" (Tyrtaeus)

The Army

In the Mycenaean age, the army was made up of aristocrats. The decisive role was played by noble warriors equipped with costly armor who raced onto the battlefield on chariots, clashing in a scattered pattern. The mass of common soldiers, armed haphazardly, did not count for much. Starting in the eighth century BC, a revolution in military science took place contemporaneous with the birth of the *polis*, as the values of civic solidarity that fostered the new democratic institutions were extended to the battlefield. The heart of the Greek army was now composed of hoplites, infantrymen in heavy armor who fought in tight formation—the phalanx—where each soldier was protected by his neighbor's shield (*hoplon*). The hoplites were flanked by the peltasts who wore a lighter armor and by the cavalry; the latter was used primarily for reconnaissance and pursuit, since the mountainous terrain and the lack of stirrups or saddles made it difficult for them to be involved in direct combat.

The draft system varied according to the laws of each city-state. All citizens were required to serve, but in critical times freemen like Sparta's Perioeci who had no civil rights were also drafted, as were slaves. The upper census classes supplied the cavalry and the heavy infantry which they armed themselves, while the light infantry drafted from the lower classes was fitted at the state's expense.

Related entries
Lycurgus, Cleisthenes, Themistocles, Pericles, fleet, sports, Sparta

▼ Statue pediment with a chariot led by charioteer and carrying a warrior, and hoplites on foot, from the walls of Athens, late 6th century BC. Athens, National Archaeological Museum.

On eighth century BC vases found in the Athenian necropolis of Dipylon, the warriors are always depicted with a unique type of shield known as the "Dipylon shield."

The "8"-shaped shield that protected the body down to the knees, had wide upper and lower sides and a narrow center.

The shape of the shield was probably derived from an ox skin sown onto a wooden frame, with the four hooves protruding from the corners; it is the typical shape of the large Mycenaean shields that protected the entire body.

▲ Krater 990 from Dipylon (detail), ca. 750 BC. Athens, National Archaeological Museum.

This statuette is characterized by a "Dipylon type" shield carried on the shoulders, of an even more bizarre and impractical shape than those depicted on the vases of the Athenian necropolis.

This warrior has no armor except for a wide metal belt that was perhaps used as protection over the regular tunic.

Probably this shield was no longer in use in the eighth or seventh century BC; this would explain why the artists exaggerated its shape since they no longer understood its origin; it was the memory of a Mycenaean shield that had become an attribute of the epic age heroes.

► Bronze statuette of a warrior, from Karditsa (Boeotia), 7th century BC. Athens, National Archaeological Museum.

The hoplon, *the round shield from which the heavy infantry, the hoplites, took their name, had an approximate 40-inch diameter and a slightly convex shape. It was made of wood with a reinforced bronze rim or, in some rare cases, sheathed entirely with bronze.*

The shield was equipped with a loop to secure it to the forearm, a leather belt fastened at the rim to hold it, and a shoulder strap.

Because the round shield only protected the body down to the thighs, sometimes hoplites wore greaves to protect knees and shins.

The greaves were made of thin bronze sheeting contoured to the shape of the leg so that they required no fastening; they were lined with fabric sewn to the small holes along the border.

▲▶ Bronze hoplite shield and greaves, from Olympia, late 7th century BC. Olympia, Archaeological Museum.

This Corinthian-type helmet, sometimes topped by a crest, was initially the most common model. Fashioned from a single sheet of hammered metal, it covered the head almost entirely from the collarbone up.

Because it narrowed the field of vision and covered the ears limiting hearing, during the fifth century BC this model was gradually replaced by regional variants such as the Ionic, Illyrian, and Calchidean helmets.

The jaw protectors projected forward and the nose cover left open only a T-shaped slit for eyes, nostrils and mouth.

The bronze bell-shaped cuirass, of which this is the earliest example that has survived, consisted of two parts with holes to lace them to each other along the sides.

The Greeks adopted this type of cuirass from other European populations. Perhaps because of the climate, metal-sheet armors were never used in the East.

▲ Corinthian-type helmet from Agia Paraskevi, ca. 500 BC. Thessalonica, Archaeological Museum.

► Back side of cuirass, from Olympia, late 7th century BC. Olympia, Archaeological Museum.

This is the only surviving illustration of the hoplite phalanx battle tactics: because the hoplon only protected the left side, the phalanx advanced in closed ranks so that each warrior was protected by the shield of the warrior on his right.

The defensive armor consisted in the Corinthian helmet, the bell-shaped cuirass, greaves, and shield; the offensive equipment was a raised spear ready to strike and a back-up spear held in the left hand.

The phalanx moved to the sound of the flute (aulos) while the orders to charge or to retreat were given by sharp trumpet blasts that even the hoplites, almost deaf on account of the helmets, could hear.

▲ Corinthian *oinochoe*, known as "Chigi olpe" (detail), from Veio, late 7th century BC. Rome, Museo Nazionale Etrusco Romano di Villa Giulia.

The soldier's equipment was completed by a high-crested Corinthian helmet, greaves, and a round shield in a traditional style.

Toward the end of the sixth century BC, the heavy bell-shaped cuirass was replaced by a new type of metal cuirass that was anatomically shaped, and by "composite" breastplates formed by several quilted layers of leather, linen and rope reinforced by bronze sheeting.

The composite breastplates were worn by fastening the buckles in front and passing the wide straps over the shoulder, tying their laces to the plate.

Below the waist the cuirass became a short skirt made of leather strips worn over the traditional soldier's chiton.

▲ Attic red-figure *kylix* by Douris (detail), *Warriors Dressing*, from Cerveteri, early 5th century BC. Vienna, Kunsthistorisches Museum.

The peltasts had no armor and instead of the helmet wore a leather cap.

The hoplite infantry was flanked by the light infantry known as peltasts. Like the hoplites, they took their name from their shield, the pelte, which had a moon crescent shape and was made of woven wicker covered with leather.

Starting in the sixth century BC, the Greek army began to use slingmen and archers, for the most part Scythian mercenaries who, like other Steppes tribes, were highly skilled in shooting arrows from a galloping horse.

The peltasts were equipped with javelin and sometimes the sword, plus a long spear.

The Scythian archers had no metal armor or helmet, only quilted protective garments and a leather head covering.

The Scythians stored their thin, short-pointed arrows in a large quiver where they also kept their bow.

▲ Attic red-figure *kylix* (detail), *Peltast*, end of the 6th century BC. Leipzig, Antikenmuseum der Universität.

▶ Attic red-figure *kylix* by Oltos (detail), *Scythian Archer*, 525–500 BC. Paris, Musée du Louvre.

The double-curved bow required extensive training and unusual skills even for just stringing it and pulling it taut.

"Should a war later break out, I know that they will force you to pay for fitting out the triremes and to pay taxes so high that they might not be easy to bear" (Xenophon)

The Fleet

In ancient Mycenae, the same ships were used in times of peace and for war, also because their main use in warfare was to ferry troops. Starting in the Geometric age, warships proper were born: the shape became narrower and more pointed, allowing for higher speed, the prow was fitted with bow rams to strike at the keel of enemy ships, and the number of oarsmen was increased and arranged on several levels, eliminating wind propulsion during attacks. Warships were perfected in the seventh century BC, when the trireme, which probably originated in Corinth, first appeared. With a length of one hundred to one hundred and twenty feet, equipped with one hundred and seventy rowers arranged on three levels and twenty navy soldiers (*epibatai*), some sailors to work the sails, and the officers (the *trierarch*—the ship's commander, the *proreus* who issued course instructions from the prow, and the steersman), the trireme remained the most advanced warship until the end of the fourth century BC, when ships with five levels of oarsmen began to appear.

Organization and management of the fleet was entrusted to magistrates elected for this purpose, the *neoroi*, who drew up statements of account, kept inventories of all the triremes docked in the military ports, and were in charge of keeping them at full efficiency. Each commander had to fit out his ship and provide a trained crew at his own expense and was responsible for damage to the ship.

Related entries
Themistocles, army, roads and transportation

▼ Miniature clay merchant ship, from Amatunte (Cyprus), 9th–8th century BC. London, British Museum.

The two warships are depicted
navigating with unfurled sails;
both are equipped with a
powerful rostrum in the shape
of a wild boar's head and the
stern ending in a swan figure.

Seated at the stern, the
steersman moves the two
directional oars. The ladder
at his back was used in
landing and perhaps also
to beach the ships.

The rowers are not visible;
the portholes along the side
suggest two levels of rowers,
with the lower one just
above the waterline.

▶ Attic black-figure *kylix* by
Nikosthenes (detail), *Warships*,
from Vulci, 530–520 BC. Paris,
Musée du Louvre.

Atop the forecastle, behind a rail, stands the proreus, *the prow officer. Because the ship had no deck or bridge, supplies were probably stowed under the forecastle's platform.*

This scene depicts what could be a pirate warship attacking a merchant ship, probably to board it instead of sinking it.

The warship is recognizable by the narrow, pointed hull, the prow spur used to strike enemy ships and sink them, and the mixed propulsion by sail and oar.

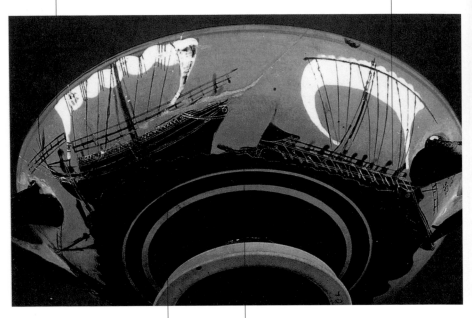

Merchant ships had tall hulls with probably a bridge and a covered deck, a trellised bulwark and wider sails. The steersman sat astern with the directional oars.

In military attacks where the aim was to sink the enemy, the ships used only rowers, for after piercing the enemy ship with the rostrum, they had to reverse course in order to let the water fill the leak.

▲ Attic *kylix* (detail), *Warship and Cargo Ship*, ca. 510 BC. London, British Museum.

The tangle of oars along the side of the ship suggests
that this was a trireme. To increase the ship's speed
without lengthening it too much (which would make
the hull unstable), the oarsmen were arranged on
three superimposed rows.

The rowers in the two lower rows
moved the oars through rowing
portholes that were open in the
ship's side and arranged in staggered
rows so that the paddles did not
knock against each other.

The oars had different lengths: the
oarsmen on the upper row used the
longest ones, those on the lowest
the shortest ones.

▲ Bas-relief with trireme and
oarsmen, late 5th century BC.
Athens, Acropolis Museum.

Divinities and Religion

◄Votive relief, *Athena Pensive*,
ca. 460 BC. Athens, Acropolis
Museum.

*"Zeus of the loud thunder holds the purpose of all that exists
arranging it as he pleases ... we live like beasts, ignoring how
the god will bring each thing to conclusion" (Semonides)*

Zeus and Hera

Related entries
Phidias, Poseidon,
Athens Acropolis,
Olympia

The highest divinity in the Greek pantheon, Zeus, belongs to the second generation of gods. The son of the Titan Cronus and of Rhea, he was born in Crete and hidden from his father who was wont to swallow his own children fearing that one of them might dethrone him. Once he became adult, Zeus forced his father to bring up the children he had swallowed and with help from the Cyclopes defeated him. He then divided the kingdom with his brothers assigning the sky to himself, the sea to Poseidon and the netherworld to Hades.

Originally, Zeus was the god of the bright sky, of atmospheric phenomena and of mountaintops, as we can deduce from his attribute, the thunderbolt, from the epithet "gatherer of clouds" that identifies him in the Homeric poems, and from the altitude of some of the shrines dedicated to him. As the arranger of the cosmos, his powers also extended to keeping order and to justice, social hierarchy, and political institutions. He was worshiped as the Agoraios (protector of assemblies) in many a city square, and as Polieus (defender of the *polis*) on acropolises.

▶ Bronze statuette,
*Zeus Hurling a
Thunderbolt,*
from Dodona,
ca. 470 BC. Berlin,
Antikensammlung.

Notwithstanding his many loves, both divine and human, and his numerous children, with his sister and bride, Hera, Zeus represents the divine couple by definition, the heavenly archetype of "just marriage." In fact, Hera is the custodian goddess of the bonds of matrimony and of family institutions, celebrated in the wedding month in ceremonies that staged representations of her sacred union (*hieros gamos*) with Zeus.

Ganymedes, a young Trojan prince, was considered the handsomest of all mortals. For this reason Zeus took a fancy to him and kidnapped him, taking him to Mount Olympus where he was granted eternal youth and became the cupbearer of the gods.

The cock Ganymedes holds in his right hand was a traditional courting gift that Greek men gave to their young male lovers.

Zeus, here appearing in human form, is running holding in the right hand a knotty club and in the left Ganymedes. According to another version of the myth that became popular starting in the fourth century BC, to kidnap the youth Zeus transformed himself into an eagle.

▲ Polychrome terracotta, *Zeus and Ganymedes*, from Olympia, ca. 470 BC. Olympia, Archaeological Museum.

This terracotta composition was reconstructed in the nineteen-seventies from fragments found during about eighty years of excavations, from 1878 to 1952.

This twenty-inch marble head crowned by a polos with lush foliage belonged to a cult statue that was found in the cell of an archaic temple dedicated to Hera. It is one of the very few examples that have survived of this type of statue.

This statue depicts Hera seated on a throne; a statue of Zeus stood at her side, wearing a helmet and a shield.

As was often the case with archaic cult statues, the head sat atop a barely sketched out body made of wood that was covered with fabric clothes and various ornaments.

▲ Colossal head of a cult statue from the temple of Hera at Olympia, 600–580 BC. Olympia, Archaeological Museum.

According to Pausanias who was a witness, every four years sixteen women wove a new peplum for the goddess to celebrate her festival, the Heraea.

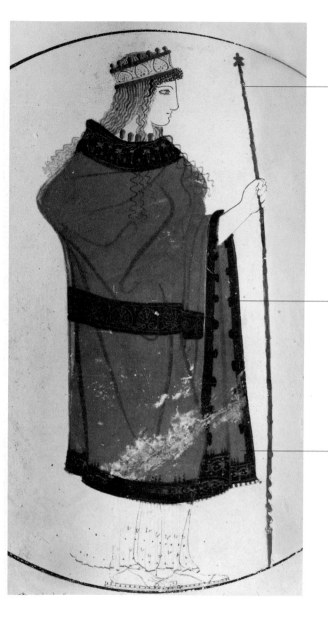

According to Greek mythology, Hera was a demanding wife ready to assert her legitimate spousal rights; she was also irascible and violent and showed little motherly affection. Thus this goddess embodied the legal aspect of marriage, but was certainly not an example to be imitated by mortal women.

Married Greek women took inspiration from Hera only when defending their marriage rights; at the same time, they had to be lovers like Aphrodite and mothers like Demeter.

The goddess is covered in a wide cloak; under it, the densely pleated chiton is visible; she wears a crown and carries a scepter, both symbols of royalty.

▲ Attic *kylix* with a white background by the Sabourov Painter (detail), *Hera Wearing a Mantle*, 470–450 BC. Munich, Antikensammlung.

Turning toward her spouse, Hera is caught raising her veil. This gesture, a recurring one in Greek iconography, was typical of married women and symbolized the union legitimized by marriage.

Hera was often represented seated on a throne and equal in dignity to Zeus, not because she was his wife, but because they were also brother and sister and her birth was as noble as her husband's.

One of the appellations frequently used for the goddess was Teleia, i.e. "perfect," a specific reference to the fullness of legal marriage, which was the goal of all women.

▲ Eastern Parthenon frieze, *Zeus and Hera*, 447–432 BC. London, British Museum.

▶ Attic red-figure krater by the Syriskos Painter, *Poseidon Enthroned with His Son Theseus and a Nereid*, from Agrigento, 480-470 BC. Paris, Cabinet des Médailles.

"A sanctuary called Erechtheum stands on this acropolis ... an olive tree and sea water is there ... Poseidon and Athena vying for dominion over the country placed them there to prove their power" (Herodotus)

Poseidon

Linked to water, the sea in particular that became his kingdom after his father Cronus was defeated, to the Greeks Poseidon was also the god of earthquakes and seaquakes which he caused with a strike of the trident, his most characteristic attribute. A brother of Zeus, like Hera, Hestia, Demeter, and Hades, he had been devoured by their father and freed by Zeus who had forced Cronus to bring up the children hidden in his stomach.

As with Zeus, numerous love affairs were attributed to Poseidon, which he consummated through metamorphoses and kidnappings; divine creatures and heroes such as the mythical Theseus were born from these couplings, depending on whether the beloved was a goddess or a plain mortal. Although Poseidon is not a frequent subject in art, including vases, he was worshiped throughout Greece; his sanctuaries were located in the countryside where they could be reached by sea also, and were preferably set on headlands, islands, or isthmuses, where the elements of earth and water, of which he is lord, come patently in contact.

The leading cult site of this god was in Isthmia. Already active in the eighth century BC, it was born as a shrine of Corinth outside the city walls but gradually became Pan-Hellenic thanks to its location on the road linking northern Greece and the Peloponnesus and because it could be reached by sea from both the Saronic and the Corinth gulfs. From the end of the sixth century BC, competitions comparable to the Olympian Games were held there.

Related entries
Zeus and Hera, Demeter and Persephone, sports, Athens Agora, Olympia

The Cape Sunium promontory lies at the southeastern tip of Attica, and was therefore an important navigation point in antiquity.

Cult activity at this site probably dates back to the Mycenaean age; some of the earliest kouroi *were dedicated to the sea god in this very ancient shrine, in the years between 625 and 600 BC.*

This Classical Age temple was erected on the site of an older, Late Archaic temple that stood incomplete after it was destroyed by the Persians in 480 BC while still under construction.

This peripteral Doric temple, dating to the middle of the fifth century BC, was believed to be the work of the same architects who erected the temple of Hephaestus in the Athens Agora, the Nemesis temple at Rhamnous, and the temple to Ares in the Acharnae deme.

The temple to Poseidon rose on the highest point in a shrine area which one entered through a monumental entrance, with porticoes to shelter the pilgrims. During the Peloponnesian war, the promontory was surrounded by fortified walls that were successively restored until the middle of the third century BC.

▲ Temple to Poseidon on Cape Sunium, 450–440 BC.

The god is about to throw an object, now lost, with his right hand. The position of the fingers, weighing as they do the weapon to gauge the strike, seems more adapted to the trident than a thunderbolt, which is usually held with the entire hand.

This bronze statue was found in 1928 in the sea around Cape Artemisium, in Euboea. It was part of a cargo of Greek sculptures on a merchant ship that sank there between the end of the first century BC and the beginning of the following century.

Poseidon's iconography is very similar to that of Zeus, both when depicted sitting on a throne or in the act of throwing a thunderbolt or the trident. Without any identifying attributes, differentiating between the two gods is often difficult.

▲ Bronze statue of Poseidon from Cape Artemisium, 460 BC. Athens, National Archaeological Museum.

"[Zeus] generated bright-eyed Athena from his head, / a tremendous stirrer of turmoil, the undefeated leader of armies, / a mistress who loves uproar, wars, and combat" (Hesiod)

Athena

Related entries
Phidias, Zeus and
Hera, Ares, Heracles,
female religiosity,
Athens Acropolis,
Epidaurus, Sparta

As reflected in her many, varied epithets, Athena is a multi-faceted figure. Sprung from the skull of her father, Zeus, already fully armed, she is first of all the virgin warrior (Parthenos, Promachos) who battles the Giants, fights alongside Heracles in his adventures and actively participates in several episodes of the siege of Troy, exercising cunning and tactical skill against the bloody frenzy of Ares, the god of war.

As Polias, guardian of the city and its institutions, Athena is a peaceful deity, worshiped on the acropolises of Athens and many other cities such as Sparta, Argos, and Epidaurus. Finally, her attribute of Ergane, industrious, marks her as the guardian of woodworking, shipbuilding, horse training, spinning, weaving, and the arts and crafts in general. Having introduced the cultivation of the olive tree to Greece in a contest that she won against Poseidon for dominion over Attica, she is also a tutelary deity of agriculture.

Depicted fully armed, the goddess Athena was also known as Pallas, the "Palladium" being a rough wooden statuette that apparently Athena herself had carved in memory of her comrade in arms Pallas, whom Zeus had killed by mistake. The city that held the Palladium was guaranteed to be invincible; for this reason the Greeks stole it from the temple of Athena at Troy and subsequently many cities boasted of possessing it.

▶ Bronze statuette,
*Athena with Little
Owl*, known as the
Elgin Athena, ca. 450
BC. New York,
Metropolitan
Museum of Art.

Athena was born an adult and fully armed with spear, helmet, shield with the Gorgon's head in the center, and the aegis, a sort of protective leather cuirass.

Hephaestus, equipped with a double axe, has just struck open Zeus's skull, allowing Athena to be born. As a reward, he is given the goddess in marriage but having been brought to the nuptial chamber, Athena, who has always been represented as a virgin maiden, disappears.

The appellation of Pallas, referring to the armed goddess, is of uncertain origin. According to one, perhaps late, version of the myth, the name refers not to the goddess but to a sort of warrior "double," the virgin daughter of Triton who was her mate in military training.

According to Greek mythology, Athena is the daughter of Zeus and of his first wife Metis ("cunning"). Although Zeus, fearing a prediction that the child born of this union would become a king of gods and men, had swallowed a pregnant Metis, Athena was born nevertheless, delivered from her father's skull.

▲ Attic red-figure *pelike* by the Painter of Athena's Birth (detail), eponymous vase, from Vulci, ca. 450 BC. London, British Museum.

Athena here wears the Corinthian helmet but her mantle is knotted at the waist, in craftsman fashion; she is shaping the clay statue of a horse on a pedestal.

Among the activities placed under Athena's protection was also horse care and training; the goddess herself was believed to have introduced the bridle.

Originally only the patroness of spinning and weaving, Athena gradually became the guardian deity of all crafts and was credited with inventing many tools including the potter's wheel and the shuttle.

A mass of clay lies at the feet of the goddess; she takes pieces from it, adding them gradually to the statue.

▲ Attic red-figure *oinochoe* from the Berlin Group 2415 (detail), *Athena Shaping an Equine Statue*, from Capua, ca. 470 BC. Berlin, Antikensammlung.

"Serious ailments / he cures ... the cithara he gave to man and gives / to those who ask, the powerful Muse; / ... she brings about / justice in the hearts and rules over / the prophetic penetralia" (Pindar)

Apollo

Apollo is the son of Zeus and Leto and the twin brother of Artemis. While still pregnant, Leto was persecuted by a jealous Hera who ordered that no place on dry land shelter her when her time to give birth came. Hence the twins were born on a moving island which, as a reward, was anchored to the bottom of the sea. Because in the *Iliad* Apollo is the guardian god of Troy, scholars surmise that the cult may have originated in Asia Minor.

In any case, the manifold skills of this god suggest that he assimilated, by way of syncretism, the powers of other deities; for at the same time he is a pastoral, agrarian god, the guardian of flock and harvest; a warring, exterminating god who kills from afar with bow and arrow; a redeeming divinity who can lift man from the evils of religious impurity; a god who protects civilization from barbarism; the inspirer of the laws and the protector of contracts and oaths; a patron of music and the bestower of poetic inspiration.

After killing the snake Python and taking possession of the Delphi oracle, Apollo became the main oracular deity in Greece; as such, his pronouncements could affect the religious and political life of the entire country, and he was the only god who could issue the rules for ritual purification from crimes and sacrilege.

Related entries
Praxiteles, Zeus and Hera, Artemis, divination, Delphi, Olympia, Delos

▼ Silver coin of the Delphic Amphictyony, *Apollo seated on the omphalos*, 336 BC. Athens, Numismatics Museum.

This statuette, dedicatetd in a shrine, is one of the earliest surviving artifacts that undoubtedly portray Apollo.

The triangular face with large eyes and the braids falling on the shoulder already foreshadow the later "Daedalic" art.

The complex composition of this statue with the triangular bust counterposed to the trunk-like neck is still characteristic of Geometric art, but the rendering of the different parts of the body are a first attempt to follow the anatomy.

The inscription carved on the legs reads: "Mantiklos offers me as a tithe to the Striker from Afar with the Silver Bow [Apollo]; do you, oh Phoebus, grant me good luck in return..."

▲ Bronze statuette, *Mantiklos Apollo*, from Thebes, 700–680 BC. Boston, Museum of Fine Arts.

This statue was discovered in 1959 during channeling and dredging work in the Piraeus, in a cache with other bronze and marble statues that were probably a Roman ship's cargo that had sunk before it left the port.

Perhaps in his right hand, palm facing up, the god held a cup that was about to be filled.

The identification of this statue with Apollo is given primarily by the broken cylindrical object the statue is holding in the left hand, widely understood to be part of a bow.

The Piraeus Apollo is totally hollow inside, and is the earliest statue that has come down to us to have been cast with the "lost wax" technique.

▲ *Piraeus Apollo*, bronze statue, 520–510 BC. Athens, National Archaeological Museum.

Of all the god's attributes, this representation exalts Apollo as the guardian of order and the embodiment of rationality overcoming chaos.

The western pediment of the temple of Zeus depicted the struggle between Lapiths and Centaurs; the latter had crashed Pirithous's wedding feast to kidnap the bride. The characters, placed in groups of two or three to the left and right of Apollo, are shown in a frenzy of movements, their faces distorted and contracted by the fight.

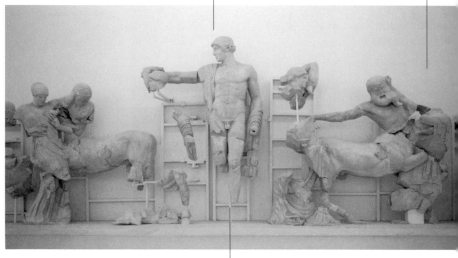

Apollo is at the center, perfectly still, his right arm extended in a gesture that seems to imperiously put an end to the fight.

▲ Western pediment of the Temple of Zeus at Olympia, *Apollo and the Centaur*, ca. 460 BC. Olympia, Archaeological Museum.

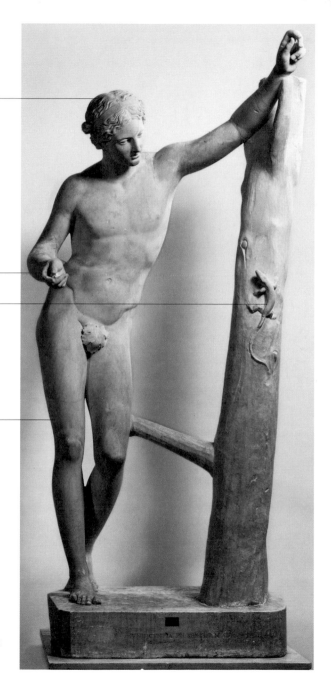

Apollo "the Lizard Slayer" is a well-known statuary type thanks to the survival of about twenty copies. The original is attributed to Praxiteles who made the statue on commission from a city in Asia Minor.

The god most likely held a small arrow in his right hand and was about to strike the lizard almost playfully.

Apollo is here depicted as an adolescent, resting gently on a tree trunk on which the lizard is climbing.

Among Apollo's attributes were also Alexikakos and Epikourios—rescuer from disease and helper—for which reason people prayed to him in times of contagion and epidemics. This statue most likely represented this aspect of the god; in keeping with the light touch typical of Praxiteles, disease is symbolized by the small, harmless reptile.

▶ *Apollo Sauroktonos* (the Lizard Slayer), Roman copy of an original by Praxiteles from ca. 360 BC. Vatican City, Musei Vaticani.

"She even upset the common sense of thundering Zeus / whose power towers over all, the most honored of the gods, / and yet, at her bidding … consorted he with mortal women" (Hymn to Aphrodite)

Aphrodite and Eros

Related entries
Praxiteles, Zeus and
Hera, Hermes

▼ White-background
Attic kylix by the
Lyandros Painter
(detail), *Aphrodite
with Erotes*, from
Cesa, 460 BC. Florence,
Museo Archeologico.

Aphrodite, the goddess of love, beauty, and fertility, was a powerful deity in Greek religion. According to Hesiod, she was one of the generating principles of the cosmos who oversaw the continuity of life on earth, but could also upset the equilibrium of both gods and men; for this reason, she often quarreled with Hera, the guardian of conjugal love. Because she ensured births, thus guaranteeing the survival of the *polis*, in addition to being worshiped at three vast shrines outside the city, such as the central one on the island of Cyprus, she was also worshiped inside city walls, on acropolises next to the agoras.

Even Eros, whom a widespread tradition describes as the son of Aphrodite and Hermes, was originally a feared divinity, worshiped in specific places dedicated to him; it was his prerogative to shoot love arrows from his bow against gods, men, and animals alike. Starting in the Classical age his iconography gradually changed to that of a graceful boy, Aphrodite's child servant, or was multiplied into a swarm of mischievous *putti* playing at the feet of the goddess. His cult gradually lost importance but came back in the Hellenistic age in groups close to Orphism that revived the concept of Eros as a cosmic force born of the primordial, life-generating egg.

The theme of the Judgment of Paris is the central episode of the myth of Aphrodite and was a popular vase-decorating subject.

During the wedding of Peleus and Thetis, attended by all the gods, Eris, the goddess of discord, threw a gold apple into the crowd of guests intending it for the most beautiful goddess, thus stirring up a contest among Aphrodite, Hera, and Athena.

Paris, a Trojan prince, son of Priamus and Hecuba, was exposed to the elements at birth, atop Mount Ida, because a prophecy had foretold that he would one day cause the destruction of Troy. There he was found and raised by shepherds.

Because Zeus had ordered an end to the quarrel, Hermes took the three goddesses atop Mount Ida, where the handsome Paris would award the beauty prize to one of them.

Aphrodite, depicted as usual with a retinue of erotes, was awarded the golden apple by Paris; in exchange, she granted him the love of Helen of Sparta, thus causing the Trojan war.

▲ Attic red-figure *kylix* by Macron (detail), *The Judgment of Paris*, from Vulci, 500–485 BC. Berlin, Antikensammlung.

Over twenty copies of this statuary type have survived; it is generally identified as the Aphrodite Sosandra *(savior of mankind), a work of Calamis. The author Lucian described the smile of this veiled statue as "pure and hallowed."*

This chaste representation of the goddess, totally shrouded by a heavy, shape-hiding mantle that covers all her body, is unusual with respect both to previous iconographic tradition and later art.

In the vase repertory, the prevailing image of Aphrodite portrays her at the mirror busy adorning herself, assisted by a train of erotes; *after Praxiteles made the* Cnidian Aphrodite, *she was often represented naked or semi-naked.*

▶ *Aphrodite Sosandra*, Roman copy of an original by Calamis from 470–460 BC, from the Baths of Baia. Naples, Museo Nazionale.

"As the huntress Diana goes forth upon the mountains ... to hunt wild boars or deer ... [she] stands a full head taller ... and eclipses the loveliest of the wood-nymphs." (Homer, Odyssey, VI)

Artemis

Artemis, daughter of Zeus and Leto and sister to Apollo, is a divinity in whom extremely ancient, pre-Greek religious elements survive. In the Archaic age she was Potnia Theron, the mistress of animals, and was often represented with wings or on mountaintops, holding one or two wild animals in her hands. In the Classical era her iconography changed and her youth was exalted along with her passion for the hunt and her skill with the bow. Still, a number of attributes from her earlier incarnation as a nature and fertility goddess survived, for while she is an untouchable virgin, she is also the guardian of women in childbirth, to whom new mothers offer their childbirth linens, and of wet-nurses, for mothers bring their newborns to her, that she may protect their growth.

Her shrines, such as Brauron's near Athens or that of Artemis Orthia near Sparta, were usually located near cities or close to springs, rivers, or marshes, on mountains or by the sea. In fact, although over the centuries Artemis lost part of her attributes of wilderness goddess, she did guard the boundaries between nature and civilization mediating between the two realms and punishing man's excesses against nature. Hence her role as an educator of boys, their escort in the passage from the wildness of childhood to entry into civic life, to whom the boys dedicated their toys upon leaving puberty.

Related entries
Zeus and Hera,
Apollo, female
religiosity, Sparta

▼ Volute krater by
Ergotimos and Kleitias,
known as the "François
Vase" (detail), *Artemis
Mistress of Animals*,
from Chiusi, ca. 570
BC. Florence, Museo
Archeologico.

Her bow taut and ready, Artemis is about to shoot the arrow that will strike a mortal blow to Actaeon.

The hunter Actaeon had offended Artemis by daring to gaze at her as she was bathing naked in a spring. The goddess turned him into a deer and sent his dogs into a frenzy: not recognizing him, they tore him to pieces.

In Greek mythology, Artemis is portrayed as a ruthless, vindictive deity whose rage fells many victims. Mindful of the death of Actaeon and the giant Orion who had been punished for killing too much game, Greek hunters never failed to honor Artemis, dedicating to her votive gifts to propitiate her for a successful hunt.

In vase decorations, Actaeon is often portrayed with his human features, to make the myth more easily identifiable and distinguish it from a regular hunting scene.

▲ Attic red-figure krater by the Pan Painter, *Death of Actaeon*, ca. 470 BC. Boston, Museum of Fine Arts.

"Do not come whining here, Sir Facing-both-ways ... for you always fight and make mischief. You have the intolerable and stubborn spirit of your mother Hera ..." (Homer, The Iliad, *V)*

Ares

Ares, son of Zeus and Hera, was the Greek god of war par excellence. Unlike tales of other warrior gods who display wisdom and tactical intelligence in battle, the myths are somewhat hostile toward Ares: he is a stormy, litigious god, so blinded by his bellicose frenzy as to be sometimes defeated even by mortals. He is rarely invoked by epic heroes or by everyday soldiers, who consider themselves his slaves rather than his protegés or emulators. The negative connotation of this deity also extends to the demons that accompany him, born of his adulterous affair with Aphrodite: Eris (discord), Deimos (terror), and Phobos (fear).

The cult of Ares, which probably originated in Thrace, was only moderately active in Greece with the exception of Sparta and Thebes. Still, the hill where the Areopagus tribunal stood was dedicated to him, the name being derived from Ares, for that was the place where the god himself had been tried by a divine jury and acquitted of having killed Halirrhothius, a hero son of Poseidon whom he had caught raping his own daughter Alcippe. This god's unpopularity is also seen in the rarity of artifacts that portray him: when they do, it is as a regular hoplite with no particular divine attributes.

Related entries
Zeus and Hera,
Poseidon, Athens
Agora, Sparta

▼ Volute krater by
Ergotimos and Kleitias,
known as the
"François Vase"
(detail), *Ares,* from
Chiusi, ca. 570 BC.
Florence, Museo
Archeologico.

Dressed in a chiton and with her head veiled, Aphrodite carries an oinochoe *in her right hand from which she pours wine into a cup that Ares is offering her.*

Aphrodite's gesture of raising her veil in the presence of Ares symbolizes their union, which was adulterous since the goddess war married to Hephaestus.

This representation of Ares is probably derived from a cult statue, the work of Alcamenes, that stood in the temple of Acharnae, near Athens, one of the few places were Ares was actually worshiped. This type of statuary has traditionally been identified as the "Borghese Ares" which is at the Louvre.

Ares is wearing greaves and a body-hugging cuirass over a short *chitoniskos; the shield is resting by his side.*

The worshiper, here represented in a smaller scale, seems to witness the scene, though in reality he is the one offering the libation.

▲ Attic votive relief with a cult scene of Ares and Aphrodite, late 5th to early 4th century BC. Paris, Musée du Louvre.

The temple stood in the center of the Agora where it had been moved at the time of the Roman Emperor Augustus by the Acharnae deme, where it originally stood. It was dismantled piece by piece and reassembled.

The phenomenon of the "wandering temples" is typical of the Roman imperial age, when classical buildings were moved into cities from abandoned Attic villages, perhaps to be used to worship the deified emperors.

While the foundations were built in the early Roman Empire, the architectural blocks are from 475 to 500 BC and have markings made by the Roman masons to facilitate their reassembly.

This temple is a Doric peripterum and was originally decorated with pediment sculptures and acroteriums very similar to the Hephaesteion, perhaps the work of the same architect.

▲ Temple of Ares, Athens Agora.

"You rascal, you heart is full of tricks; ... / For this shall be your honor, among the already blessed Gods, / to be known for all times as the king of knaves" (Hymn to Hermes)

Hermes

The child of Zeus's secret liaison with the nymph Maia, Hermes is an anomalous divinity, a unique blend of vices that are more human than divine; though he possesses no great powers, he has a manifold array of skills. On the day of his birth, in a display of extraordinary technical skills he rose from his crib, found a turtle, emptied it and built the first lyre with it. Later, on the Pieria mountains he stole fifty cows from Apollo's herds, was the first ever to light a fire and show how it is done, and sacrificed two heads of cattle to the gods, thus inventing a way of placating their wrath and founding the ritual of sacrifice.

When his brother Apollo discovered the theft, he protested his innocence and successfully bartered the lyre for the cows, befriending

Apollo who gave him the gift of the caduceus, the staff he had used to lead his herds. This staff becomes Hermes' principal attribute, a symbol at once of his prerogative as herald of the gods and as the guardian god of shepherding. A thief and a cheat, and therefore the lord of theft and of perjury, Hermes was also worshiped in the gymnasia as an example to boys for his intelligence and eloquence. His speed in taking advantage of situations and his physical speed make him the guardian and guide of travel, including passage to the other world, and the messenger of the gods, while his quick bartering and negotiating skills make him the god of commerce and merchants. But he is also the mediator between the human and the divine sphere.

► Bronze statuette of Hermes Criophorus (bearer of a sacrificial ram), 520–510 BC. Boston, Museum of Fine Arts.

The guardian god of journeys, Hermes is dressed in typical traveling garb with the petasos on his head to protect him from the sun and inclement weather and a mantle wrapped around him and fastened on the right shoulder.

This statuette depicts Hermes in his most characteristic iconography, one that will be adopted unchanged for the Roman god Mercury.

The leather purse filled with coins characterizes Hermes as the god of trade and at the same time the patron god of thieves and swindlers.

In his left hand the god holds the caduceus, a gift he had received from Apollo and the typical staff of shepherds and heralds, whose guardian he was; the top of the staff, ending in two snakes that symbolize the netherworld, suggests his role as an escort of the souls into Hades. The two outspread wings that sometimes decorate the sandals or the petasos symbolize his speed and his role as messenger of the gods.

▲ Bronze statuette of Hermes with caduceus and money purse, 4th century BC. Paris, Musée du Louvre.

This marble lekythos, used to mark a grave, reproduces the shape of the more common terracotta lekythoi, offerings that were placed full of scented salves on top of tombs.

Myrrhine, the young girl whose name is inscribed above her figure, is depicted crossing the river Acheron escorted by Hermes who holds her by the hand.

In the left corner are the grieving parents taking leave of the deceased.

The guardian god of travel and of passages also filled the role of Psychopomp, the guide who accompanied the souls in their last journey to the netherworld. The chlamys, a short mantle worn by travelers, and the winged sandals identify him immediately.

▲ Marble *lekythos* with relief, *Hermes Psychopomp*, from Athens, ca. 420 BC. Athens, National Archaeological Museum.

The god Hermes, here naked, carries the chlamys on his left arm and wears a winged petasos on his head, a characteristic attribute.

The oratorical gesture of the right hand seems to identify him with the god of eloquence worshiped in gymnasia as a role model for boys.

Algardi, who restored this statue in 1631, added the caduceus in the right hand and the coin purse in the left, thus mitigating the statue's oratorical pose; they were removed in the early nineteen-hundreds. Determining whether these attributes were actually part of the original Greek statue (some scholars believe it to be an early work of Phidias) is not easy.

▲ *Hermes Logios*, Roman copy of an Attic original from the mid–5th century BC, from the Boncompagni Ludovisi Collection. Rome, Museo Nazionale Romano di Palazzo Altemps.

The priest overseeing the sacrifice is drinking from a cup and pours the wine on the altar.

A young servant carries on the palm of his right hand the kanoun, *a ritual basket containing the sacrificial tools and the cereal grains to be sprinkled on the altar. The second helper is roasting the victim's meat on the fire, using a long skewer.*

The sacrifice takes place before a herm, a four-cornered pillar topped by the half-length portrait of the god complete with a large phallic symbol.

Herms are the most ancient representations of Hermes, from whom they take their name. Originally they were imageless and sometimes consisted of just a stone or small stone piles placed at the border of fields or at crossroads to place them under the guardianship of the god who protected property, boundaries, thresholds, and passages.

In the Classical age, the herms dedicated to Hermes Agoraios and Propylaios became popular. They were set at the entrance of agoras or near monumental propylaea (temple gates). Over time, the word "herm" was applied to the half-length statues of any deity.

▲ Attic red-figure krater by the Pan Painter (detail), *Sacrifice Before a Herm*, from Cuma, ca. 460 BC. Naples, Museo Archeologico Nazionale.

"Sacred to Asclepius are different kinds of snakes, including yellowish ones that are harmless to man and are found only in the region of Epidaurus" (Pausanias)

Asclepius

According to the myth, Asclepius was not initially a god but a hero, a son of Apollo and Princess Coronis. Saved from the funeral pyre of his mother who had been killed while Asclepius was still in her womb by Apollo whom she had betrayed, the child was raised by Chiron, a centaur: from him Asclepius learned medicine and surgery. He became so skilled that he could revive the dead, and for this reason Zeus killed him with a thunderbolt. However, Apollo requested that instead of being plunged into Hades, Asclepius be transformed into Ophiucus, the Serpent Bearer constellation; thus he began to be worshiped as a god.

The first cult site was a cave in Tricca, Thessaly; from there it spread to Epidaurus that became the center of the cult; to Kos, where the Asclepiadae who were believed to be descendants of the god and were devoted to medicine practiced; to Athens, to Corinth, and throughout the Hellenic world.

Usually, his sanctuaries were located outside of cities, in healthy, pleasant locales where water was present and where the pilgrims traveled in search of healing. After a period of purification based on fasting and baths, the cure was done by "incubation": at night, the pilgrims slept in the shrine's dormitories where the god appeared to them in a dream and either healed them or suggested a therapy through a vision that was interpreted by the priests. As they left, the patients left ex-votos as a sign of gratitude, and the story of the healing was carefully recorded on stone tablets.

Related entries
Zeus and Hera, Apollo, offerings and ex-votos, medicine, Epidaurus

▼ Marble head of the god Asclepius, Roman copy of a Greek original from the 4th century BC, from Palatine Hill, Rome. Rome, Museo Antiquario del Palatino.

The Piraeus, where this relief was found, was the seat of an important shrine to Asclepius in the fourth century BC. The cult of this god was officially introduced to Athens in 420 BC after a great epidemic that ravaged the Peloponnesus.

The god practices his art in the presence of the young girl's relatives, who are rendered in a smaller scale. Often the family escorted the sick on their pilgrimage, which sometimes required a long stay at the shrine.

▲ Marble votive relief, *Healing While Asleep*, from the Piraeus, 4th century BC. Athens, Piraeus Archaeological Museum.

Among the finds uncovered in Epidaurus are several wood and stone game tablets, perhaps consecrated by the sick who used them to pass the time during their stay at the shrine.

Asclepius is depicted as a physician who works directly on the patient and heals him by touching the diseased part or applying a remedy.

The god is assisted by his daughter Hygieia, the personification of health, who played an important role in her father's worship. People prayed to her to ward off disease and to preserve them in good physical condition.

The patient lies asleep on a couch, indicating that the healing takes place in a dream or a vision, in keeping with the practice of "incubation."

A group of faithful—perhaps an entire family—appears before the god as suppliants. As was frequently the case for votive reliefs, the faithful were rendered according to a "hierarchical perspective" that shrinks the size of the characters depending on their lesser degree of relevance in the composition.

The god is escorted by his four daughters— Hygieia who personifies health, Panacea who heals all diseases, Iaso, and Aglaea, and by his sons Machaon and Podalirius who were physicians in the Trojan War. The dynasty of the Asclepiadae, to which Hippocrates also belonged and which descended from the two sons, transmitted the secret principles of the healing art from generation to generation.

Asclepius is recognizable by his leading attribute, the staff with the coiled serpent; because it sheds its skin, the serpent symbolizes rebirth; this is the same reptile that brought him the miraculous herb with which he brought back to life Hippolytus, son of Theseus. The cock, symbol of the dawn and of a return to life, was also sacred to the god and was sacrificed to him on his feast days.

▲ Marble votive relief, *Asclepius and the Faithful,* from the Thyrea area, ca. 360 BC. Athens, National Archaeological Museum.

"I believe those Greeks do well who build double shrines to Heracles: they sacrifice to one as if he were immortal ... and to the other they pay funeral honors as if he were a hero" (Herodotus)

Heracles

Heracles, son of Zeus and Alcmene, a mortal woman, was hated by Hera but had the privilege of drinking her milk, which gave him immortality. Since childhood he displayed extraordinary strength, for example by strangling the snakes that Hera had placed in his crib, but also an untamable rage that would one day ruin him, driving him to kill his music teacher for no reason. Having murdered, in a fit of madness, his own children, he must now undergo the twelve labors: he is forced by the Delphic oracle to atone for the murders by working for his cousin Eurystheus, king of Mycenae, and under his command will cross the entire known world, wiping out monsters and evil beings, founding cities, experiencing slavery and sullying himself with sacrilege and betrayal, until Zeus will step in and carry him to Olympus, thus rewarding him for his grievous, tormented life.

Heracles is the most popular hero of the Greek world, for his myths mirror the predicament of the human condition. The core of his legend cycle probably hails back to the Neolithic age, when the figure of a young hero who puts the world in order began to be formed; new episodes were then added from time to time, accompanying the stages of Greek expansion in the Mediterranean, though the twelve-labors cycle may have become set only in the fifth century BC when it was fully portrayed for the first time in the temple of Zeus at Olympia.

Related entries
Euphronius, Exekias,
Zeus and Hera,
Delphi, Olympia

▼ Attic black-figure
amphora by the
Nessus Painter
(detail), *Heracles Kills
the Centaur Nessus*,
from Athens, 620 BC.
Athens, National
Archaeological
Museum.

Having murdered Iphitus, Heracles had to travel to Delphi to undergo purification rites. Because the Pythia refused to question the oracle on his behalf, Heracles stole the tripod which symbolized the cult of Apollo.

This scene portrays Heracles and Apollo, to whom the Pythia had turned for help, fighting for the tripod.

Standing between the two rivals, Zeus tries to quell the furious quarrel. The Pythia was to inflict an exemplary punishment for the murder and the profanation of the temple by sending Heracles into slavery, exposing him to the lowest of human conditions.

The myth of Heracles contains frequent episodes in which the hero succumbs to the darker side of his semi-human nature to the point of committing sacrilegious acts.

▲ Eastern pediment from the treasury of the Siphnians in Delphi, *Quarrel between Heracles and Apollo for Possession of the Tripod*, ca. 525 BC. Delphi, Archaeological Museum.

Armed with a sword and covered with the leonte—the hide of the Nemean lion killed during his first labor—Heracles confronts the triple-bodied giant and kills him in order to seize his herds.

The giant Geryon, here rendered as a three-headed monster with triple lower limbs, lived on the island of Erytheia, located in faraway western lands which some believe to be Epirus, and others Cadiz, in southern Spain.

The herdsman Eurytion, who guarded Geryon's cattle, lies at the hero's feet, pierced by an arrow.

▲ Attic black-figure amphora by Exekias, *Heracles and Geryon*, from Vulci, ca. 540 BC. Paris, Musée du Louvre.

After removing the lion skin, Heracles floors the giant and is choking him, at the same time being careful to keep him raised from the soil to avoid his touching Mother Earth, which would restore his invincible strength.

The giant Antaeus, son of Poseidon and Gaia (the Earth), terrorized Libya, forcing travelers to fight him and then offering the spoils to his father's temple.

As the giant's right hand lies lifeless on the earth, the bodies are clutched in one last shudder, offering the painter an excuse for daring anatomical details.

The meeting between Heracles and Antaeus preceded the hero's last labor, when he seized the gold apples from the garden of the Hesperides in northern Africa.

▲ Attic red-figure krater by Euphronius, *Struggle between Heracles and Antaeus*, from Cerveteri, ca. 510 BC. Paris, Musée du Louvre.

Heracles ascends to Olympus on a chariot pulled by horses, with Nike (Victory) at his side.

At the end of his labors, Heracles is accepted into the divine community after being poisoned by his jealous wife with the tunic she had received from the centaur Nessus and being in such atrocious pain that he wished for death to the point of ordering that his funeral pyre be lit on Mount Oeta.

While in the Greek tradition the figure of Heracles expressed aristocratic ideals such as a passion for solitary adventure and the will to overcome one's own limitations, the theme of his final apotheosis was resurrected by early Christian authors as a metaphor for man who can reach heaven through suffering and endurance.

▲ Attic red-figure krater (detail), *Apotheosis of Heracles*, ca. 400 BC. Vienna, Kunsthistorisches Museum.

Of the more than twenty-five copies that have survived, the Farnese Heracles, so called because for a long time it stood in the courtyard of the Farnese Palace, is the most celebrated. The original, a bronze statue by Lysippus, was also reproduced on many coins.

The hero still holds in his right hand, behind his back, the fruit of his last adventure, the golden apples stolen from the garden of the Hesperides with Atlas's help.

Heracles is portrayed at the end of his labors as he leans on a rock on which he has laid down his club and his lion skin.

The signature of the sculptor, Glycon, second century AD, who copied the statue, is carved visibly on the rock, below the club.

▲ Farnese Heracles, 2nd century BC copy of a bronze original by Lysippus from the late 4th century BC, from Rome, Baths of Caracalla. Naples, Museo Archeologico Nazionale.

This image of Heracles that catches the hero in a state of rest, is a novelty from the Archaic and Classical traditions that always represented him at his labors, and humanizes him by highlighting his pained expression.

"Let us drink. Why wait for the oil lamps? / ... take the large colorful cups, / because the son of Zeus and Semele / gave wine to men / that they might forget their sorrows" (Alcaeus)

Dionysus

The god of wine and inebriation who drives Maenads and Satyrs to orgiastic frenzy is a god in apparent conflict with the value system prized by Greek society: he encourages not order, but an excess that breaks down social barriers and erases roles. This "diversity" is already expressed in the myth of his birth: like Athena, he was not born of a woman but from his father Zeus, and not from a noble part of the body such as the brain, but a lower one, the thigh. From this came his sensual and irrational nature, which was foreign to the canons of Greek manhood and was perceived as effeminate. Furthermore, he was raised by nymphs in the woods, far from the civilized world, and for this reason he is also the god of vegetation and of fertile nature, and as such is often represented with a phallic image.

In Greece, the temples to Dionysus were not located in cities, though he was worshiped in important city-sponsored festivals in which transgression was controlled by channeling the orgiastic rituals into symbolic performances with dance and song. Over time, these rituals were replaced by musical and poetic competitions, comedies and tragedies, whose subject was no longer Dionysus but that preserved the quality of a religious celebration performed on the feast days dedicated to him. For this reason, when theaters became permanent structures starting in the fourth century BC, they also became places of worship of this god and often had altars dedicated to him.

Related entries
Zeus and Hera, mystery cults, female religiosity, theater

▼ Attic red-figure amphora by the Cleophrades Painter (detail), *Dionysus and Maenads*, from Vulci, 500–490 BC. Munich, Antikensammlung.

Dionysus

In the myth set down by Hesiod, Dionysus is the son of Zeus and Semele, a mortal woman who, being pregnant and having demanded that he reveal his true heavenly nature, was struck to death at the sight of her divine lover.

To save the unborn child, Zeus extracted it from the maternal womb and sewed it into his thigh; at the end of the period of gestation, he gave birth by undoing the laces that had tied up his leg. For this reason, Dionysus was also called dissotokos *(born twice)* or dimetor *(with two mothers)*.

Hera, here solicitously witnessing the birth, was in reality responsible for Semele's death: out of jealousy, she drove her to make the demand that would cause her death, and will persecute Dionysus relentlessly by forcing him to gain his return to Olympus only after demonstrating his true divine nature by roaming the earth for a long time.

▲ Apulian red-figure krater by the Painter of Dionysus' Birth (detail), eponymous vase, 400–380 BC. Taranto, Museo Archeologico Nazionale.

This cup, the work of Exekias, depicts an episode from the myth of Dionysus that rarely appears in the iconography and refers to his earthly wandering before returning to Olympus.

To escape the pirates, Dionysus turned their oars into snakes and filled the ship with grapevines.

Crowned with a wreath of vine leaves, Dionysus reclines on the deck in a pose typical of a banquet guest.

Equipped with a rostrum in the shape of a boar's head, the ship belonged to Tyrrhenian pirates who had captured the god, whose identity they did not know, planning to sell him as a slave.

The music from invisible flutes drove the crew to madness, they jumped into the sea and were immediately turned into dolphins.

▲ Attic black-figure *kylix* by Exekias, *Dionysus and the Pirates*, from Vulci, 540–530 BC. Munich, Antikensammlung.

"For nine days the sovereign goddess roamed the earth, carrying lit torches; grieving, she refused ambrosia and disdained nectar, the honey-sweetened drink" (Hymn to Demeter)

Demeter and Persephone

Related entries
Zeus and Hera,
mystery cults, female
religiosity, Eleusis

▼ Attic red-figure
hydria (detail), *The Winged Chariot of Triptolemus Between Demeter and Persephone*,
ca. 450 BC. Vienna,
Kunsthistorisches
Museum.

Demeter was the goddess of vegetation and agriculture; most likely an extremely ancient divinity, she was added to the Olympic pantheon as the daughter of Cronus and Rhea. In both the myth and the cult, her figure is closely linked to that of her daughter Persephone, often called simply Kore (young girl), begotten with her brother Zeus.

The central episode in the myth is the kidnaping of Persephone by Hades, king of the Infernals, after which Demeter wandered long and wide to find her daughter, then forced the gods to do her justice by depriving the earth of fertility and sending a deep famine. But because Persephone had tasted a pomegranate—the fruit of the dead—she was prevented from returning forever to Olympus and was fated to remain one third of the year (the winter months) in the Underworld.

Satisfied, Demeter allowed the fruits of the earth to be reborn and in sign of gratitude to Eleusis that had welcomed her during her wandering, she gave Triptolemus, a young Eleusinian, the gift of agriculture that he might introduce it to humankind, and taught the local girls sacred rituals. Thus, Eleusis became the center of worship of these deities; in fact, a shrine was in place there already in the eighth century BC. The cult rituals included the Great Mysteries procession that each year wound its way for twenty kilometers from Athens to the shrine, complete with a cart that carried the objects sacred to the goddesses.

The character who leads the way for Persephone holding two torches in her hands is Hecate, the guide of the dead who guards over the roads at nighttime, and to whom it was customary to leave food offerings near crossroads.

Lit torches were part of the Eleusinian mystery rituals that took place at night to commemorate Persephone's nighttime journey from the Underworld.

Persephone rises from the Netherworld through a fissure in the earth. Hermes is already on the surface: he escorted Persephone through Hades, a land he knows well because he guides the souls of the dead.

On the far right, Demeter anxiously waits to embrace her daughter again.

▲ Attic red-figure krater by the Persephone Painter, *Persephone Returns from Hades*, ca. 440 BC. New York, Metropolitan Museum of Art.

In her left hand Demeter holds her customary attribute, a long scepter that resembles the pilgrim's staff she had leaned on during her long search.

According to the more common version of the myth, Triptolemus was the son of Celeus, the king of Eleusis whose family had warmly welcomed Demeter in their home even without recognizing her. In another version, Triptolemus is the youth who had warned Demeter that her daughter had been kidnapped.

Identifiable from the tall torch, Persephone holds her hand over Triptolemus, perhaps to crown him with a wreath.

Young Triptolemus is at the center of the scene: from Demeter he receives a spike of wheat, which he is to make known to men. Triptolemus is frequently depicted on a winged chariot, a gift from the goddess to help him quickly complete his mission.

▲ Marble relief, *The Mission of Triptolemus*, from Eleusis, second half of the 5th century BC. Athens, National Archaeological Museum.

The kernos *was a ritual vase for multiple offerings, used especially in the cult of Demeter.*

Each small container in this vase was filled with different fruits, seeds and cereals in memory of Demeter's gift of farming to mankind.

A late literary source described in detail the offerings that filled the kernoi for Demeter: *"Grains of wheat and barley, peas, vetch and bitter vetch grains, sage, white poppies, lentils, fava beans, oats, preserved fruits, honey, oil, wine, milk, sheep's wool."*

▲ Terracotta *kernos*, from Eleusis.
Eleusis, Archaeological Museum.

"The mighty monster hobbled off from his anvil ... he gathered / his tools ... donned his shirt, grasped his strong staff / and limped towards the door" (Homer, Iliad, *XVIII)*

Hephaestus

Related entries
Zeus and Hera,
Athena, Heracles,
Dionysus, Athens
Agora

▼ Attic red-figure *kylix*
by the Ambrosius
Painter (detail),
*Hephaestus on a Winged
Chariot*, from Vulci,
510–500 BC. Berlin,
Antikensammlung.

Born of Hera alone, who had challenged Zeus who begat Athena alone, Hephaestus is the god of the element of fire and of metallurgy. Like other mythical figures linked to technology, he has a physical deformity: he limps. For this reason he is a marginal figure, almost inferior in the society of gods. According to Homer, Hera was ashamed of this deformed, ungainly son and right after his birth hurled him down Mount Olympus. These characteristics liken Hephaestus to the blacksmiths of other ancient societies who were often marginalized and feared because of their skill in dominating changing, fluid forces such as fire, the wind, or minerals.

Far from Olympus, the god learned the secrets of heating and shaping metal, becoming a skilled builder of traps and devices. Taking revenge on his mother, he sent her a gold throne that trapped those who sat on it. Many gods then tried to bring Hephaestus back to Olympus in order to free her, but only Dionysus succeeded: he inebriated him with wine and brought him back among the gods, riding a donkey. Once he regained his seat, Hephaestus continued to work as a blacksmith and created masterpieces such as Zeus's thunderbolts, the Sun's chariot, Heracles' gold corselet and Achilles' weapons. The cult of Hephaestus was especially strong in Athens, where his temple dominated the Agora and he was worshiped as the patron of craftsmen together with Athena.

Brought back to Olympus by Dionysus in a festive procession of Satyrs and Maenads, a drunken Hephaestus lolls on a mule and carries in his right hand the double axe symbol of his craft.

Notwithstanding his clumsy appearance that in many episodes provokes laughter among the other gods, Hephaestus was linked to extraordinarily beautiful goddesses such as Charis (one of the Graces), his wife in the Iliad, *and even Aphrodite, his wife in the* Odyssey.

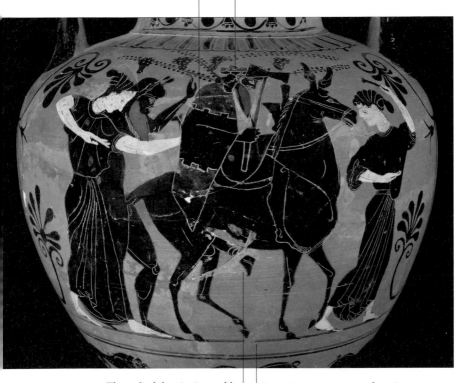

The god's deformity is noted by the fact that one foot is turned backward, for which reason he went back and forth while walking like a crab, an animal linked to him and whose name (karkinos) is also that of the blacksmith's tongs.

Even Homer reports two diverging traditions about the cause of the god's deformity: in one the god was born lame, for which reason Hera cast him into the sea; in the other, the culprit was Zeus who threw him down from Olympus to earth on the island of Lemnos because he had taken his mother's side in a marital spat.

▲ Attic black-figure amphora (detail), *Hephaestus Returns to Olympus*, 550–500 BC. Vienna, Kunsthistorisches Museum.

The nymph Thetis, one of the fifty Nereids, was the mother of Achilles born from her marriage to Peleus, a mortal. Because she had rescued Hephaestus from the sea, she asked him to make weapons for her son.

The myths refer to various locations as the seat of Hephaestus's forge. Only Homer placed it on Mount Olympus; later authors placed it at the feet of a mountain on the island of Lemnos, which was the god's favorite earthly abode, or inside vulcanoes in Southern Italy.

▲ Attic red-figure *kylix* by the Forge Painter (detail), *Thetis receives from Hephaestus Achilles' Weapons*, from Vulci, 490–480 BC. Berlin, Antikensammlung.

Hephaestus is here depicted working in his forge. Sitting on a bench, he wears a short work tunic and finishes with the hammer Achilles' helmet while Thetis examines the shield and the spear; the greaves hang from the wall.

"Demeter gave us two supreme gifts: the fruits of the earth … and the initiation into the mysteries, which ensure to participants the sweetest of hopes, both for the end of one's life and for eternity" (Isocrates)

Mystery Cults

To Classical age Greeks, the *mysteria* (from *myein*, to close one's mouth) were a part restricted to the initiated, of the open, public cults that were attended by large crowds of faithful. For the Athenians, the mysteries par excellence were the festivals celebrated at Eleusis to honor Demeter. Some rites honoring Dionysus and those linked to Orpheus and to the Cabiri (sons of Hephaestus) also had mystical features; these last were worshiped on the island of Samothrace.

Because anyone who revealed the mysteries was punishable by law, only a few sources that discuss them exist, except for the denigrating testimony of some Christian authors. One common feature of the mysteries was an initiation ceremony in which the candidate imitated in a ritual, formulaic manner the sufferings that the deities had experienced. For Demeter, it was probably her desperate search for her daughter Persephone, while in the Dionysian mysteries it was the dismemberment of the child god by the Titans and his rebirth from his own heart which had survived intact. Once initiated, the elect were made privy to secrets, usually centered around the hope for a personal salvation, and were allowed to view symbolic objects such a spike of wheat "harvested in silence" for Demeter, or the toys of the child god Dionysus. Often, the ceremonies ended in ecstasies or orgies in which communion with the divinity was achieved.

Related entries
Dionysus, Demeter and Persephone, Hephaestus, female religiosity, Eleusis

▼ Terracotta bust, *Dionysus with an Egg and a Kantharos*, from Boeotia, first half of the 4th century BC. Vienna, Kunsthistorisches Museum.

Dionysus and Demeter replaced the traditional couple of Hades and Persephone on account of the popularity of the mystery cults of which they were the protagonists.

Seated on a lion-footed throne, Dionysus and Demeter are identifiable by their attributes: the kantharos, *a two-handled wine cup, and the pomegranate that was at once the food of the Netherworld and a symbol of fertility and abundance.*

The large snake climbing the back of the throne identifies the two deities as lords of the world of the dead, for reptiles, being chthonic animals tied to the earth, were always associated with infernal cults.

The cock, the lotus flower and the eggs offered by the small couple—parents of the deceased—to the gods to propitiate the soul's entry into the Netherworld, are symbols of rebirth and regeneration and of passage, as documented by the cults that promised an afterlife to the initiated.

▲ Funerary marble relief, *Demeter and Dionysus Enthroned*, from the necropolis of Chrysapha (Laconia), 550–540 BC. Berlin, Antikensammlung.

Here Eurydice takes leave with great sadness from her husband Orpheus, while Hermes already grasps her wrist to lead her back to Hades.

The poet and musician Orpheus, dressed in the traditional Thracian mode, had succeeded in leading his wife back to earth after moving the infernal deities to tears, but was unable to keep his promise not to look back at her until he had reached the sunlight.

"Orphic" groups attributed to the mythical Orpheus a unique doctrine about the nature of man who was stained with an original fault, having been born from the ashes of Titans (who had been burned to the ground by Zeus for having devoured Dionysus), and who must undergo purification before being released from the cycle of rebirth and find his place among the gods.

▲ Marble relief, *Orpheus Takes Leave of Eurydice*, Roman copy of a Greek original from the 5th century BC. Naples, Museo Archeologico Nazionale.

The spread of Orphism is documented archaeologically starting in the fifth century BC, from several gold-sheet tablets found in tombs, inscribed with comforting words and instructions for the initiated. Also, in a Derveni (Macedonia) tomb some papyrus fragments were found that contained a commentary to a poem attributed to Orpheus.

"When I was seven I was in the Arrephoria; at ten, I ground wheat ... then I was a she-bear in the Brauronia, and when I was all grown up and lovely, I became a kanephoros" *(Aristophanes)*

Female Religiosity

Related entries
Athena, Aphrodite
and Eros, Artemis,
Dionysus, Demeter and
Persephone, sacrifice

In Greece women took an active part in the celebration of the leading religious festivals, though in marginal roles. Young girls wove the peplum and carried it as an offering to Athena during the Pan-Athenaea, and in many cities it was the girls' duty to wash and dress cult statues. However, being excluded from political life, women were not allowed to perform violent sacrifices and to share in meat eating: that was reserved to adult males who enjoyed full citizenship. Only in rare cases were women the protagonists in communicating with the gods.

In the Thesmophoria—the sowing feast dedicated to Demeter and Kore—married women went to the temple and celebrated a sacrifice, with a man present only for the slaughtering. In the Lenaea and the Anthesteria dedicated to Dionysus, when the new wine was unsealed and consecrated, they drank wine, danced recklessly, and performed rites from which men were excluded such as the ritual marriage of the queen (the wife of the archon king) to Dionysus. In the Adonea, which were private cults, they commemorated the premature death of young Adonis. The rituals that took place at the temple of Artemis at Brauron were reserved to young girls between the age of eleven and fourteen who were invited to serve the goddess as "little she-bears" to compensate her for the death of a sacred she-bear that had been killed because it had scratched a little girl.

▶ Attic red-figure *lekythos* by the Icarus Painter, *Bearer of Sacrificial Basket Near an Altar*, ca. 480 BC. Paris, Musée du Louvre.

This statuette depicts a young girl holding a baby rabbit, and is one of many found in Brauron. They were consecrated by the "little she-bears," the young girls who before marriage spent some time in the shrine serving the goddess Artemis.

The race probably took place during the Brauronian feasts; it was a rite of passage in which little girls said goodbye to the "wild" side of their youth.

Some small vases dedicated in the same shrine portray little girls, naked or dressed in short dresses, running surrounded by dogs, deer, and adults wearing bear-like masks in a sort of ritual hunt.

► Terracotta statuette, "Little She-Bear," from the shrine of Artemis in Brauron, 4th century BC. Brauron, Archaeological Museum.

A woman, perhaps Aphrodite, is on a step-ladder and receives from Eros a broken amphora turned upside down, containing young plants.

This scene illustrates a typical ritual of the Adonis festivals, when women placed vases with seeds of wheat and lettuce on the roofs of their homes. They let the sprouts dry up and die under the heat, in memory of the premature death of the very handsome Adonis, who was Aphrodite's lover killed in jealousy by Ares.

The cult of Adonis, which perhaps originated in the East, was believed to have been founded by Aphrodite herself. The rituals were the exclusive province of women who gathered during the Adonea wearing mourning and grieving together.

The feminine dimension of the cult is highlighted by the fact that scenes such as these were depicted almost exclusively on perfume vases used by women.

▲ Attic red-figure *lekythos*, *The Gardens of Adonis*, ca. 390 BC. Karlsruhe, Badisches Landesmuseum.

The effigy of Dionysus consisted in a bearded mask and a short, belted chiton on a wooden pole stuck in the ground. The round disks on each side of the head are perhaps flat loaves of bread, offered to the god by arranging them in the branches behind the effigy.

Bacchants approach dancing, playing the double aulos *and a tambourine, and holding the thyrsus and a tall, lit torch.*

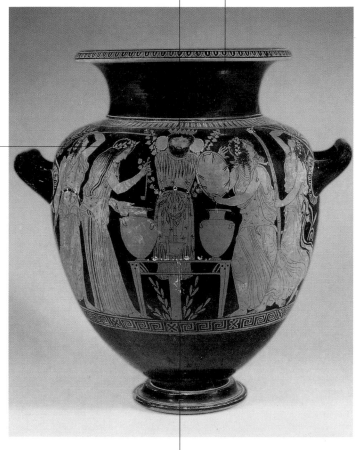

A woman with the hair loose on her shoulders and an ivy wreath draws wine from a stamnos *placed on a table and is about to pour it into a skiphos.*

This scene portrays one of the night celebrations to which only women were allowed, that took place during the Lenaea, the feast when the wine was consecrated to Dionysus.

▲ Attic red-figure *stamnos* of the Dinos Painter, *Sacrifice to Dionysus*, from Nocera, 425–415 BC. Naples, Museo Archeologico Nazionale.

"Those who interrogate the gods about those matters for which the gods gave man the power of discrimination ... are out of their mind" (Xenophon)

Divination

▼ Attic red-figure
amphora by the
Cleophrades Painter
(detail), *Reading the
Entrails Before the
Warrior's Departure*,
from Vulci, 490–480
BC. Würzburg, Martin
von Wagner Museum.

Under the definition of "divination" are grouped all the techniques used to predict the future or divine the favor of the gods. Scrutinizing animal entrails, the liver in particular, was quite common in Greece, especially when weighing the appropriateness of taking action. Other signs could be found by carefully reading the shape of the oil dropped in a basin of water, or the plumes of smoke spiraling upward from an incense fire on the altar. In the great oracular shrines, prophetic divination took place in which the god's response was given directly through a man who spoke on his behalf. In some shrines the spirits of the dead were questioned, a practice known as necromancy; sometimes, these apparitions were aided by "scenic devices" or by ingesting hallucinogenic substances, as scholars discovered when they excavated the shrine of Ephyra, in Epirus near the river Acheron, where Odysseus had summoned the spirit of Tiresias from Hades to consult him.

Oneiromancy—the interpretation of dreams—was practiced especially in the sanctuaries dedicated to Asclepius, where

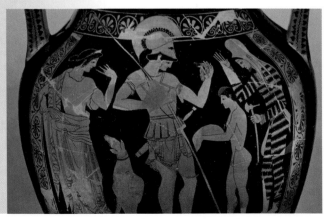

the god came to the sick in a dream suggesting to them the therapy to be adopted. A very popular method of divination was the "drawing of lots" in which small items such as pebbles, sticks, dice, or astragali where used, mixed and chosen at random.

The female figure seated on the tripod and answering the question, a cup in one hand and an olive branch in the other, is not the Pythia but the goddess Themis who personified order and the law and who was believed to have invented rituals and oracles. According to one myth, she had taught Apollo the art of divination.

The bearded man crowned with a laurel wreath is consulting the oracle. He is Aegeus, the mythical king of Athens, father to Theseus and the hero who gave his name to one of the Attic tribes.

In the historical age, the oracle of Delphi issued its pronouncements through the Pythia, a local girl chosen for her moral integrity and not because she possessed prophetic gifts. Sitting on a tripod she shook an olive branch and ranted, possessed by the god, uttering noises and screams that were interpreted by the priests who then pronounced the oracle.

In other oracular sanctuaries different processes were followed, for example, listening to the rustling branches of a specific tree, or to the chirping of birds.

The shrine to Zeus at Dodona contained more than 150 short texts engraved on lead tablets and dated from the sixth to the second century BC, containing questions for the oracle. They were all written in binary form, so that the answer could be either just affirmative or negative.

Attic red-figure *kylix* by the Kodros Painter (detail), *Consulting the Oracle*, from Vulci, 450–425 BC. Berlin, Antikensammlung.

"Were the sacrifices offered by the wicked more welcome to the gods than those offered by the just, men would not find life worth living" (Xenophon)

Sacrifice

Related entries
Offerings and ex-votos, temples and sacred buildings, public banquet halls, porticoes

To the Greeks, the sacrifice was the central act of the cult, and it could be private or public. To sacrifice meant to honor the gods, to placate them or beseech a favor from them, consecrating to them victims that were slaughtered and burnt. Collective sacrifices took place during periodic sacred festivals and were generally preceded by processions in which the faithful reached the sacred enclosure carrying with them the ritual tools and the animal victims. After reaching the altar, which was usually built outdoors near the temples, the sacrifice was marked by a series of ritual acts, from prayers to the slaughter of the victim, to roasting the meats. After reserving to the immortal gods the bones wrapped in fat and burned, the men shared the comestible meat, for the final act of the sacrifice consisted in the banquet, which preferably took place inside the sanctity of the shrine and was an important time of renewal of the citizenship covenant in which all freemen participated.

Unlike public sacrifices, private ones were held at all times of the year, using either the spaces around the temples or less monumental structures, or even household altars. Sometimes there was no banquet and the meats were either completely burned or discarded without being eaten.

▶ Bronze votive axe-head dedicated to Hera. From the Kyniskos sacrificial mound of Sybaris, mid–6th century BC. London, British Museum.

A private citizen who sacrificed a head of cattle made a large commitment since the animal had a high economic value.

The Moschophorus (man bearing a sacrificial calf), a statue found while excavating the Persian landfill, was dedicated to Athena by an offerer named Rhombos; it is the best-known representation of a bearer of a sacrificial animal.

While some divinities received the sacrifice of only certain kinds of animals, such as the suckling pigs offered to Demeter during the Thesmophoria festival, the feast honoring Athena included the trittoia, the triple sacrifice of a bull, a sow, and a sheep.

Quantitative studies of epigraphic texts that report public sacrifices and of victims depicted on vases and votive reliefs show that the most frequently sacrificed animals were lambs, sheep and rams.

Moschophorus, from the Athens Acropolis, 570–560 BC. Athens, Acropolis Museum.

Rising atop a stepped base, the altar to Zeus was made from the solidified ashes of animals sacrificed over the centuries, mixed with water from the Alpheus river. The victims were slaughtered on the altar base, while the animals' haunches were roasted on top of the mound.

Visiting the Olympia sanctuary in the second century AD, Pausanias counted at least seventy sacrificial altars used to worship various deities; the central one dedicated to Zeus was about 20 feet high and had a circumference of about 100 feet.

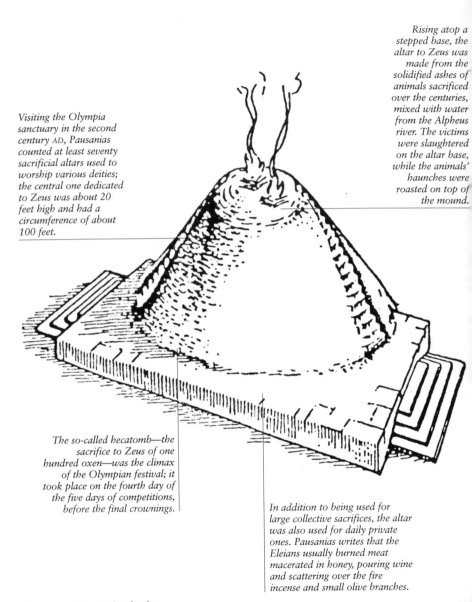

The so-called hecatomb—the sacrifice to Zeus of one hundred oxen—was the climax of the Olympian festival; it took place on the fourth day of the five days of competitions, before the final crownings.

In addition to being used for large collective sacrifices, the altar was also used for daily private ones. Pausanias writes that the Eleians usually burned meat macerated in honey, pouring wine and scattering over the fire incense and small olive branches.

▲ Drawing reconstructing the altar of ashes at the temple to Zeus at Olympia (from Settis 2002, Atlante).

This scene illustrates one phase of the meat offering after slaughtering the victim; the vine and the ivy form a sort of arbor, suggesting that this sacrifice was to Dionysus.

The animals' entrails were the first parts to be extracted, roasted and eaten by the priests near the altar: here they are being roasted on skewers.

A young man draws wine for the altar libation from an amphora.

The bones, the tail, and all the non-comestible parts of the animal were wrapped in fat, covered with barley flat breads and offered to the gods, while the quarters were roasted or boiled and shared by the participants.

Offering a sacrificial banquet was expensive. With time, it was offered more and more often by private citizens who used it for political promotion, extending the distribution of the sacrificial meat also to foreigners and slaves.

Ionic black-figure *hydria* (detail), *Roasting Meat at the Altar*, 525–500 BC. Rome, Museo Nazionale Etrusco di Villa Giulia.

This is the best preserved of a group of four painted wooden pinakes *(tablets) found in Pitsa inside a cave dedicated to the cult of nymphs.*

Three women dressed in blue peplums and red mantles approach the altar carrying myrtle branches. Next to two of them we read their names, Euthydike and Euqolis.

▲ Wooden tablet portraying a sacrificial procession, from Pitsa (Corinth), 540 BC. Athens, National Archaeological Museum.

Two boys walk in the procession as aulos *and lyra players, while a third leads a sheep tied with a red rope, symbolizing its consecration to the gods.*

The Pitsa tablets are rare surviving examples of a wood painting technique similar to wall frescoes. The vividly painted figures were drawn on a white gesso background that was also used for writing official documents on wood.

The woman closest to the altar holds a small ewer in her right hand and carries on her head the kanoun, a ritual basket filled with sacred barley grains to be sprinkled on the altar and on the victim's head before immolation. Hidden under the barley is the slaughter knife.

"At the time of her wedding, to you Timareta dedicated her tambourines, the ball that she loved, the net that held her hair, and her dolls" (Palatine Anthology)

Offerings and Ex-Votos

Related entries
Apollo, Artemis, Asclepius, sacrifice, sacred temples and buildings, porticoes, Epidaurus

A typical expression of ancient religiosity was the offering to a deity which took on different forms depending on whether it was public or private and on the offerer's social rank. The offers of first fruits to be laid out on the altar or burned were made at the time of the sacrifice. One popular private offering consisted in dedicating to the deity the symbols of a phase of one's life that had ended, such as the locks of children now adults, or their toys, or a bride's virginal clothes. Another common type of offering were statues or other images of the gods of that particular shrine, ritual objects, or artifacts representing cult acts, from monumental sculptures to humble clay objects. While the precious artifacts became part of the sanctuary's treasure and were carefully inventoried and protected, sometimes by constructing stoai and *thesauroi* (treasuries), the humble offerings that accumulated near the altars were periodically removed and discarded into pits.

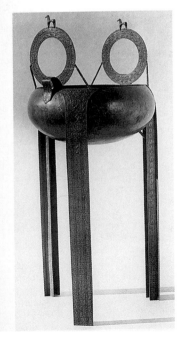

► Modern reconstruction of a votive bronze tripod with embossed decoration. Olympia, Archaeological Museum.

One characteristic offering was the ex-voto, a gift to the deity who had granted a wish implored in a time of need or danger. In times of war, cities usually offered the tenth part of the spoils, such as weapons or works of art paid for with the proceeds from the sale of the spoils. In private life, anatomical ex-votos in the shape of the body parts or limbs healed by the god were quite common.

On the temple walls hang women's wear such as a pair of shoes, a chiton, and rectangular, fringed pieces of fabric and a peplum, also reported in great quantity in the inventories of the shrine of Artemis at Brauron and identified as the clothes worn by women in childbirth.

This relief narrates a private sacrifice dedicated to Artemis upon the presentation to her of a newborn child. Although she was a young, virginal goddess, Artemis was also the guardian of newborns and of childbirth.

The offerers are all women and carry different kinds of gifts for the goddess: the first carries a basket full of fruits on her head while the second, her head veiled perhaps because she is the family's matriarch, holds a small box whose contents has not been identified.

The actual sacrifice of the animal during the visit to the temple—here, a young man is about to slit the ox's throat—is of lesser importance in this scene, hence the figures are in a smaller scale.

▲ Drawing reconstructing a votive marble relief, *Offerings to Artemis*, from Echinos, late 4th century BC. Lamia, Archaeological Museum (from Settis 2002, *Atlante*).

Anatomical ex-votos were a common type of offering especially in the temples dedicated to health divinities.

In addition to clay reproductions, often life-size, of diseased limbs that had been healed, internal organs were also represented, offering us useful information about the anatomical knowledge of the time.

Anatomical ex-votos were usually made of clay; rather than being custom-made for the buyers, they were probably produced, on an almost industrial scale, by specialized workshops that flourished around temples, where the faithful could choose from a large selection of mold-produced types the one that fit their needs.

▲ Anatomical ex-votos from the shrine of Asclepius at Corinth.

This head of a man, with glass eyes intact, has long hair divided in two side bands ending in curls.

The two heads were perhaps part of the statues of Apollo and Artemis. They were found in 1939 in a votive storeroom underneath a repaving layer of the Sacred Way that led to the temple of Apollo at Delphi.

This ivory female head is crowned by a tall diadem made of embossed gold-sheet; on her ears are two rosette earrings decorated with the same technique. The hair has disintegrated.

Because the heads were finished at neck height, they were probably set on a wooden frame draped with fabric clothes. The ivory feet fragments found in the same pit end below the ankle, at the hem, suggesting that only the visible parts were made of the precious material.

Because there was a ban on destroying the gifts to divinities, in order to make space in the temples for new ex-votos, the older offerings that crowded the area were periodically buried in votive pits.

▲▶ Gold and ivory heads from Delphi, mid–5th century BC. Delphi, Archaeological Museum.

Daily Life

◄Attic red-figure *hydria* (detail),
Musician, from Rhodes, 440–430
BC. London, British Museum.

"The Phoenicians who came with Cadmus ... brought new knowledge to the Greeks, including the letters of the alphabet that, to my knowledge, the Greeks had not known before" (Herodotus)

Script

Related entries
School and education

The alphabet was brought to Greece by the Phoenicians in the eighth century BC. The Greeks made important adaptations to it such as signs to denote vowels which did not exist in the Phoenician alphabet. However, the resulting script was not uniform throughout Greece since each region made its own modifications, and the local variants survived for a long time. At the close of the fifth century BC, the most perfected alphabet was the one used in Miletus and the Ionic cities of Asia Minor. For this reason, it was adopted by Athens and from then on became the official alphabet of the entire Hellenic world.

For a long time, it was believed that the adoption of an alphabet-based writing system was motivated primarily by commercial reasons such as the taking of inventories or the recording of transactions. Since none of the earliest inscriptions are of a commercial nature, but are in fact votive and are in verse, a new, alternative theory holds that writing was introduced in a literary context, to take down verses, in particular epic poems, whose texts, after centuries of being handed down orally from generation to generation, had become sufficiently stabilized to suggest that they might be recorded as an aid in declaiming them by heart.

▶ Bronze tablet with the Greek and Phoenician alphabets, from Cyprus, 8th century BC. Oslo, Schøien Collection.

The oinochoe *was a type of pitcher used for pouring wine primarily at banquets.*

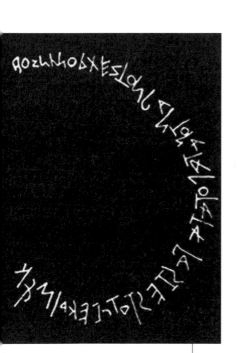

Etched around the vase is the oldest Attic inscription that has been dated; written in hexameter verses, it relates to the prize for a dance contest, the prize being perhaps the vase itself.

According to some scholars, this and other inscriptions would seem to confirm that the first use of the written language took place at banquets, to write down poetry or exchange jokes or professions of love.

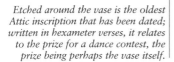

▲ *Oinochoe* from Dipylon, ca. 740 BC. Athens, National Archaeological Museum.

By the sixth century BC, writing was commonly used on vases to indicate their use, their owner, their dedication to a god, or the names of the characters depicted.

The inscription between the figures, applied before the vase was baked, identifies the double aulos player as "Polyterpos" and says that the vase belongs to Pyrrhias, "choir master" or "first dancer."

▲ Corinthian black-figure *aryballos*, from the temple of Apollo at Corinth, ca. 580 BC. Corinth, Archaeological Museum.

Pyrrhias is probably the figure jumping with raised arms, facing the three pairs of dancers. Perhaps he had received the vase as a prize.

"Socrates counseled that one should be wary of foods or drinks that are appetizing even if one is neither hungry nor thirsty; ... they are bad for the stomach, the head, and the soul" (Xenophon)

Food and Table

Until the sixth century BC, the Greeks ate sitting down. In the Homeric poems the main food are meats, usually roasted over a fire, and large loaves of bread. It is likely, however, that since this was a sheep-rearing society, cheese was also important together with fish, fruits, and wild vegetables. They used no dishes or flatware, only cups for drinking and knives for meat carving. They drank generous amounts of wine, by then already probably diluted with water. The habit of dining reclining on tricliniums was introduced in the sixth century BC from Persia. From then on, dining in a sitting position became a sign of subjection: that is how women ate at home—family dinners being the only ones to which they were allowed—along with children and "stool men," i.e., parasites.

Also starting in the sixth century, agriculture was greatly improved, adding new crops to the traditional cultivation of cereals, making for a more diversified diet, so that legume soups and barley or spelt mush became the food staples of the lower classes. By the fifth century, the sources describe rich and elaborate banquets where boiled or roasted meats were preceded by appetizers served in small bowls, accompanied by fish, shellfish, and mollusks and side dishes of vegetables, salads, fruits, and desserts of all kinds. Wine was not drunk during dinner, but afterwards during the symposium.

Related entries
Sacrifice, symposium, public banquet halls

◀ Terracotta, *Butcher Killing a Suckling Pig*, from Thebes, 500–475 BC. Paris, Musée du Louvre.

The character depicted here, waiting on a customer, is not a common fishmonger but a seller of tuna steaks: equipped with a large knife, he cuts the fish on a chopping block letting the scraps fall to the floor.

▲ Campanian kalyx-krater, *Fishmonger*, 380–370 BC. Cefalù, Museo della Fondazione Culturale Mandralisca.

While ceramic artifacts from Mycenae were often decorated with stylized drawings of fishes and octopuses, Homeric poems never mention the consumption of seafood, which was considered a food of the poor, thus unfit for heroes.

In the Classical age, the consumption of fish and seafood of all kinds was documented in comedies. Recipe books described in detail the elaborate preparation of fish dishes fried, roasted, stewed, and in sweet-and-sour sauces.

Grilling, described in the Iliad and the Odyssey as the only method for cooking meat, was also used for fish and vegetables.

At home, grill roasting was usually done outside on fire pits or on stoves located in the yard.

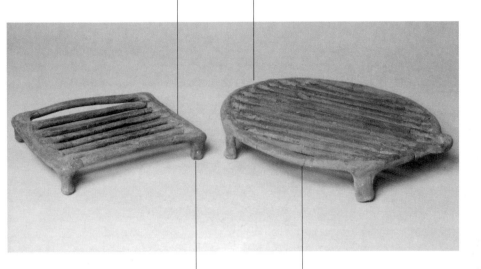

In the city markets one could buy cooked food, sausage roasted while you waited being the most popular type of meat.

Roasting was also typical of sacrificial banquets, which were often the only time when men ate meat.

▲ Grills for cooking on a fire, from the Athens Agora, 5th–4th century BC. Athens, Agora Museum.

Boiling was the most common cooking method. For this, terracotta or metal pots were placed on small portable stoves that were filled with blazing embers or directly on the fire, on supports.

Boiling was used primarily for soups and mush made with cereals and legumes, a basic food staple of the lower classes.

This type of pot-shaped stove was used by filling the bottom with blazing coals through the square opening, and placing the cooking pot on top.

▲ Terracotta oven, from the Athens Agora, 5th–4th century BC. Athens, Agora Museum.

Bread was the basic staple of the Greek diet; called *maza*, it was usually made of barley or mixed cereals; bread made entirely of wheat (artos) was more refined and cost more.

In bakeries, the bread was cooked in ovens; at home, portable terracotta ovens were used, or braziers, which produced a thin, soft, spongy bread that was dunked in sweet wine.

Bakeries were plentiful, as many preferred to buy bread at the market instead of baking it at home. Home baking was more prevalent among the wealthy, aristocratic households that sometimes hired their own bakers, those from Lydia and Phoenicia being much appreciated and in great demand.

In addition to the usual loaves, bread was baked in many other shapes: the cubos, *shaped like a loaf bread, the* boletinos *shaped like a mushroom and sprinkled with poppy seeds, and flower-shaped rolls and braids made with oil, lard, and pepper.*

▲ Terracotta with women bakers working the dough at the sound of the flute, from Thebes, 525–500 BC. Paris, Musée du Louvre.

Although the sources do not mention it often, perhaps because it was a food of the poor, cheese must have been a regular part of the Greek diet.

Adding grated cheese to wine was a common practice; this is supported by the finds in some tombs, which included graters among the metal implements used for symposia.

Wine mixed with grated goat cheese was used as a powerful tonic and was given to the sick and the wounded already in the Iliad *and the* Odyssey.

▲ Terracotta statuette of a man grating cheese, from Ritsona, 6th century BC. Thebes, Archaeological Museum.

"Now ... everyone's hands / and the cups; now someone crowns his head with wreaths ... a krater filled with joy sits in the center, / and more wine is ready to be poured from amphoras" (Xenophanes)

The Symposium

The symposium was the final part of the banquet and was restricted to adult men: the guests, reclining on dining couches (*klinai* or *tricliniums*), drank and engaged in conversation and games, sang convivial songs, listened to the poems of celebrated bards or watched dances and other performances. The symposium began after the dinner remains were cleared from the *andron*, the hall used for this entertainment, and the precious dinnerware for serving wine was brought in. After ritual ablutions, the guests prayed and made offerings to the gods. Then one of the guests was elected king of the symposium and charged with deciding the number of toasts, the percentage of water to be used to dilute the wine, and the activities.

Although drunkenness and the presence of *hetaerae* and adolescent boys must have made for a far less refined ambience than what the poets describe, the symposium was not just a time for drinking and playing together, but an important moment in the community life of the nobility, when politically active groups came together. The choice of guests was not random: the participants referred to each other as *hetairoi*, comrades, they felt connected by a similar life style and were often bound by oaths of loyalty. With the advent of democracy, the symposium lost much of its political function and became primarily an environment conducive to poetry and philosophy.

Related entries
Food and table, homes

▼ Corinthian krater with studs, known as the "Eurythios krater" (detail), *Banquet Guests Reclining on Klinai,* from Cerveteri, ca. 600 BC. Paris, Musée du Louvre.

The psykter *was a vase used as a wine cooler: after being filled, it was placed in a krater full of ice or snow leaving only the upper decorated part showing.*

The name written next to each hetaera is evidence of the notoriety they could reach in Athenian society.

Hetaerae *are shown drinking wine from large cups, playing the flute or engaged in the game of* kottabos: *with the last drop of wine remaining in the cup, they tried to hit a target outside the scene.*

In keeping with the function of the vase, this scene portrays four hetaerae *at a symposium: naked, they recline on dining couches* (klinai) *draped with embroidered blankets and pillows.*

▲ Attic red-figure *psykter* by Euphronius, *Hetaerae at a Symposium*, from Cerveteri, 515–510 BC. Saint Petersburg, Hermitage.

The kalpis *was a large jug used at symposia to store the water used to dilute the wine.*

Perhaps wine had a higher alcohol content than the ones produced today, for which reason it was drunk pure only rarely, since it was believed to be harmful.

The most common dilution rates were five or three parts (three parts water to two parts wine or two parts water to one part wine).

This scene depicts two servants busy pouring wine from an amphora into a krater to which water will be added. The third figure is a flute player, suggesting that the symposium was in full swing.

▲ Attic red-figure *kalpis* by Euthymides, *Preparing the Wine,* from Vulci, 480–470 BC. Vatican City, Museo Gregoriano Etrusco.

This scene depicts the final act of a symposium: a maid helps one of the guests who is throwing up the excess wine he has ingested.

This scene painted inside a wine cup seems to admonish the drinker against excesses.

Although sympotic poetry praised moderation and modesty as aristocratic values, scenes such as these must have been rather frequent; there are also comic vase scenes and descriptions about the use of the chamber pots that were placed under the dining couch.

▲ Attic red-figure *kylix* by Douris, *Drinking Excesses*, from Vulci, 480–470 BC. Vatican City, Musei Vaticani.

"She put on a wondrous robe ... / put on a girdle that had a hundred tassels ... / and threw a lovely veil over her hair ... / She bound her sandals to her feet" (Homer, Odyssey VI)

Clothing

The Greeks wore very plain clothes that were similar for both men and women, mostly homemade of homespun fabrics, usually wool, though vegetable yarns such as hemp and linen were also in vogue. For women, the rarest and most refined garments were made of byssus or "sea silk," a fabric woven with the filaments of certain mollusks. Cotton and silk became fashionable only in the Hellenistic age. The dominant colors were white for men and strong colors such as saffron yellow and crimson red for women. Embroidery, in the Archaic age especially, was popular, being used primarily to decorate the hems of women's garments.

Clothes were classified in two large groups: the *endumata* which were cut and sewn dresses worn on the skin, and the *epiblemata* which were overgarments consisting of rectangular lengths of cloth adapted to the body with draping and brooches. The most common dress was the chiton, a plain tunic with applied sleeves or simple openings for the arms. Men frequently wore a short chiton, especially when doing work that required a lot of movement, while women wore it long to the ankles. The most popular overgarment was the *himation*, a wide, square or rectangular mantle that was wrapped around the body in several fashions. The *chlamys* on the other hand was a short men's cape fastened on one shoulder, typically worn by soldiers and travelers.

Related entries
Hair styles and make-up

▼ Volute krater by Ergotimos and Kleitias, known as the "François Vase" (detail), *Wedding of Peleus and Thetis, The Embroidered Peplums of the Horai*, from Chiusi, ca. 570 BC. Florence, Museo Archeologico.

This kore *unearthed in 1886 is known as the "peplum* kore*" because it was believed it was the only statue from the Acropolis that wore the archaic Doric dress, unlike the other* korai *dressed in the Ionian fashion.*

The peplum consisted of two lengths of woolen cloth sewn along one or both sides, and folded over the bodice to form a wide flounce, the apoptugma, *fastened at the shoulders with large brooches.*

Recent studies about the statue's surviving colors have uncovered graffiti that had been etched on the marble before applying the colors, retracing an earlier waistband decorated with a frieze of sphinxes ibexes and lions.

In Ionia, overgarments that recalled the Doric peplum embellished with multicolored decorations, were reserved for priests and divinities, thus suggesting that this kore *is the statue not of an offerer but of a goddess.*

▲ *Kore 679*, from the Persian landfill, ca. 540 BC. Athens, Acropolis Museum.

Instead of being applied, the sleeves were shaped from the width of the fabric and sewn in several points along the top.

This kore is wearing a long ankle-length chiton deeply draped on top and held at the waist by a belt that forms a rich swelling effect, a bouffant known as a kolpos.

The chiton, originally an Eastern garment, became popular starting in the second half of the sixth century BC. In the Classical age, it almost completely replaced the Doric peplum which continued to be used only in the very traditional Spartan society.

Kore 670, from the Persian landfill, ca. 520 BC. Athens, Acropolis Museum.

This kore *is a refined example of Ionic sixth-century fashion popular with the young daughters of influential families who dedicated their statues to the deity.*

This pleated chiton made of thin fabric is covered with a himation, *a thicker cloth draped around the body so as to create a diagonal flounce in front, and is pinned on the right shoulder.*

This statue's garments are still covered with paint that also reproduced the mantle's embroidery.

▶ *Kore 675*, from the Persian landfill, ca. 520 BC. Athens, Acropolis Museum.

Clay statuettes of this type are known as "Tanagrines" from Tanagra, the Boeotian city where great quantities of them were found in 1872–73 when over eight thousand tombs were sacked and their contents flooded the European antiques market.

Tanagrines were produced on a mass scale in a great variety of types; they mostly portrayed young women dressed in the fashion of the times.

This figurine is wearing a long chiton that reaches the floor and a wide mantle that covers the head; over it she wears a strange "top-shaped" hat; in her right hand she holds a heart-shaped fan.

The clay of these statues was typically covered with a white base, here still visible on the face, on which rich colors, including gold foil, were applied.

▶ Terracotta statuette, *Woman with Hat and Mantle*, from Tanagra, 325–300 BC. Berlin, Antikensammlung.

Oedipus has just reached
Thebes: he is portrayed in the
typical traveler's attire, busy
answering the Sphinx's enigmas.

The petasos, a
wide-brimmed hat
fastened with a
ribbon under the
chin, protected the
traveler from the
sun and the rain.
The side flaps
could be folded
downwards to
cover the ears.

The short mantle
fastened on the
chest or at the
shoulder with a
fibula is a
chlamys, also
worn by soldiers
over their cuirass.

Travelers as well as hunters wore
these types of boots cross-tied
with laces, often with hobnailed
soles to make them sturdier since
they were used for long marches
on unpaved roads.

▲ Attic red-figure *kylix* by
the Oedipus Painter (detail),
Oedipus and the Sphinx,
from Vulci, ca. 460 BC.
Vatican City, Musei Vaticani.

Balm containers were used to store perfumed unguents to rub on the body.

This type of woman's sandal had thin strips between the toes and metal trim.

This naked young girl, her head covered by a sort of kerchief, has just washed herself in the basin at her feet; she holds a pair of bootees in her hands.

Sandals were the most basic type of footwear: they were made of a thin leather or cork sole fastened to the foot with laces or strips.

▲ Balm container shaped like a sandaled foot, from Samos, 6th century BC. London, British Museum.

▶ Attic red-figure *kylix* by Epictetus (detail), *Bootees*, 520–510 BC. Athens, Agora Museum.

This type of closed, short boot that reached mid-calf was used only by women; a shorter version that barely covered the ankles was unisex.

"Their eyebrows are too thin? They paint them with lampblack. Too dark? They cover them with grease paint. A courtesan with too-white skin will use rose-colored powder" (Alexis of Thurii)

Hair Styles and Make-Up

Related entries
Clothing

The Greeks arranged their hair in the most varied fashions and each epoch had its favorite styles. In the Archaic period, both men and women wore their hair long, framed by ringlets on the forehead and longer curls that fell on the shoulders. Later, men began to wear their hair short and to shave their beards in the Macedonian fashion, while free women continued to wear their hair long. In the Classical age, simpler styles were favored, with the hair gathered on top or braided and wound around the head. In the Hellenistic period, curls, waves, and ringlets became popular, including the use of hair pieces. Because blond hair was highly prized, women dyed their hair, though doing so was deemed unbecoming for proper women.

Even the use of cosmetics was often stigmatized: Solon tried unsuccessfully to forbid them and Lycurgus banned the perfume makers from Sparta. Nevertheless, the personal grooming of both men and women called for a large selection of unguents and fragrances. Starting in the seventh century BC, Corinth became the fragrance-manufacturing center exporting perfumes everywhere, packaged in precious, finely decorated ceramic containers, the *aryballoi* and *alabastra*. In addition to perfume, powders called *diapasmata* were used: sprinkled on linens and clothing, they deodorized and acted as anti-perspirants.

▼ Cosmetics holder made from a carved shell, Syrian-Palestine manufacture, 700–600 BC. London, British Museum.

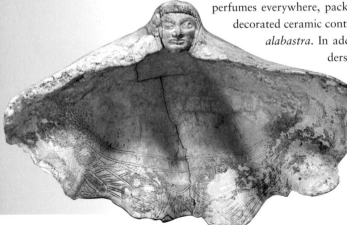

Apollo is always depicted as a beardless youth. Here he has a particularly youthful hair style with long, wavy hair.

Two locks are brought up to the forehead from each side and knotted in a high knot, the krobalos. Soldiers and athletes also favored this hairdo.

The eyes of the statue, now lost, were originally made of vitreous paste, marble, or ivory. The bronze plates that held them from the inside projected outside to form the lashes.

▲ Bronze head of Apollo, known as the "Chatsworth Apollo," from Tamassos (Cyprus), ca. 460 BC. London, British Museum.

This head, 18 inches high, belonged to a colossal kouros *found in 1916 in the Athenian necropolis of Dipylon, where it marked an aristocratic tomb.*

The hair is held in place by a ribbon, the tenia, *that girds the forehead and is knotted in the back.*

The hair falls heavily on the shoulders forming a compact curtain of rows of ringlets; short bangs of smaller curls frame the forehead.

This type of hairdo, used in both the kouroi *and* korai *of the Archaic period, is called "pearl" or "small snail" style.*

▲ Colossal head from the Dipylon, ca. 600 BC. Athens, National Archaeological Museum.

Both Apollo and Poseidon wear their hair short and curly, in Classical age fashion, but Poseidon has the long beard that marks adult men and is a symbol of dignity. The custom of shaving the face was introduced by Alexander the Great and became widespread in the Hellenistic age.

Artemis has her wavy hair pulled into a soft chignon covered with a fabric kerchief that was used in the fifth and fourth century BC, the kekryphalos.

As usual, Apollo is beardless. The Athens Agora had many flourishing barbershops, which the comic authors referred to as gossip factories.

▲ Eastern frieze of the Parthenon, *Poseidon, Apollo, and Artemis*, 447–432 BC. Athens, Acropolis Museum.

181

The older soldier, bearded and with a mustache, is caught cutting a lock of his hair with his unsheathed sword. It was customary for soldiers to dedicate a lock of hair to the god from whom protection was being sought in battle. Brides and grooms also performed this ritual right before their wedding, and would-be travelers as well.

The warriors prepare for battle by inspecting their weapons and donning body-fitting armor and greaves.

The younger soldiers shaved their beards and wore their hair short and curly, "garden style."

▲ Attic red-figure *kylix* by Macron (detail), *Warriors Arming Themselves*, from Capua, ca. 480 BC. Paris, Musée du Louvre.

Mirrors were common toiletry items; usually made of bronze, the reflecting surface was silver-washed. The humbler versions had no decorations and sometimes no handle.

This elaborate mirror has a handle shaped like a female figure joined to the supporting bar by two winged sphinxes.

The female figure is a goddess, perhaps Aphrodite, and is probably the adaptation to a popular luxury item of models of much larger statues.

The small, lion-shaped base suggests that this mirror was not hand-held but was a standing model to be placed on top of a surface.

► Bronze mirror with female figure and sphinxes, Spartan or Corinthian manufacture, mid–6th century BC. Athens, National Archaeological Museum.

Combs made of wood, bone, or ivory were popular grooming items used by both sexes.

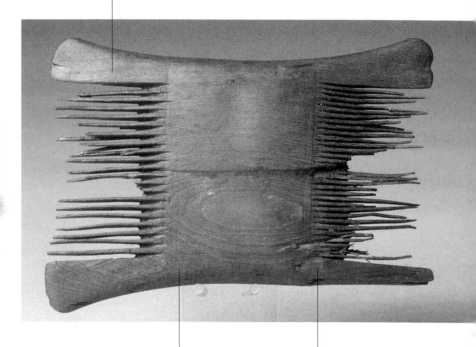

The many gynaeceum scenes depicted on vases show that since shelves or furniture with shelves or drawers did not exist, toiletry items such as mirrors, combs, and pomade containers were hung from walls or placed on the floor inside small wooden caskets or ceramic vessels.

The most common type of comb was this one with two opposite rows of teeth arranged on either the short or the long side.

▲ Wooden comb from the Athens Agora, 6th century BC. Athens, Agora Museum.

"What remedies will not cure, iron will; what iron will not cure, fire will; what fire will not cure must be deemed incurable"
(Hippocrates)

Medicine

Since the eighth century BC, medical practice in the Greek world was sharply divided: on one hand were the religious healers who practiced in the temples; on the other, the "lay" physicians who followed methods based on experience and were treated as lowly craftsmen. The transition to a medical science with its own field of knowledge and techniques is attributed to Hippocrates, who was born in Kos around 460 BC and under whose name the theories of a number of philosophers and doctors from his own time or from earlier ages were probably collected.

Related entries
Asclepius, Epidaurus

Although he belonged to the Asclepiadae clan that boasted to be descended from Asclepius and traditionally practiced medicine in the temples, Hippocrates separated the discipline from religion and gave priority to the experimental method and to diagnostics based on symptoms and on the patient's personal history, thereby refusing to attribute a sacred origin to some diseases. He also drew up a vast catalogue of recipes that included purgatives, diuretics, astringents, and sedatives. He is also credited with the Hippocratic oath, which sets down the rules that the physician must observe in exercising his profession. Starting in the fifth century BC, in the cities under democratic rule medicine developed by leaps and bounds; Athens even organized a health corps of physicians, surgeons, dentists, and oculists paid by the state and selected through an exam of their qualifications and skills given by the *ekklesia*.

▼ *Aryballos* by the Clinic Painter (detail), *Physician Performing a Bloodletting,* 480–470 BC. Paris, Musée du Louvre.

From the implements found in the sanctuaries dedicated to Asclepius, we learn that the doctors who practiced there did not just prescribe cures based on diet or medicaments but also performed surgery.

Because dissection was not practiced, anatomical knowledge was based primarily on external observation and on wounds. Most of the surgery performed was on bone injuries, to reduce fractures and limb dislocation.

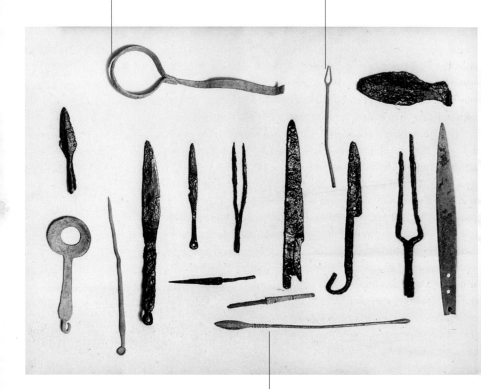

The two typical surgeries were "cutting" and "burning"; bloodletting was thought to be effective for many pathologies and was done by applying heated leeches to incisions.

▲ Surgical instruments from the shrine of Asclepius in Corinth. Corinth, Archaeological Museum.

"The writing-master first draws lines with a stylus for the use of the young beginner, and gives him the tablet and makes him follow the lines ..." (Plato, Protagoras*)*

School and Education

Ancient Greece had no public schools, only private institutes directed by teachers who were paid by the families. Even though the number of pupils was high, elementary instruction was still the privilege of a select few, except when some generous benefactor decided to finance schools making them accessible to all freeborn children.

Instruction began at the age of seven and included gymnastics, language, writing, and music. Through these subjects that nourished the spirit and harmonized the body, the ideal of *kalokagathia* was pursued—a pleasing physical aspect coupled with solid morals (what the Romans would call "mens sana in corpore sano"—a sound mind in a healthy body). Lessons were normally held in the teacher's home and lasted from sunrise to sunset. There were no desks, only stools; waxed tablets were used for practicing writing, the letters being drawn with a stylus. Only rarely were pupils allowed to write with pen and ink on papyrus rolls.

Once they reached puberty (*ephebia*), between the ages of eighteen and twenty, the boys began to attend the gymnasium where they were molded into citizens. There was a one-year draft-like period in which the youths received military training and learned hoplite combat and hunting. Literary instruction also continued at the hands of a *grammatikos* or *philologos*, and there was instruction in the oratorical art by a rhetorician, and in mathematics and the sciences.

Related entries
Writing, music and
dance, sports,
gymnasia and palestrae

▼ Red-figure *kylix* (detail), *Pupil with Closed Writing Desk*, 475–450 BC. New York, Metropolitan Museum of Art.

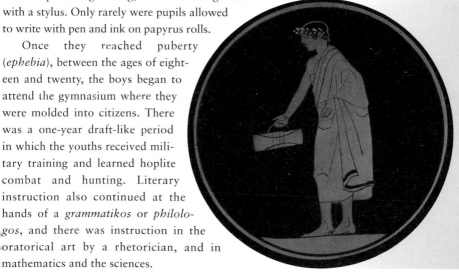

This cup by Douris is the most complete surviving representation of instructional activities in an Athenian school, divided into the three subjects of music, language, and writing.

At the extreme left is a music lesson: the teacher (kitharistes) and the pupil are seated facing each other and play the lyre together, while a double aulos lesson is depicted on the opposite side of the cup.

Wooden tablets on which a thin layer of wax was applied were used as exercise books; also, inexpensive everyday materials such as pottery shards and polished stones.

▲ Attic red-figure *kylix* by Douris (detail), *School Scenes*, from Cerveteri, ca. 480 BC. Berlin, Antikensammlung.

The most common type of writing stylus was a reed stalk, the kalamos, that was regularly sharpened, but bone styluses were also common. Ink was made with metal pigments such as copper, iron, or lead.

On the stretched roll we see the typical opening lines of an epic poem, "Oh Muse, find for me on the shores of the Scamandros / the subject matter of this my song."

The pupil stands before the teacher and recites the poem by heart as the teacher checks the words against the written text. On the right, the senior school director, known as didaskalos, carefully supervises the lesson.

Books began to appear in Greece in the middle of the seventh century BC, mostly written on papyrus rolls; linen and parchment rolls were rarer. The book was usually wound around itself starting from the end, sometimes around a thin wood or bone stick that ended in knobs at each end.

> *"[The teachers] make harmonies and rhythms familiar to the children's souls ... that they may learn to be more gentle ... for the life of man ... needs harmony and rhythm"* (Plato, Protagoras)

Music and Dance

In Greek culture, the term *mousike* did not simply denote the art of sounds, but also poems and dance, and the musician often composed the melody, the lyrics, and the choreography as well. Originally, singing or recitation was accompanied by instruments that followed it, playing in unison. Over time, the scores became more complex and large orchestras were formed. In all likelihood, music began to be written down between the fifth and the fourth century BC using an alphabet-based script that distinguished between annotations for voice and for instruments. Still, composition and transmission continued to be mostly oral. The more popular instruments to accompany the bard's song and the tragic choirs was the *lyra*, consisting of a sound box made of turtle shell with gut strings stretched over it, and the *aulos*, a sort of two-pipe flute.

Ancient Greeks believed that music was an effective tool for teaching morals and civics to citizens, thus they made it part of the school curriculum. In Athens it was one subject of primary education, together with writing. In Sparta, young people received musical instruction because the rhythmic cadence of the choirs was deemed to train them for battalion discipline, since the army's movements were dictated by the *aulos* and by chants. In the gymnasia, training was done to the sound of the flute. Finally, all public ceremonies, whether political or religious, were accompanied by music.

► Bronze statuette, *Rattles Player*, Spartan manufacture, ca. 530 BC. New York, Metropolitan Museum of Art.

According to a myth, Hermes was credited with inventing the lyre; in turn, he gave it to Apollo to compensate him for the theft of the Pierian cows, thus making him the guardian god of music.

The goddess Athena was credited with inventing the flute, but after she saw in a reflection in a stream that playing it deformed her face, she promptly discarded it, threatening terrible punishments on whoever would pick it up.

This myth reflects the opposition often remarked by ancient authors, between the bewitching power of music, symbolized by the flute and linked to Dionysus and orgiastic rituals, and the music that accompanies song or recitation, represented by the lyre and linked to the Apollonian realm of rationality.

This scene depicts Marsyas still playing, in a desperate attempt to win the contest while Apollo, the lyre on his lap, watches him ironically and a figure dressed in the Phrygian mode already clutches the knife that will flay the Satyr alive for having dared to challenge a god.

The Satyr Marsyas found the flute in Phrygia and was so spellbound by it that he challenged Apollo to make sounds just as beautiful with the lyre.

▲ Relief base of a statue, *Musical Contest Between Apollo and Marsyas*, from Mantinea, ca. 320 BC. Athens, National Archaeological Museum.

A young student named Euthymides plays the lyre following the teacher's suggestions; he is observed by another student and an elderly figure.

Originally, the lyre was made out of a turtle shell, the sound box, to which two animal horns were attached, one at each side, joined on top by a yoke from which the strings were stretched to the body. The strings, usually seven, were made from animal tendons or gut.

The musician used a plectrum or plucked the strings with the right hand while adjusting the strings' tautness and vibration with the left. The teacher is tuning the instrument by adjusting the strings' tension on the yoke.

An inscription behind this figure identifies him as Smikythos, a famous teacher at the time.

▲ Attic red-figure *hydria* by Pinthias (detail), *Music Lesson*, from Vulci, ca. 510 BC. Munich, Antikensammlung.

The salpinx *was a bronze trumpet with a straight pipe and round sound box, played by holding it diagonally towards the ground. It was used primarily by the military: its shrill sound gave the armies the signal to march, to attack, and to retreat, and announced the commander's orders.*

A leather strip tied at the nape brought the trumpet's cup-shaped opening to the mouth, allowing some freedom of movement to the hands.

This Scythian archer is wearing their characteristic costume: vividly colored, padded but without metal protection, the leather headdress shaped like an inverted funnel.

The double-curved bow projects from the quiver, where it was stored together with the arrows.

Attic black-figure *kylix* by Psiax (detail), *Archer Playing the Salpinx*, 520–500 BC. London, British Museum.

Here the double aulos player steps on a podium to begin his performance. Around him the judges sit on stools.

The aulos was made of sycamore, maple, or plum wood and varied in length between 8 and 32 inches, depending on whether it played soprano, alto, tenor, baritone, or bass. When two auloi were played together one sounded the melody, the other the basso continuo

Musical competitions often took place alongside sports and theater performances at the major religious festivals. There is plentiful evidence of them on Attic vases starting from the middle of the sixth century BC; in all likelihood, therefore, they were already part of the Pan-Athenaean festival program when it was first instituted in 566 BC.

Flute and kithara performances were either played solo or with a choir; the two instruments also accompanied the recitation of epic poems and singing contests.

▲ Attic red-figure kalyx-krater
by Euphronius, *Musical Contest,*
from Cerveteri, 520–510 BC.
Paris, Musée du Louvre.

A wrestler, a discus thrower, and a javelin thrower train in a gymnasium to the sound of the flute.

The sound of the flute was considered appropriate for all situations, from competitions and war to the symposium, the theater, sacrifices, or funeral ceremonies.

The Greeks believed that music created a positive environment for sports training and military exercises, because it soothed the soul and promoted concentration.

▲ Attic red-figure *kylix* by Epictetus (detail), *Athletes Training to the Sound of the Flute,* from Vulci, 520 BC. Berlin, Antikensammlung.

This vase depicts a succession of lively scenes including dances and acrobatic exercises, very popular at the time, performed to the sound of flute and rattles.

The warrior on the left is dancing the pyrrhic, an armed dance performed before the battle, which mimed the movements for striking the enemy and avoiding his blows. The pyrrhic, probably born in Crete, was very popular, especially in Sparta where it was an important part of military training.

The acrobat on the table is a contortionist: after doing a vertical, he now does a complete dorsal arch and is about to drink from a cup in this position.

This young male dancer, after arranging three swords vertically on the floor, dances or jumps over them.

▲ Attic red-figure *hydria* by Polygnotus, *Musicians, Dancers, and Acrobats*, from Nola, 430 BC. Naples, Museo Archeologico Nazionale.

"Gymnastic exercises should be employed in education, and for children they should be lighter, avoiding severe diet or painful toil, lest the growth of the body be impaired" (Aristotle, Politics, I)

Sports

The Greeks always understood sport as a competition or "agon," and it occupied such an important place in their culture that the earliest date in Hellenic history of which we are sure, 776 BC, sets to memory not the date of a battle or a political event, but the name of the first winner of the Olympian Games. In addition to being a fundamental aspect of education, sports competitions had an intrinsic religious significance; at first, the agons took place at the funerals of important personalities, as one way of honoring the deceased. Probably some of the major Pan-Hellenic Games were also first instituted to commemorate some heroic figure whose death was being mourned, such as Oenomaus at Olympia. In the historical age, the funerary significance of the games began to fade as they became spectacles organized to please the gods, part of the periodic religious festival programs, like processions and sacrifices; each *polis* organized them autonomously and participation was limited to the citizens of that city.

Over time, for political and religious reasons some of the cult cities chosen as agon sites such as Olympia, Delphi, Nemea, and Isthmia began to take on an importance that extended beyond the city borders; gradually, the group of participants admitted to the games was extended to include other cities, then other regions, until the games became "Pan-Hellenic" that is, open to all of Greece, an acknowledgement so important that all war activities were suspended while the games were in progress.

Related entries
School and education, music and dance, funerals, gymnasia and palaestrae, stadiums and hippodromes, Delphi, Nemea, Olympia

◄ Bronze statuette, *Runner at the Starting Line*, from Olympia, ca. 480 BC. Olympia, Archaeological Museum.

197

Racing was the first competition introduced at Olympia in 776 BC, and the only one for the first thirteen years. Initially, the race was 192.27 m long, corresponding to one stadium (an ancient Greek and Roman unit of length, the Athenian one corresponding to about 607 feet); later, the diaylos, 2-stadiums long, was introduced, and later the long race called dolichon whose length varied from 7 to 24 stadiums.

The contest known as hoplites in which the racers ran wearing bronze helmet, shield, and greaves, was the only one where the athletes were not naked. Twenty-five bronze shields ready to be used by the athletes were stored at all times in the temple of Zeus at Olympia.

Pan-Athenaean amphoras full of oil were given as prizes at the Great Pan-Athenaean Games that took place in Athens every four years. The state commissioned their production and they continued to be decorated with black figures even after this technique had been discarded in regular pottery production.

One face of the vase always had a picture of Athena in arms, while the other illustrated the sports specialty of the athlete who would receive the vase as prize. This amphora has been dated exactly because starting in the fourth century BC the name of the archon in office was inscribed next to Athena.

▲ Amphora of the Pan-Athenaean Games from the Nikomachos series (detail), *Hoplite Race*, from Bengasi, 323–322 BC. Paris, Musée du Louvre.

The torch race, known as *lampadedromia, was not an Olympian sport but was part of the opening ceremonies of the Pan-Athenaean Games; it also took place at the Hephaestian and the Promethean festivals.*

Participating in the race were the teams that represented the various Athenian tribes; in the race, a courier carried the torch from the Academy, where the altar dedicated to Prometheus, the Titan who had stolen fire from the gods and given it to mankind, was located, to the altar of Eros on the Acropolis.

▲ Attic red-figure *oinochoe, Race with Torches,* mid–5th century BC, Paris, Musée du Louvre.

The modern tradition of lighting the torch at Olympia just before the opening of the games and carrying it in a relay race to the site where the games will be held is not a properly "Olympian" tradition but an Athenian one.

This bronze statue portrays the driver of a quadriga (a two-wheel chariot drawn by four horses harnessed abreast) and was part of a statuary group dedicated by Polyzalos, tyrant of Gela, for a victory at the Pythian Games in 478 or 474 BC.

Because the winners of these races were not the charioteers but the chariot owners, even a woman, Cynisca, daughter of the king of Sparta Archidamus II, was proclaimed twice the winner at Olympia.

Based on the surviving fragments, this composition included, in addition to the charioteer standing on the chariot driven by four horses, two more horses on each side, either mounted or led by the bridle by two servants. The statue depicted the honor lap around the stadium after the victory.

The young charioteer has eyes of semi-precious stone and copper lips. He wears the long linen garment typical of the charioteers, held at the chest by thin suspenders and cinched above the waist by a belt. He wears a headband decorated with a wavy motif inlaid with silver.

Chariot races were the most prestigious and enthralling of the Pan-Hellenic Games, also because of the risk involved; they were monopolized by the powerful men of the various cities, the only ones who could afford to train and support teams of horses and crews of charioteers, grooms, and servants.

▲ *Delphi Charioteer*, ca. 478 BC.
Delphi, Archaeological Museum.

The Nikai—winged victory goddesses—bring honor ribbons to the young winning athlete.

At the Olympian Games, the winners went to receive their prize wearing red woolen fillets wound around the head, the forearm, and the thigh.

The winners of the Pan-Hellenic Games received symbolic prizes: at Olympia they were crowned with wreaths from the branches of an olive tree that grew behind the great temple of Zeus; at Delphi, the winners of the Pythian races received laurel wreaths; in Isthmia the wreaths were made of pine boughs, and in Nemea, of wild celery.

Once they returned home, the athletes were rewarded with more substantial prizes such as sums of money, a life-long state pension, places of honor at performances, and other material benefits.

▲ Attic red-figure *kylix* by the Briseides Painter (detail), *Nikai and Winning Athlete*, from Vulci, ca. 480 BC. Paris, Musée du Louvre.

This equestrian statue was reassembled by joining a head held at the Louvre to torso fragments held at the Acropolis Museum and here reproduced by cast. The reassembly was suggested by Payne in 1936.

The wreath of oak leaves that the rider is wearing identifies him as the winner of one of the four "crown" games whose prize was a wreath, although the oak leaves are specific neither to Olympia nor to Delphi, Nemea, or Isthmia.

Horse races were the most prestigious and popular races in the Pan-Athenaean Games as well, horse raising being the hobby of just a few wealthy aristocratic Athenian families.

▲ *Rampin Rider*, from the Athens Acropolis, ca. 560–550 BC. Athens, Acropolis Museum / Paris, Musée du Louvre.

Horse races were part of all the Pan-Hellenic Games and were run on an approximately one-kilometer (3280 feet) track. At Olympia there were eight equestrian competitions: horse and mare races, biga and quadriga *pulled by horses*, biga *pulled by she-mules*, biga *and* quadriga *pulled by colts*, and colt race.

This athlete is holding alteres, *which were stone or metal dumbbells carried forward in the run-up and take-off to increase the jumping rush.*

▲ Attic red-figure *kylix* by the Euergides Painter (detail), *Athlete Preparing for the Long Jump*, from Vulci, ca. 510 BC. Paris, Musée du Louvre.

The long jump was not a separate specialty; together with racing, discus throwing, javelin throwing, and wrestling, it made up the pentathlon, *the most complex and complete of the ancient sports disciplines.*

According to the Greeks, wrestling was the most ancient sport, born out of the need for survival. The palaestrae where athletes trained in all specialties, in fact, took their name from pale, the Greek word for wrestling.

Wrestling was one of the five pentathlon specialties; it had very strict rules: starting from a standing position, the wrestlers fought head to head extending their arms and trying to floor their opponent; for victory to be declared, there had to be three knock-downs.

▲ Relief base of statue, *Wrestling Scene*, from the Wall of Themistocles, 510–500 BC. Athens, National Archaeological Museum.

The match took place on a square of soft earth, the skamma, *where the wrestlers could fall without hurting themselves too much. Before the fight the dirt was worked a bit with the feet to soften it.*

Wrestlers could hold the opponent only above the waist, though tripping to destabilize him or make him fall was allowed. Here the referee holds a long cane so he can step in in case of irregularities.

Discus and javelin throwing were both part of the pentathlon. The disks that have survived vary in weight from 3.3 to 13 pounds. Because most of them are ex-votos, disks that the winning athletes dedicated to sanctuaries, they might not be not faithful reproductions of the disks actually used in the games.

Here the athlete is shown at the end of the run-up as he is about to throw the javelin, his right arm pulled back. The javelin was 8 feet long and was thrown by giving it a rotating movement with a slip knot set in the center.

The disk was thrown from a space marked by lines in front and on each side, using the technique illustrated in vase paintings and in sculptures such as the famous Discobolus *(Discus Thrower) by Myron.*

▲ Bronze disk, *Javelin Thrower,* from Aegina, ca. 470 BC. Berlin, Antikensammlung.

Boxing was a demanding discipline,
with rules different from today's: there
were neither rounds with rest periods
in between, nor time limits; since there
was no victory "on points," it lasted
until one of the boxers collapsed.

Boxing gloves were
used, but not to
soften the blows.
At first, simple
leather strips
(himantes) were
used to protect
fingers and wrists;
in the fourth
century BC the
infamous
"penetrating"
gloves were
introduced: they
had a sort of wool-
padded
reinforcement on
the forearm and
big, hard leather
rings around the
phalanges.

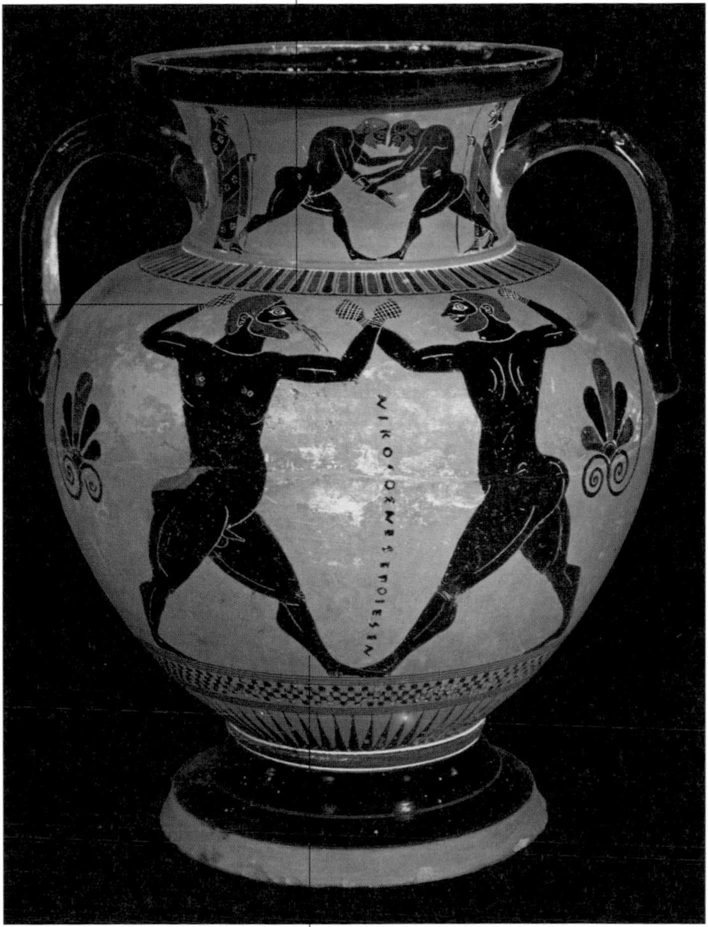

Apparently punches were
mostly to the face; the
other parts of the body
were not usually hit.

▲ Attic black-figure amphora,
Boxing Scene, 550–525 BC.
London, British Museum.

"The ball ... the boxwood castanets so rich in sound, and the dice, his passion, with the rhombus that turned and turned ... Philocles did place his old toys before Hermes" (Palatine Anthology)

Toys and Games

Related entries
Symposium, sports

The Greek took a keen interest in games, and even wrote books to describe the rules, but unfortunately most of them have been lost. Most of the surviving information has been garnered from vase iconography and from the toys found in excavated temples, where boys and girls dedicated them once they reached adulthood or were about to be married, or in necropolises, as part of children's tomb furnishings. Infants were entertained with animal-shaped feeding bottles, rattles, and bells of various shapes. Older children played with animal toys on wheels and small carts, which they received for the Anthesteria feast, on which a child could sit and be pulled by another. As they grew, boys played primarily skill games such as the spinning top, the hoop, spools used as yo-yos, and kites made of cloth, while girls played with dolls.

Group games played by both boys and girls were blind-man's-buff and *ephedrismos*, throwing walnuts or astragali—tiny animal knucklebones also made of clay, bronze, or precious metals. Adults played with astragali in a complicated game of chance in addition to morra and dice. Quiet games were those played with pieces on checkerboards, as documented by many game tables, but the rules are not clear to us. A typical symposium game was the *kottabos*, which consisted in hitting a target with the last drops of wine from one's cup.

▼ Terracotta statuettes, *Girls Playing Astragali*, 330–300 BC. London, British Museum.

Dice, here thrown without the dice shaker, were manufactured from the most varied materials, from clay to gold. The game was played with three dice and the different combinations had names: three 6's was a "Venus shot" while three 1's was a "dog shot."

According to Pausanias, the game of dice was invented by Palamedes, a Greek warrior, to fight boredom during the siege of Troy.

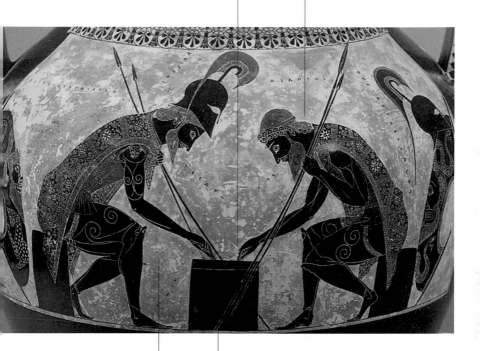

The numbers "three" and "four" written in front of the players are evidence that they are surely playing a game of dice, whose faces are usually numbered from 1 to 6.

This topic will be represented by many other artists, some of whom will depict the heroes playing a table game recognizable from the small balls used as pawns.

▲ Attic black-figure amphora by Exekias, *Achilles and Ajax Playing Dice*, from Vulci, 540–530 BC. Vatican City, Musei Vaticani.

The earliest surviving Greek dolls were manufactured in Boeotia in the second half of the eighth century BC. Made of terracotta and up to 20 inches high, they had jointed legs and a typical bell-shaped skirt decorated with fishes, birds, or geometric motifs. Their weight and size suggest that they may have been used mostly for funerary or votive reasons.

In antiquity, dolls were not like today's baby dolls, but always portrayed marriage-age girls. During the Daedalea celebrations, terracotta dolls dressed in bridal gowns were carried in procession.

▶ Terracotta doll with trousseau, late 5th century BC. London, British Museum.

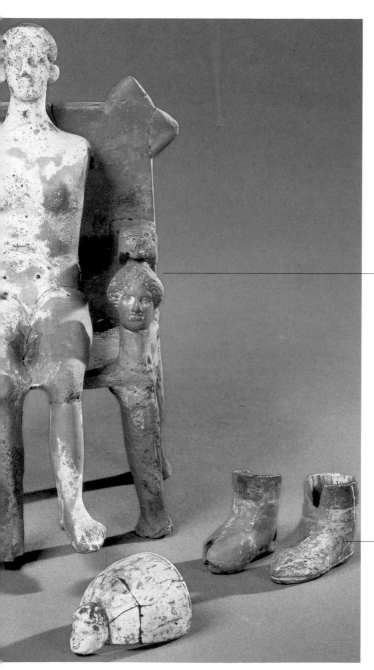

The most common materials used for dolls were terracotta and carved wood. Rag dolls must also have been popular, since they could be made at home, and some examples from the Roman period in Egypt have survived.

This terracotta doll with jointed arms sits on a chair whose arms are supported by female protoms. Her trousseau consists of a pair of short boots, a krater on a high pedestal, and an epinetron, a device used to spin wool while in a sitting position.

A bronze pole was used to play the game of kottabos: *on the top of the pole was a loosely set disk, the* plastinx.

A drunken Dionysus is supported by a satyr as he is about to throw wine on the kottabos, *which a woman has just rearranged.*

▲ Attic red-figure *kylix* (detail), *Dionysus About to Play Kottabos*, late fifth century BC. Florence, Museo Archeologico.

A second perforated disk, the lekane, *was set at about two-thirds down the pole. The game was played by causing the small dish on top to fall on the* lekane *from the weight of the wine thrown from the cup or even sprayed with the mouth.*

According to ancient sources, the kottabos *originated in Sicily in the sixth century* BC, *later spreading to Greece and Etruria. Because we have no evidence that the Romans played it, it was probably out of fashion already in the Hellenistic period.*

Sometimes used as a penalty in a throwing game, this game probably consisted in carrying the winning mate on the shoulders to the goal, following the verbal instructions of a third player.

The term ephedrismos *means carrying someone piggyback in games and team matches of various kinds.*

A boy is carried *by a friend on his shoulders and covers his eyes with the hands.*

▲ Attic red-figure *oinochoe* by the Shuvalov Painter, *Game of Ephedrismos*, from Nola, 430–420 BC. Berlin, Antikensammlung.

The third playing mate *is squatting on the floor and points to a target, a stone stuck in the earth.*

Two young men play ball
with long sticks bent at
one end, as their
teammates watch.

Ball games, whether one-on-one or
in teams, for children or adults, are
amply documented in literary and
iconographic sources.

The small, hard ball
used was probably a
harpaston *and was
made of wool or tow.*

These sticks are very similar to
those used in contemporary ice
or roller-blade hockey, however
we know neither the dynamics
nor the rules of the ancient game.

▲ Relief base of statue, *"Hockey"
Players*, from the Wall of
Themistocles, ca. 510 BC. Athens,
National Archaeological Museum.

"Your son's bride will come to you on a cart / carried to your house by sturdy-footed mules. / She will spin the cloth resting her feet on amber" (Pseudo-Homer)

Marriage

Ancient Greek marriages were complex, multi-phased rituals. The two salient passages were the formal contract between the bride's father and the groom, sealed with the delivery of the dowry, and the transfer of the bride to the groom's house during a night procession of relatives and friends. Because marriage was considered a private affair, it was not governed by laws and there was no official religious ceremony, but only a set of rituals: the future bride prepared for the wedding by offering her childhood toys to Artemis; offerings and sacrifices were made to the guardian gods of marriage; on the wedding day, the couple took purifying baths; sometimes a banquet at the home of the bride was held, at which she participated, her face hidden behind a veil. Then the procession to the groom's house set out, which included de rigueur some characters with specific roles: a guide, an escort for the couple, the bride's mother carrying torches, and a child with living parents as a token of good luck. Not all these phases are documented in images or artifacts. Betrothals and banquets were never depicted, as the artists concentrated on the preparatory aspects such as scenes of the bride surrounded by girlfriends as she perfumes and adorns herself, or the house-to-house procession.

Related entries
Zeus and Hera, Artemis, female religiosity, sacrifice, offerings and ex-votos, houses

▼ Black-figure, footed *dinos* by Sophilos (detail), *Wedding of Peleus and Thetis*, 580–570 BC. London, British Museum.

The procession to the groom's home leaves from a house with a door ajar, behind which we see a woman, probably the bride's mother.

Because the procession took place at night, the bridal couple is preceded and followed by torch bearers.

The group is led by Hermes, the guardian god of travel and passages and of commercial transactions.

The two women are carrying a lebes gamikos used for the bride's ritual ablutions, a wooden coffer and a large pot. These objects symbolized the transfer of goods that went hand in hand with marriage and was a key part of it.

The veiled bride already stands on the chariot while the husband is about to reach her. The chariot is an improbable addition to a fifth-century urban procession, perhaps an archaic memory of the mythical wedding procession of the hero Peleus and the nymph Thetis.

▲ Attic red-figure pyx by the Marlay Painter (detail), *Door-to-Door Procession*, ca. 430 BC. London, British Museum.

Often, the vases
decorated with
wedding scenes
were gifts to
the bride: the
loutrophoros
and the lebes
gamikos were
used for water
for bathing; the
pyxes contained
cosmetics or
jewels; the
lekuthoi and the
alabastra, scented
unguents, and
the kraters were
used at banquets.

A maid (or the
bride's mother)
arranges the folds
on the bride's
gown as she
leaves her home.

Already walking, the groom
turns to the bride and takes
her by the hand. By placing
his hand on her wrist, the
man is symbolically taking
possession of the woman.

◄ Attic red-figure pyx by the
Wedding Painter, *Nuptial
Cortège*, 470–460 BC. Paris,
Musée du Louvre.

Arts and Crafts

Related entries
Potter's art, Athens
Agora

Greek culture did not glorify work and was marked by a radical lack of appreciation for manual labor, deemed unworthy of free citizens. The only productive activity that was not disparaged was land ownership of small or medium estates, because the attachment to the land was seen as a guarantee of patriotism and working the land was considered a manly pursuit, like bearing arms. Nevertheless, the economy of cities such as Athens or Corinth turned largely on commercial and craft businesses that were organized on an almost industrial scale in sectors such as construction, shipbuilding, and weapons manufacturing, and gave work to small workshops that specialized in crafts such as carpentry, rope-making, sails, leather, and woodwork.

One key element of all kinds of work was slavery. It is true, however, that slaves were allowed to manage their own independent workshops, as long as they paid a fixed percentage of their gain to their master. Still, a good part of the specialized craftsmen were freemen who worked independently or for hire, and they constituted the most dynamic, and therefore less controllable and more feared, social class. The rare images, on vases primarily, that depict arts and crafts, were made on the specific request of the patron who practiced that particular craft and probably reflected his professional pride.

▶ Attic black-figure amphora by the Taleides Painter (detail), *The Weighing of Goods*, from Agrigento, ca. 540 BC. New York, Metropolitan Museum of Art.

Commercial activities appear only rarely in the vast vase-painting repertoire. Generally discredited by society, these scenes were probably depicted only when the patron requested them specifically.

This fishmonger is going to the market carrying a pole with two baskets filled with fish. His head covering and attire are those of the humblest of manual laborers.

The dog is perhaps waiting for fish scraps to soothe its hunger.

The squatting man is busy selecting or cleaning fish.

Attic black-figure amphora from the Hypobibazon Class (detail), *ishmongers*, 520–510 BC. Berlin, Antikensammlung.

The shoemaker's shop is furnished with two stools, a table, and a tool shelf.

A shoemaker's shop was discovered near the Athens Agora thanks to an abundant find of iron nails and bone eyelets for laces. The name of the likely owner, Simon, was scratched on a ceramic cup found on the floor; he was probably a friend and disciple of Socrates.

The boy who needs new shoes has climbed on top of the workbench so that the shoemaker can custom cut the leather sole around the foot's contour.

The basin under the table was either used to collect scraps or filled with water to soften the leather.

▲ Attic black-figure *pelike* by the Eucharides Painter, *The Shoemaker*, from Rhodes, 500–490 BC. Oxford, Ashmolean Museum.

This young carpenter is finishing an unidentified piece of wood with a type of hammer held by a shoulder strap.

Carpenters did not have their own shops; they mostly worked on private or state construction sites, in the large dockyards or in arsenals where fleet maintenance work was done.

Attic red-figure *kylix* by the Carpenter Painter (detail), eponymous vase, from Chiusi, 510–500 BC. London, British Museum.

Two forge workers are busy near a cylindrical smelting oven with the fire lit underneath a crucible. One of them sits on a stool and fires an object, holding it with a pair of tongs; the other blows on the fire with a pair of bellows.

A worker is assembling the separate pieces of a life-size statue.

Heads and other anatomical parts hang from the walls awaiting assembly; the small paintings of animal or human figures were perhaps used as models.

Two workers are smoothing out and putting the finishing touches on a colossal warrior statue.

The two supervising men, here represented on a larger scale, were probably the owners of the business.

▲ Attic red-figure *kylix* by the Forge Painter, eponymous vase, from Vulci, 490–480 BC. Berlin, Antikensammlung.

Work is done under the supervision of Athena, the guardian deity of crafts, and of the likely owner of the shop, whose status as boss is made clear by his sitting position and the olive wreath on his head.

A worker is sculpting a horse using an awl and a small hammer.

In the southwest corner of the Athens Agora were several sculptor's shops, as documented by the unearthing of semi-finished statues and blocks of marble, and lead, bronze, and bone tools, smoothing tools made with abrasive stone, bowls still full of emery for polishing, and layers of marble dust and chips.

▲ Attic red-figure *kylix* by the Forge Painter (detail), *The Sculptor*, from Vulci, 490–480 BC. Munich, Antikensammlung.

"Come to me, Athena, and lay your hand over the kiln, / let cups and chalices come to a good end, / let them bake at the right point, and let good money be paid for them" (Pseudo-Homer)

The Potter's Art

Related entries
Euphronius, Exekias,
arts and crafts

Like all manual workers, potters did not enjoy a good reputation in Greece and ancient sources mention them infrequently. Most of the information we have about this craft and its production processes has been garnered from studying the vases that still bear traces of the labor that went into them, from the artist's signature to the representation of shops, and from finds such as ancient kilns.

Because ceramic-making discharged dust and smoke, the shops were usually located on the outskirts of settlements, in places with plentiful water that were easily reached by clay and fuel suppliers. Many of the processes involved in this industry, such as preparing and decanting clay, were done outdoors, thus the shops needed large courtyards where the kiln was also located. Covered, light-filled, and airy spaces were required for shaping the vases and drying them. Most of the shops were probably family owned and operated, perhaps with the assistance of a slave or two; however it is possible that in times of prosperity and expansion of pottery manufacturing, large specialized factories existed. The signature, followed by "epoiesen" (made this) for the potter, and "egrapsen" (drew this) for the painter, tell us that the two roles were distinct and that the potters, who signed their work more frequently, were considered more important that the painters.

▼ Attic black-figure *kylix* by the Lesser Masters (detail), *Potter Centering the Clay on the Wheel*, ca. 550 BC. Karlsruhe, Badisches Landesmuseum.

The mobile potter's wheel originated in the ancient East; its use in Greece is documented starting in the second millennium BC.

Large vases taller than an arm's length were often shaped in separate pieces and assembled by gluing the pieces together with an extremely fine, muddy clay.

The potter's wheel was a wood, stone, or clay disk that rotated on a fixed axis set in the ground, and was moved manually.

To shape small vases on the wheel, the potter moved the wheel; for the larger wheels used for amphoras and kraters, he used an apprentice to whom he gave the rotating time and speed.

▲ Siciliot red-figure kalyx-krater (detail), *Turning a Large Vase*, 5th century BC. Caltagirone, Museo Regionale della Ceramica.

Once the clay, carefully smoothed with a leather rag, had dried sufficiently and taken on a leathery consistency, the vase was painted. This was a slow process with the vases stored in shaded, cool places.

Athena and two Nikai crown the painters with honor wreaths. Probably the painter who decorated this hydria *reproduced his own shop with professional pride and as a homage to the guardian goddess of craftsmen.*

Sitting on a chair, the shop "master" decorates a large kantharos *by dipping a brush in the small color bowl placed on a nearby stool; at his feet are more vases waiting to be decorated.*

The three figures reproduced in a smaller scale, including the woman, were either servants or apprentices busy creating ornamental bands around the vase.

▲ Attic red-figure *hydria* by the Leningrad Painter (detail), *Ceramic Makers at Work*, ca. 470 BC. Milan, Collezione Torno.

The pinakes *from Penteskouphia (Corinth) are painted clay tablets dedicated by the Corinthian potters to the local shrine of Poseidon and Amphitrite, as ex-votos for the success of their work. They document all the phases of clay processing, from extraction to kiln firing.*

On top of the kiln is the draught hole. Kilns were made of stone and lined with clay or dried clay bricks that baked as they were used, thus strengthening the kiln.

Several pinakes *reproduced the firing of pottery, the riskiest part of the ceramist's work. The* pinakes *were probably placed inside the kiln with the objects to be fired, as propitiatory items, and then consecrated in thanksgiving.*

An amphora and several jugs stand in the oven on a perforated shelf supported by a small pilaster. The most valued ceramic piece was placed at the center where the heat was more uniform.

The full kiln is here seen in a cutaway view with the perforated floor turned over to reveal the artifacts to be fired.

The fuel-feeding chamber is full of charcoal. Probably the missing part of the pinax *portrayed the potter lighting the fire.*

▲ Terracotta *pinax*, *Kiln*, from Penteskouphia (Corinth), 6th century BC. Berlin, Antikensammlung.

Painters and ceramists work inside the shop. The figure on the left, probably the "master," is putting the finishing touches to a vase he just turned, while his assistants on the right put vase pieces out to dry.

The column separates the indoor space—a room or a portico—from the courtyard where the kiln was located.

Only rarely have archaeological digs unearthed the ruins of premises that were clearly those of potter's workshops, also because these locales did not have unique or easily identifiable architectural features and were often built with humble and perishable materials such as unbaked clay or wood.

The monster masks hanging from the kiln had an apotropaic function, to ward off the danger of a faulty firing that could inflict economic loss; the olive branches were probably hung to attract the guardian deities.

▲ Attic black-figure *hydria* (detail), *Ceramist's Shop*, 510 BC. Munich, Antikensammlung.

"Tell me also about the inns, the bakeries, the brothels, the drinking shops, the detours … and the innkeeper where you found the fewest fleas" (Aristophanes, The Frogs)

Roads and Transportation

Over-the-land conveyances were of little use for long-distance transportation in the Greek territory, mountainous as it was, divided into innumerable cities often at war with each other and lacking the financial resources to develop a widespread network of roads; in fact, long-distance shipping was done by sea, since roads often were little more than paths cut into the rock. Only city streets were paved in stone or at least had gravel beds, as well as the routes that ensured the transportation of food staples from the country to the city and those that led to the major sanctuaries visited by many pilgrims. Even rarer were the "wheel track" roads along which wagons moved with greater stability inside the ruts cut at a set distance corresponding to the length of the axle between the wagon's wheels. A unique case was the road that linked Athens to the Pentelic marble quarries that was laid out with double tracks for the simultaneous passage of heavily loaded wagons traveling in both directions.

Road signs were almost nonexistent; sometimes they were replaced by herms erected to attract the protection of Hermes on the road, which also bore rudimentary directions. People usually walked, or traveled on mule or donkey back; horses were reserved for war and hunting. The most common vehicles were light, two-wheeled carts with an open bed or an arched roof; heavy loads were transported on four-wheel wagons pulled by pairs of oxen.

Related entries
Hermes, fleet

▼ Paved section of the Pan-Athenaean Road in Athens.

The road from Athens to the sanctuary of Apollo at Delphi is one rare example of a "wheel track" road with two ruts about 3-4 inches deep cut at a set distance of 55 inches corresponding to the axle of the wagons' wheels.

The last section of the road, inside the sacred perimeter, was called the Sacred Way and was paved with regularly shaped stone blocks. The paving was redone several times until the Romans took over Greece.

Participation in the Pan-Hellenic celebrations involved mass travel. As with today's Olympics, it was not just the athletes and the spectators who traveled to the festival, but the official delegations of the various poleis as well who were in charge of attending the ceremonies and were a reference point for their compatriots who traveled to the shrines.

The cost for the construction and upkeep of roads leading to sanctuaries was shared by the poleis that participated in the cult.

▲ The Sacred Way in the sanctuary of Apollo at Delphi.

*The driver uses a stick instead
of reins to guide the animals.*

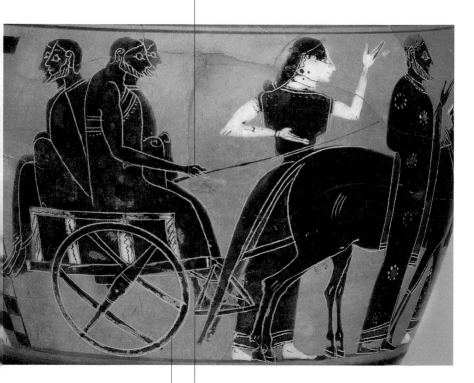

*This wheel has a thicker crossbar
and two thin parallel ones placed
crosswise; it evolved from the
filled wheels used in archaic
times and in turn would soon
be replaced by spoke wheels.*

*This small, light wooden cart
is pulled by a pair of mules;
one passenger sits facing
forward and two facing the
back. Carts such as these
must have been a normal
means of transport used for
short distances.*

▲ Attic red-figure *lekythos* by the
Amasis Painter (detail), *The Nuptial
Cart*, ca. 540 BC. New York,
Metropolitan Museum of Art.

Weights and Measures

Related entries
Athens Acropolis,
Athens Agora, Eleusis

In antiquity, length measures always referred to parts of the human body. In Greece, the basic unit was the foot and until the Hellenistic period it varied in size from region to region. To measure capacity, containers of predefined shape and size were used and their standards were kept at official sites where they could be scrupulously copied. The weight unit for solids, the talent, corresponded at first to the load that a single man could carry, or about 57 pounds; later it was calculated as a cubic foot of water.

The excavation of homes and shops, especially near the agoras that were true commercial hubs, have often unearthed measuring containers and objects. The largest group of these artifacts is from Athens, where containers and weights with the inscription "demosion Athenaion" (public property of the Athenian people) were found both on the Acropolis and in the Agora. Bronze weights were also marked with inscriptions bearing the unit or the fraction and a visual symbol next to it: an astragalus for the stater (28.6 ounces), a shield for the quarter-stater and a turtle for one-sixth of a stater. The set below, according to a decree that has survived, was probably kept with others in the Acropolis *tholos*, in Eleusis, and at the Piraeus for public reference.

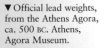

▼ Official lead weights, from the Athens Agora, ca. 500 BC. Athens, Agora Museum.

The liquid measures used in Attica were the metretes, *equal to about 41 quarts; the* chous, *equal to about 3.43 quarts, and the* kotyle, *equal to about .29 quarts.*

The letter "delta" painted on the ewer's neck marks it as state property (demosion, i.e. public).

This ewer is a unique example of the smallest liquid capacity measure, the kotyle.

▲ Ceramic liquid capacity measure, from the Athens Acropolis, 5th century BC. Athens, Agora Museum.

The most common dry weight capacity measure was the choinix: *corresponding to 1.08 liters (1 U.S. dry quart), it was the daily wheat ration for an adult man.*

Under the rim is a lead seal bearing an official mark.

Dry weight measuring containers were cylindrical, making it easier to level the contents on top. The first measures 3 choinikes, *the other two 1.5* choinikes.

In addition to the usual inscription "demosion," this container is marked with a seal bearing a little owl and the head of Athena, similar to the seals on coins.

▲ Ceramic dry weight measures from the Athens Acropolis and Agora, 5th–2nd century BC. Athens, Agora Museum.

This tile measure was found intact on site outside the ruins of public office buildings. Probably it was not used by private citizens, but by city officials to inspect the large supplies of tiles that the city ordered for public works.

Although this measure is from the Roman period, flat and bent roofing tiles of the same size as this were also used in the fifth century BC, evidence of the advanced standardization of production.

▲ Official marble tile measure in the Athens Agora, 1st century BC.

ΗΓΗΣΩ ΠΡΟΞΕΝΟ

The World of the Dead

The Funeral
Rites and Offerings
Markers
Public Monuments

◀ Grave stele of Hegeso, from the Athens Ceramicus, late 5th century BC. Athens, National Archaeological Museum.

The Funeral

Related entries
Sports, rituals and offerings, markers, public monuments

Most of the information we possess about funeral ceremonies is drawn from vase imagery, which focuses especially on the laying out of the corpse (*prothesis*) and the removal to the cemetery (*ekphora*). Only rare images exist of the washing of the corpse, the lowering of the coffin or the burial; our knowledge of these rituals is mostly from written sources.

When someone died, the women were assigned the chore of washing the body, anointing it with balms, dressing it and laying it out on beds covered with rich bedspreads, the head resting on a pillow. The following day, a dirge was held with the participation of friends and relatives. While in the Archaic age both men and women wailed, starting in the Classical period a clear distinction of roles emerged: the women wailed inside the home, while the men came from the outside to pay their final respects, a symbol of social recognition.

At the dawn of the third day, a procession took the body to a necropolis where it was either buried or burned on a pyre, depending primarily on family tradition, although for a long time the aristocratic classes favored incineration because it was a hero's funeral, as described in the Homeric poems of yore. The burial of the body or of the ashes was accompanied by offerings of food and libations. After the funeral, friends and relatives were invited to a funeral banquet at the house of the departed.

▼ Amphora No. 804 from the Dipylon (detail), *Laying Out the Dead*, ca. 750 BC. Athens, National Archaeological Museum.

The same scene is repeated on both sides of the vase neck: a woman wails and pulls her hair while another carries a loutrophoros identical to the one on which this image appears. This vase carried the water used to wash the corpse and was also placed before the house door in sign of mourning.

Men and women are visibly separated groups. The men stand at a set distance from the funeral bed and stretch the palms of their hands upwards in a farewell gesture that also symbolizes separation from the departed.

The deceased lies on a bed shrouded in a sheet, the head resting on a pillow, the jaw supported by a bandage. Next to him, the women who laid him out for the prothesis cry and tear their hair.

The knights drawn on the lower register probably mark the social status of the deceased or escort him to the necropolis.

▲ Attic red-figure *loutrophoros* by the Cleophrades Painter, *Funeral Lamentation*, ca. 480 BC. Paris, Musée du Louvre.

Men and women walk before as well as behind the cart, their hands to the head in the typical sign of mourning that appears in vase imagery already in the Geometric age.

A beardless youth and a woman, most likely the immediate family of the deceased, sit next to the corpse on a two-wheeled cart pulled by a pair of mules.

The corpse was taken to the necropolis either on foot or on a cart. When on foot, sometimes it was placed in a coffin. When carried on a cart it was usually laid out on a litter.

▲ Attic black-figure *kyathos* (detail), *Transporting the Dead*, from Vulci, 525–500 BC. Paris, Cabinet des Médailles.

"[Solon] did not allow the sacrifice of oxen in honor of the dead, nor did he allow more than three garments to be buried in the grave, nor visiting the tombs of strangers, except for the funeral" (Plutarch)

Rites and Offerings

The Greek funeral rite called for several offerings of food and libations to honor the deceased and propitiate his or her passage to the other world. These rituals began at the burial. If the body was incinerated, the vases carrying food and balms were placed on the pyre while the body burned, and often the ashes were put out with the libations and then collected and placed in the grave together with the funerary furnishings. A similar ritual was held for burials when the body was lowered in a grave, as documented by the numerous findings of shards, especially of drinking and pouring vessels, next to graves.

Nine days after the funeral it was customary for family and friends to meet at the necropolis to repeat the funeral ceremony; more rituals marked the thirtieth day after the funeral. Subsequently, each visit to the grave and each anniversary of the death—an important duty—was marked by many offerings. The grave was surrounded by flower wreaths and colored strips of cloth and objects were arranged on it, including libation vessels that were regularly replaced, small perfume vases, jewelry boxes, musical instruments, weapons, even sports equipment.

Related entries
Funeral, markers,
public monuments

▼ *Lekythos* with a white background by the Sabourov Painter (detail), *Offerings on a Tomb*, 450 BC. Berlin, Antikensammlung.

241

This tomb is topped by a stele wrapped with a ribbon. On the steps are wreaths and vases, primarily lekythoi *such as the one on which this scene appears, though smaller. In addition to colored ribbons, wreaths, and vases, the steps also displayed personal items of the deceased such as jewelry caskets or musical instruments.*

The young hero who died in war stands beside his tomb and receives those who come to pay him their respects.

Large lekythoi *with a white background were typically used for funeral rites. Like the small ones, they held scented balms used to prepare the body or to anoint the tomb where they were carried as offerings; sometimes their capacity was much smaller than their size.*

▲▶ *Lekythos* on a white background by the Bosanquet Painter, *Visit to the Sepulcher*, ca. 440 BC. Athens, National Museum.

A woman carries a basket filled with leaf wreaths with which she will decorate the tomb. Visits to the cemetery and the regular placing of ritual offerings were considered typical female chores.

This stele, reused to cover a grave in the Eridanus necropolis in Athens, reproduces the funeral vases that were placed on tombs as offerings, which in turn are decorated with scenes from the life of the young man who is buried underneath.

The headband in the background, from which two alabastra hang, refers to the gym where the young man trained, to the headband he wore and the oils he applied to his body before playing sports.

The name of the deceased is written on top: it is Panaitios, from the Amaxantia deme.

The lekythos on the left portrays a boy running with the hoop, a memory of a carefree childhood.

The loutrophoros in the middle portrays the deceased in his role of ephebus. Wearing chiton and petasos, he carries a spear next to his horse and greets a child and an old man, in the customary leave-taking gesture found on Classical funerary steles.

▲ Funerary stele of Panaitios, from Athens, 400–380 BC. Athens, National Archaeological Museum.

"Instead of a woman here I lie, made of Parian marble, / in memory of Bitte, a tear-filled sorrow for her mother" (Corpus Epigrammatum Graecorum)

Markers

Beginning with Homer and the very first funerary inscriptions, the word most often used by the Greeks to mark a grave was *sema*, which means sign, understood both as a substitute for the deceased and, like him or her, carefully washed and rubbed with oils, and as a memento. Both the incineration and the burial rituals placed great emphasis on the tomb's visibility, and since necropolises were usually laid out along the roads that led out of the city, the hope was of being remembered not just by friends and family, but also by the wayfarer who perchance walked by.

Various types of markers were used; most of them were found in the necropolises of Athens and Attica. From the ninth to the seventh century BC, the use of plain steles without inscriptions or reliefs, placed on top of small mounds and flanked by large libation vases with perforated bottoms, prevailed. Starting in the sixth century BC, the large vases were replaced by monumental marble sculptures, primarily *kouroi* and figured steles. In the fifth and fourth century BC, as a result of the sumptuary laws that forbade excessive displays of luxury, both the furnishings and the outside decoration of tombs were pared down. Graves of individuals from the same family were often placed next to each other and enclosed by plain fences, and the most common markers were small marble steles that favored a private cult of the dead.

Related entries
Funeral, rites and offerings, public monuments

◀ Dipylon krater, ca. 750 BC. Athens, National Archaeological Museum.

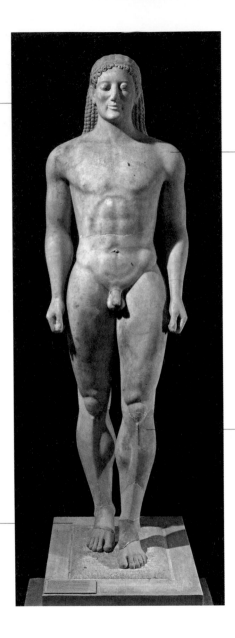

This kouros *came from a tumulus that covered several graves containing both ash urns and coffins, and was a marker for one of them located near the ancient road.*

This prestigious, larger-than-life marker suggests that the young man, Kroisos, who died in war, was the scion of a leading aristocratic family from Attica.

An inscription was carved on the original base of this kouros. *Written in verse, it addressed the wayfarer with these words: "Stop and weep before the* sema *of Kroisos dead, whom one day the raging Ares destroyed as he fought at the front line."*

The kouroi *had other functions in addition to funerary markers. Like the* korai, *they were often dedicated to divinities.*

▲ Funerary *Kouros*, from Anavyssos, Attica, ca. 530 BC. Athens, National Archaeological Museum.

The young girl Phrasikleia died before reaching marriageable age. She wears a richly decorated peplum held by a wavy-patterned sash, sandals, and a pendant necklace; a diadem sits atop her "pearl-style" hairdo.

In the necropolis of Merenda whose graves contain both ash urns and coffins, this statue was not atop a grave but in an elevated, clearly visible position near the road, suggesting that the grave's position was less important than the marker's visibility.

The inscription on the statue's base identifies it as a funerary marker, something rare for statues of women. It reads: "The marker of Phrasikleia, forever will I be called a maiden, having received this name from the gods in place of a wedding."

▲ Funerary statue of Phrasikleia, from Merenda, Myrrhinous, 540 BC. Athens, National Archaeological Museum.

The original fragments of the Megacles stele, over 12 feet high, are held at the Athens National Museum, the Berlin Museum and the New York Metropolitan. This reconstruction has cast pieces for the missing parts.

Starting in about 525 BC, this type of monumental stele became outmoded, perhaps an effect of the sumptuary laws against excessive displays of wealth, and was replaced by simple steles with plain palmette crownings.

The inscription on the base still bears the two initial letters of the deceased's name, which some scholars have interpreted as "Megacles," a name linked to the Alcmaeonidae, a powerful aristocratic family that fought the tyrant Pisistratus and whose family graves were destroyed.

The sphinx placed on top of the stele was carved in the round and still bears many traces of color. A third technique was used for the capital, decorated with drawings of scrolls and palmettes.

The young deceased, escorted by a sister, is portrayed naked and carrying an aryballos full of balm at the wrist, like an athlete. The pomegranate he holds in his left hand was at the same time a symbol of fertility and of the netherworld, perhaps symbolizing here that his death coincided with his puberty years.

▶ Grave stele of Megacles, 540–530 BC. New York, Metropolitan Museum of Art.

The area around the monumental gates of Dipylon, which later became the ceramists' district, was used as a necropolis starting in the Geometric age.

In the Archaic age, the Ceramicus became the city's leading necropolis where the funerary enclosures of the great aristocratic families were located, crowded with steles and monumental sculptures.

Starting at the end of the sixth century BC, as a result of laws passed against conspicuous displays of wealth, monumental funerary steles disappeared though the area continued to receive the tombs of famous Athenians such as Pericles and Socrates, in addition to those of private citizens and the state memorials dedicated to the fallen soldiers.

This necropolis was abandoned starting in the second half of the fourth century BC when many decaying monuments were recycled and used to fortify the city's walls.

▲ Athens, view of the Ceramicus necropolis.

The Mnason stele is one of a group of five similar steles that portray warriors in action and are made of the same stone. They were probably part of the state burials of the Theban soldiers who fell in the Battle of Delium (424 BC), when the Boeotians defeated the Athenians.

The helmet is in the Boeotian style, shaped like a metal hat with the brim turned down.

The polychrome painting of the stele is gone, but the outline of the figure is still visible carved on the stone, with the ground filled with white.

The warrior Mnason is portrayed as he attacks the enemy armed with shield and spear but without armor, dressed in a plain chitoniskos.

▲ Grave stele of Mnason, from Thebes, ca. 420 BC. Thebes, Archaeological Museum.

On the upper frame of this stele a metric-verse inscription illustrates the scene: "I hold my daughter's beloved baby in my arms. In life, our eyes both gazed at the sun's rays as I held him on my knees; and even now that I am dead and he with me, still I hold him."

Ampharete, whose name is carved on the lower frame of the stele, holds her newborn grandson and plays with him by showing him a little bird.

Funerary steles fell into disuse at the end of the sixth century BC but reappeared toward the end of the following century though in more modest styles and size and with a figurative language that fostered a domestic, private dimension of the cult of the dead.

▲ Grave stele of Ampharete and her grandson, 430–420 BC. Athens, Ceramicus Museum.

"Glorious is the fate of those who died at Thermopylae, / and bright is their destiny, their tomb an altar / ... the glory of Hellas chose to reside in this burial of the valiant" (Simonides of Ceos)

Public Monuments

Related entries
Funeral, rites and offerings, markers

Starting at the end of the sixth century BC, Athens and other cities enacted laws that imposed a reduction on the number of private funeral monuments, mostly erected by the aristocratic families. At the same time, public memorial monuments began to appear. Sometimes they commemorated just one person, whether a citizen or a foreigner, who had served the city well; some of the monuments, in the fatherland or on the battlefield, honored the war dead. Not infrequently these monuments were cenotaphs—empty tombs that, while not guarding the remains of the dead, were still meant to preserve their memory.

An exceptional case is the tumulus of the one hundred and ninety-two fallen soldiers of the Battle of Marathon, first discovered by Schliemann who also discovered Troy and began the first digs of the battle plain. In 1890 Spyridion Marinatos, who had discovered the Minoan site of Akrotiri, resumed excavation. Under the mound, perhaps originally topped by a monument, was a layer of ashes and human bones, the remains of sacrificial animals and shards of pottery that had been used for the funeral banquet. The dating of the shards to the beginning of the fifth century BC confirmed with almost total certainty that this was the place where the fallen Athenians had been cremated. Nearby, a smaller tumulus was identified under which were buried eleven males, perhaps the Plataean soldiers also killed in the battle, whose tomb is mentioned by Pausanias.

▼ Tumulus of the fallen at the Battle of Marathon.

A deceased is reclining on a kline *in the position of a banquet guest; the seated woman on the left faces him and removes the veil that covers her head in the typical gesture of the bride, while behind him a servant carries the wine he has just drawn from a large* dinos.

On the background wall hang a shield, a sword, a cuirass, and perhaps a lyre in the upper right corner.

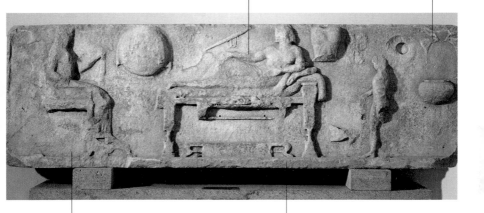

This relief was recycled and used in the Katapoliani Church in Paros, where it was found: it probably portrays the warrior poet Archilochus who was born on the island and honored there as a hero.

Several inscriptions mention the existence in Paros of a heroon *dedicated to Archilochus. The* heroa *were monuments to a deified ancestor that made of the tomb a cult site. Often these were not real tombs but cenotaphs (empty tombs) erected long after the hero's death.*

▲ Relief from the funeral monument of Archilochus, late 6th century BC. Paros, Archaeological Museum

Cities

Houses
Temples and Sacred Buildings
The Theater
Stadiums and Hippodromes
Gymnasia and Palaestrae
Public Assembly Buildings
Public Buildings and Banquet Halls
Porticoes
Water and Aqueducts

◄Athens, view of the Acropolis.

"I never spend time at home because only my wife knows how to manage what is in the house" (Xenophon)

Houses

Greek houses from the Geometric age (from the ninth to the eighth century BC) were oval-shaped huts built of wood and clay. Starting at the end of the eighth century, houses with a rectangular plan began to be built: some of them had apses, were divided into rooms, and often had a front porch. The construction materials used were stone for the foundation and unbaked clay bricks for the walls. In the Classical age, private houses began to be concentrated in residential areas, sometimes following urban plans that laid out uniform blocks bounded by parallel and perpendicular streets.

Apart from differences in size or layout, mid-level houses began to exhibit some common functional features. One recurring element was the *aule*, or inner court, where productive activities such as the processing of farm products took place. A portico (*pastas* or *prostas*) connected the yard to the inner rooms that included common spaces such as the kitchen and the bathroom, rooms for women's work (the gynaeceum) and the room reserved to the man of the house (*andron*) where he received guests and gave symposia. More modest dwellings, called *sunoikiai*, housed several family nuclei, and wealthier villas located outside of the residential neighborhoods, sometimes in the countryside, had more rooms, used especially by the servants, for productive activities and for storage.

▼ Drawing reconstructing a Late Classical age house to the southwest of the Athens Agora.

The residential districts excavated at the Piraeus are the clearest example of Hippodamic urban planning, so named after Hippodamus of Miletus, the architect who is considered its creator and who took active part in building the new districts around the port.

The principles of Hippodamic urban planning were applicable only to recently built cities: it called for residential neighborhoods clearly separated from public and sacred areas and laid out on a network of orthogonal streets that created uniform blocks of set sizes.

The Piraeus houses had two floors and were all equipped with a court and a front porch. On the main floor were the kitchen, the bathroom (though not in all houses), and the storage rooms, while on the upper story were the bedroom and the women's quarters.

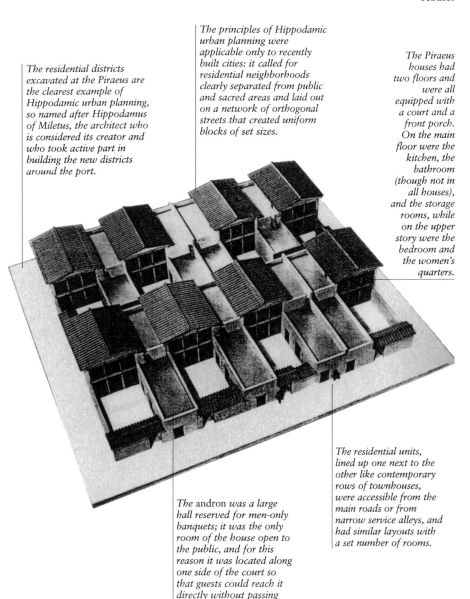

The andron was a large hall reserved for men-only banquets; it was the only room of the house open to the public, and for this reason it was located along one side of the court so that guests could reach it directly without passing through the private rooms.

The residential units, lined up one next to the other like contemporary rows of townhouses, were accessible from the main roads or from narrow service alleys, and had similar layouts with a set number of rooms.

▲ Model reconstructing a block of houses at the Piraeus, mid–5th century BC (from Settis 2002, *Atlante*).

Hanging from the wall are a metal cauldron for cooking and a grill for charcoal grilling. Both were used on the fireplace, which was frequently built flush with the floor, marked only by a row of stones; sometimes the fireplace was set in the yard.

Family members of both sexes ate their daily meals in the kitchen, which was equipped with a fireplace, food storage jars and all the cooking implements.

In this scene, the central piece of furniture is a large chest with animal-footed legs where one stored food, tableware, and cooking items. On top of the chest is a wine oinochoe and what looks like a wicker basket.

On the floor is a wine amphora leaning against the chest to stabilize it, and a large hydria full of water.

This skyphos reproduces with plenty of details the furnishings of a room that is rarely represented: the kitchen or a small pantry-storage room next to it.

▲ Attic red-figure *skyphos, Inside a Kitchen*, 5th century BC. Los Angeles, J. Paul Getty Museum.

This woman's work scene takes place in a room next to the owner's bedroom (thalamos) that can be glimpsed from the door left ajar.

The lady of the house is resting her feet on a low stool; she sits on a klismos, *an elegant chair without armrests, with a curved back and the legs bent toward the floor.*

The bed has richly decorated quadrangular legs and colored or embroidered pillows. Sleeping beds resembled banquet couches in that they were rectangular with wood or, more rarely, metal frames and a bedspring made of woven leather straps.

The seated woman is spinning wool: she holds in her hand the spindle around which she winds the wool thread. The standing maid is resting a handloom on the floor: it was used to weave small garments or as an embroidery frame.

▲ Attic red-figure pyx by the Painter of the Louvre Battle of the Centaurs (detail), *Women before the Thalamos*, ca. 430 BC. Paris, Musée du Louvre.

Lined on top of the chest are two wooden caskets for jewels and cosmetics at each end, three identical alabastra for perfumes, a wicker kalathos for spinning wool and a wine jug.

The two round loaves of bread arranged on top of the casket, the birds below and the wine jug all point to worship: all the objects, chest included, are offerings to a divinity, in all probability Persephone.

The figure in the round is a kibotos, a large chest with animal-footed legs and doors that open in front.

The scenes of brides preparing for the wedding often included chests or boxes, which the bride would fill with her trousseau and carry from her father's to her husband's house.

Chests of this type, usually kept in the thalamos, were often the only piece of furniture, in addition to the bed. People stored precious household items there, from fabrics to jewelry or weapons, and also used them to store clothing.

▲ Clay model of a chest, from Locri, 5th century BC. Naples, Museo Archeologico Nazionale.

In Greek images, spinning and weaving were symbols of woman's chores. Cooking or doing the laundry were represented only rarely.

Women's work appears often in Greek iconography; unlike male manual labor, it was never deemed unworthy; on the contrary, it was considered an asset on every step of the social ladder.

The woman on the left is twisting wool. With her left hand she holds flocks of wool, while with the right she twists them into a wick, the thick, continuous thread that falls at her feet into the kalathos, a characteristic basket with convex sides.

In the wealthier homes, a specific room, the gynaeceum, was set aside for wonen's work; often the women servants slept there on pallets. It was usually located near the thalamos, allowing the master to closely supervise it even at night.

▲ Attic black-figure *lekythos* by Amasis, *Spinning and Weaving*, ca. 540 BC. New York, Metropolitan Museum of Art.

Two standing women are weaving on a tall vertical loom using different bobbins for each color. The warp threads are knotted on top to a crossbar, the beam, and kept taut at the bottom by clay weights shaped like a truncated pyramid.

Bathrooms understood as private rooms set aside for personal grooming became common, even in mid-level homes, starting in the fourth century BC when the water supply system was improved; sometimes the room had a real bathtub made of terracotta and connected to waste water drainage canals.

This young girl carries her clothes and a bath sheet on her left arm, and is about to take a bath.

The large metal kettle contains hot water, probably heated in the kitchen that was located near the bathroom, probably also to take advantage of the heat from the fire.

Most people, men in particular, went to the public baths when they wanted to take a real bath. Washing at home was done mostly in small basins that were filled with water as needed and could be placed in any room.

The bathing vessel is a louterion, probably made of terracotta; it rests on a three-footed folding stand.

▲ Attic red-figure *kylix* by Onesimus (detail), *Woman Bathing*, 490 BC. Brussels, Musées Royaux.

Even in houses with bathrooms, toilets were rare because they required a complex drainage canal system.

When toilets did exist, they were often located in the yard. Inside the house, and especially at night, chamber pots were used.

The use of the chamber pot is documented in vase painting, even during symposia, where they are shown neatly placed under each guest's couch.

▶ Clay chamber pot from the Athens Agora, 5th century BC. Athens, Agora Museum.

Temples and Sacred Buildings

Related entries
Sacrifice, offerings and ex-votos, houses, public banquet halls, porticoes

In prehistoric times, worshiping took place outdoors around plain altars that sometimes consisted of just the ashes of the sacrificed animals. The first temples were erected in the Geometric era to protect the statues of the gods and the ritual implements; built with perishable materials, their plans reproduced those of residential houses, either rectangular or with apses, and had a front portico. During the seventh century BC, temples became monumental in size and began to be surrounded by colonnades and topped by tiled roofs: because of the weight of the tiles, the supporting wood structures had to be replaced with stone. The style, or "order" of the stone columns gradually developed with respect to the shaft, the top or capital, and the trabeation, until two regional styles became clearly differentiated: the Doric used in the Peloponnesus and the Ionic used on the islands and the cities of Asia Minor.

Even after temples began to be erected, the center of activity continued to be the altar, while the temple where the statue of the god was located was considered the god's dwelling. Even so, it was not inaccessible or without ritual function, for the steps and the porches were used as seating areas for the spectators during ceremonies; the vestibule (*pronaos*) and the area in the back (*opisthodomos*) were used to store votive gifts, and the indoor chamber was set aside for non-violent sacrifices such as libations and for depositing offerings.

▶ Small terracotta model of the temple to Hera at Argos, 8th century BC. Athens, National Archaeological Museum.

The temple of Hera at Olympia is one of the most ancient monumental temples, with a narrow, elongated shape typical of the early Archaic period, surrounded by columns arranged all around the cella or naos *(the enclosed central chamber).*

The Doric columns of the peristasis *were originally made of wood. Gradually, between the sixth century* BC *and the Roman age, they were replaced with stone columns of varying diameter and details, perhaps offered in lieu of ex-votos.*

The temple's roof has disintegrated, but the archaeologists who inspected the ruins determined that it was supported by wood beams and made of Laconian-type terracotta tiles.

Writing in the second century AD, Pausanias noted that the temple to Hera still had one oak column.

The walls of the temple, made of unbaked clay bricks, rested on a stone foundation. Inside the chamber, two rows of columns close to the perimeter walls were joined by alternating partitions creating separate chapels.

▲ Temple of Hera at Olympia, late 7th century BC.

The temple of Apollo at Corinth is one of the first built entirely of stone.

The peristyle that surrounded the temple on all sides rose above a four-tiered base and consisted of massive columns with the shafts built out of single blocks of fluted stone.

The chamber is still elongated and subdivided into three naves by two rows of columns that supported the roof.

Only seven columns are still standing, though the cavities cut into the rock to house the blocks that made up the temple's base allow us to reconstruct with precision the entire plan.

▶ Temple of Apollo at Corinth, mid–6th century BC.

In an early attempt to fill the decreasing spaces to the left and right of the central figure, the Gorgon, the artist carved two crouching panthers that fill the space but provide no narrative continuity.

The Gorgon at the center of the pediment is depicted in the typical posture of the "kneeling racer;" her head is encircled by snakes and projects from the pediment. The Gorgon-Medusa, often depicted on vases as well, was a traditional apotropaic image whose terrifying aspect was meant to protect the building.

On each side of the pediment are smaller figures depicting the murder of old Priam and the fight between a god and a giant, followed by the figures of two fallen giants in a lying position: this latter figurative device would be used frequently in ages to come.

Pindar, the poet who lived from the late sixth century to the middle of the fifth century BC, wrote that the custom of decorating the empty triangular spaces on the two short sides under a temple roof began in Corinth. Interestingly enough, one of the oldest, almost intact sculpted pediments is from Corfu (the ancient Corcyra) which was a Corinthian colony.

The small figure to the left of the Gorgon is her son Chrysaor, born from the blood the Gorgon shed when Perseus finally killed her by cutting off her head. In a symmetrical position on the other side should have been her other son, Pegasus, the winged horse.

▲ Temple of Artemis at Corcyra, pediment with Gorgon, 590–580 BC.

▶ Theater of Dionysus at Athens, first row seat reserved to the Dionysian priest.

"Aeschylus added a second actor; he reduced the importance of the Chorus, assigning the leading part to the dialogue. Sophocles raised the number of actors to three and added scene-painting" (Aristotle, Poetics)

The Theater

Areas equipped for sacred performances already existed in the Mycenaean world. However, the "Greek" theater received its defining structure only in the second half of the fourth century BC when the Dionysian theater was completed in Athens and became a model for all the others that followed. During the sixth and a good part of the fifth century BC, when the great authors of tragedies and comedies such as Aeschylus, Sophocles, Euripides, and Aristophanes flourished, temporary wooden structures continued to be used, and only a few cities had stable structures consisting of a few rows of seats in a

Related entries
Dionysus, music
and dance, public
assembly buildings

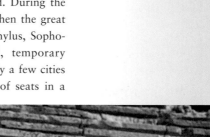

straight line or adapted to the soil configuration, but lacking an orchestra pit or a stage. Because theatrical performances were part of the feasts honoring Dionysus, many theaters were built near the god's sanctuaries and had an altar in the center, where the procession ended and where a statue of the god stood, under whose watchful eyes the performance unfolded.

The shows saw the participation of the entire citizenry: the state commissioned the play and paid the professional actors, while the expenses for the chorus (*choregiae*) were paid by the wealthier citizens, and ephebes between the ages of eighteen and twenty sang in the chorus. Competitiveness was an important ingredient in these performances, since the playwrights competed for a prize and the winner was chosen by a jury carefully selected with a view to preventing corruption or undue pressure.

The Theater

In Athens, theatrical performances were held in the Agora until 498 BC when they were moved to the sanctuary of Dionysus, on the slope of the Acropolis; there, a round wall was built to separate the central space reserved to the orchestra from the spectators who sat on the sloping hill.

The stage had projecting parts on each side decorated with columns, called paraskenia.

The transformation of the theater continued during the fifth and fourth century BC: at first the slope was arranged on a concave shape and tiers of stone steps were built, then a small building was added behind the orchestra to store stage settings, which also served as a backdrop. Finally, the stage was completed with a stone front and an arcade in the back.

The koilon where the audience sat was separated from the orchestra by a narrow, covered drainage canal, the euripos, and had a first row, the proedria, of throne-shaped seats of stone with animal-footed legs: they were reserved for personalities, and at the center sat the priest of the temple of Dionysus.

As it now stands, after the changes made by the archon Lycurgus between 338 and 326 BC, the theater's koilon holds a capacity of 14,000 to 17,000 spectators and is divided into three sections by two horizontal aisles; the radiating stairs create thirteen wedges in the lower section and twenty in the upper one.

▲ Theater of Dionysus at Athens.

The Delphi theater rose on the highest point of the sanctuary, inside the sacred enclosure; built in the fourth century BC, like many other Greek theaters it was rebuilt and renovated several times until the Roman imperial age.

The theater was used especially for lyrical and dramatic contests associated with the sports competitions of the Pythian Games.

The stage—only the foundation remains—was rebuilt in its entirety by Eumenes II in the second century BC.

The small horseshoe-shaped koilon could seat from 5,000 to 6,000 viewers; it has a 20-yard diameter and 35 tiers of steps.

The orchestra pit is paved with irregular stone slabs; it is the last reconstruction, dating to the second century AD.

▲ Delphi Theater.

The Epidaurus theater was built by taking the Athenian theater of Dionysus as model, even before Lycurgus ordered its reconstruction in the early fourth century BC. *From the outset, it was considered the most beautiful in all of Greece; it is still in rather good condition, and has maintained surprisingly good acoustics.*

The koilon *is wider than a semi-circle and can hold from 12,000 to 14,000 viewers. It is divided into two horizontal sections: the lower one, with 34 tiers, has six wedges separated by narrow staircases; the upper section has 21 tiers and twelve wedges.*

▲ Epidaurus Theater.

The actors' entrances (parodoi) *were located between the stage and the koilon's supporting wall; the actors reached the stage through tall doors framed by Ionic pilasters.*

The stage, now destroyed, had a plain rectangular shape.

The altar to Dionysus was set in the center of the round orchestra pit.

273

The actor on the left wears a long, pleated chiton and a short cape; he carries a mask.

The second actor wears a woman's mask and is dressed as a maenad with an animal skin thrown over the shoulder, a long chiton, and short pointed boots; his hair is gathered in a sakkos.

The conventional date when theater performances first began is 534 BC when Thespis of Icaria staged the first tragedy.

Until the middle of the fifth century BC there were only two actors in a play, to which a third was added later; thus masks were required because the actors played more than one role.

Although the theater was extremely important in ancient Greek civilization, plays are rarely represented on vases, and are mostly about comedies, perhaps because tragedy referred to myths, and the artists painted the myths directly.

▲ Attic red-figure krater (detail), *Theater Scene*, from Spina, 5th century BC. Ferrara, National Archaeological Museum.

Comedy appeared as a genre later than tragedy, and was partially modeled on its structure, including sung portions and recitation.

The helmets these warriors are wearing are not Attic, suggesting a foreign army.

A double-aulos *player* accompanies the dance of young soldiers in military dress who ride men disguised as horses.

▲ Attic red-figure amphora 1686 by the Berlin Painter (detail), *Riders Dancing*, from Cerveteri, 540–530 BC. Berlin, Antikensammlung.

The subject matter of comedy was political and social satire most of all. The chorus interrupted the acting and spoke directly to the public, introducing current topics and mocking the characters who were in the public eye.

The early date of this vase seems to rule out that this was a true comic chorus; rather, the type of dance and the masks foreshadow the characters of ancient comedy, where often the choruses were made up of foreigners or animals, perhaps to introduce a point of view different from that of the action taking place on stage.

"[In the Olympia hippodrome] is the Taraxippus, the horses'
terror ... when they ride before it, the horses are suddenly seized
by a violent fright" (Pausanias)

Stadiums and Hippodromes

Related entries
Sports, Delphi,
Nemea, Olympia

▼ Fragment from
an Attic black-
figure *dinos* by
Sophilos, *Funeral
Games Honoring
Patroclus*, from
Pharsalus,
580–570 BC.
Athens, National
Archaeological
Museum.

In the Archaic age, the athletic games held during the religious
festivals took place in the city's squares, with the spectators sitting on surrounding slopes or on temporary wooden bleachers.
Starting in the fifth century BC, structures called "stadiums"
were built for the Pan-Hellenic Games: the name is derived from
stadium, the unit measuring the length of the races that were
held there. Because the track was not circular, as is the case for
stadiums today, but rectilinear, the athletes had to return to the
start line every time they reached the length of one stadium
(about 607 feet).

Like the theaters, originally stadiums were built in areas with
natural contours that required little human labor, for example, by
placing a rectilinear track next to a naturally sloping terrain.
Gradually, stone steps were built for the spectators, special seats
for the jurors, monumental gates, and complex mechanisms to
regulate the athlete's take-off.

Hippodromes, in many respects just plain tracks on hard soil,
were wider than the stadiums
because they had a central strip
around which the chariots
turned; sometimes they also
had elaborate mechanisms that
set different start times for each
team. The Olympia hippo-
drome was famous for its start-
ing-line stalls laid out in the
shape of a "ship's bow" and for
a mechanism that lowered a
bronze dolphin along a pole,
simultaneously raising an eagle,
the start signal for all teams.

As was the case for theaters, the stadiums were built in natural locations that required only limited labor. The hard-soil track of the Olympia stadium was built at the foot of Cronus Hill and blocked on the valley side by an artificial embankment.

The stadium that gave the name to the sports structure where racing events took place was a unit of length of about 600 feet, though the length varied in the various Greek regions. For this reason, the Olympia stadium—the first one built ever—was 630.81 feet while the one at Delphi was 585.14 feet long.

At both ends of the track were "starting line blocks," a row of 20 stone slabs, one for each athlete, shaped with two parallel grooves that allowed a sure grip to the racers' naked feet.

Seating steps were never built at the Olympia stadium: the spectators sat directly on the grassy slopes on both sides of the stadium. Only the jurors, called hellanodikai, *had separate seats on a stone platform located on the southern embankment of the stadium.*

▲ Olympia Stadium,
early 5th century BC.

The Delphi stadium was built at the feet of the Phedriad crags and apparently had seating steps from the beginning although the final layout, with twelve rows of stone seats on the northern side against the mountain and six rows along the western curve and the south side, was the work of Herodes Atticus in the second century AD.

The starting line had ridged stone blocks as well as "cages" where the athletes took their place.

The stadium had about 7,000 seats but could hold up to 40,000 spectators if the natural surrounding slopes were occupied.

▲ Delphi Stadium, late 5th–early 4th century BC.

This stadium did not have regular stone seats. Instead, steps were cut roughly into the soft rock along the southern side and two or three better-shaped tiers built with recycled material were located along the western side, between the entrance tunnel and the start line.

The Nemea stadium was built by exploiting a natural depression between two hills on the southern side and creating artificial terraces to the north with the earth excavated on the south side.

Around the hard-soil track ran a small canal that carried fresh water to the thirsty athletes and spectators, with decanting basins and drinking fountains.

Both sides of the stadium had a start line of ridged stone blocks. Here the racers took their place standing, with arms extended.

A sort of fenced-in platform with stone chairs for the judges stood on the eastern side.

▲ Stadium of Nemea, ca. 330 BC.

In the earliest races, the starting sign was probably given by a trumpet or other instrument, although this did not ensure that all racers started simultaneously because some of them might anticipate the signal.

Many stadiums adopted start mechanisms of various kinds to prevent the racers from starting prematurely. This type of mechanism was the hysplex.

The Nemea hysplex *was particularly elaborate: made of stakes set at regular intervals between which ropes were stretched taut and twisted, it created a "catapult" effect by which the gate was suddenly lowered by a racing official.*

► Nemea Stadium, start line mechanism.

"Diving ... in this deep arena, they spray dirt on each other, and toss and scratch about like cocks in the dirt" (Lucian of Samosata)

Gymnasia and Palaestrae

Originally, gymnasia were places where freemen aged eighteen to thirty trained to fight in the hoplite phalanxes. Situated in the outlying parts of cities, they resembled well-equipped parks buried in vegetation, with hard-soil tracks for racing, fields of soft earth for wrestling, and fountains and statues. The settings included light structures either roofed or with porticoes, for undressing, rubbing oneself with oil, washing, and resting. These parks also included altars and cult sites because the gymnasia were considered sacred to Heracles and Hermes—the tutelary gods of young men—who symbolized physical strength and courage as well as intelligence and eloquence.

Gradually, these sites lost their war-like purpose and became professional athletic centers with monumental structures. The outdoor tracks were flanked by colonnaded porticoes and the wrestling fields were replaced by a new type of building, the palaestra, consisting of courtyards surrounded by colonnaded porticoes that became the focus of the gymnasium. Around it were rooms for the various athletic specialties, rooms for oiling the athletes and for immersion and steam baths. Some even had libraries and auditoriums for the philosophy schools that in the meantime had found a home there.

Related entries
Plato, Aristotle, Scopas, army, Aphrodite and Eros, Hermes, Heracles, school and education

▼ Attic red-figure krater by Euphronius (detail), *Scene in a Palaestra*, from Capua, ca. 510 BC. Berlin, Antikensammlung.

The Delphi Gymnasium is one of the earliest known to us. Designed primarily as a training site for the athletes that competed in the Pan-Hellenic Games, it occupied two terraces set one atop the other.

The lower terrace housed the loutron, an outdoor bathing area for athletes, with a round pool 33 feet in diameter and about 6.2 feet deep and ten rectangular tubs perhaps used for individual baths, set against the supporting wall of the upper terrace.

On the upper terrace was a xystos, a portico 610 x 30 feet that housed an indoor track, and a paradromis or outdoor track divided into three lanes and equipped with a start line.

To the west of the gymnasium are thermal baths built in the Roman age.

The foundations of the palaestra, and a courtyard surrounded by porticoes that led to the inner rooms, are still visible next to the loutron.

▲ Delphi Gymnasium,
mid–4th century BC.

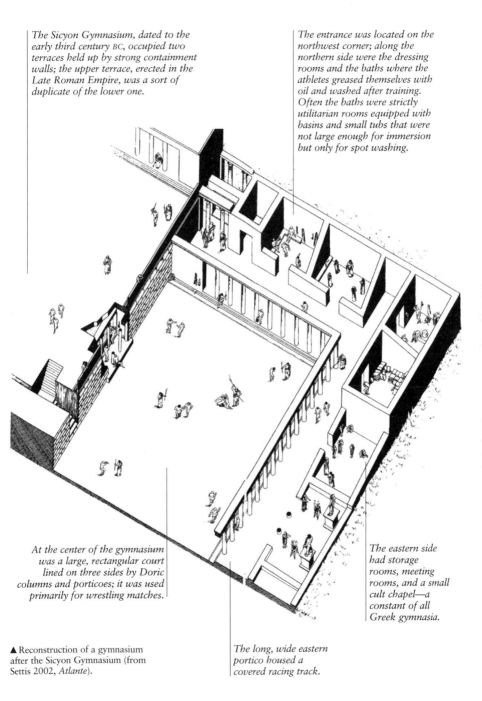

The Sicyon Gymnasium, dated to the early third century BC, occupied two terraces held up by strong containment walls; the upper terrace, erected in the Late Roman Empire, was a sort of duplicate of the lower one.

The entrance was located on the northwest corner; along the northern side were the dressing rooms and the baths where the athletes greased themselves with oil and washed after training. Often the baths were strictly utilitarian rooms equipped with basins and small tubs that were not large enough for immersion but only for spot washing.

At the center of the gymnasium was a large, rectangular court lined on three sides by Doric columns and porticoes; it was used primarily for wrestling matches.

The eastern side had storage rooms, meeting rooms, and a small cult chapel—a constant of all Greek gymnasia.

▲ Reconstruction of a gymnasium after the Sicyon Gymnasium (from Settis 2002, *Atlante*).

The long, wide eastern portico housed a covered racing track.

Pausanias narrates in the second century AD that he saw a statue of Heracles by Scopas in the Sicyon Gymnasium.

Ancient texts and archaeological findings document that the deities who were worshiped the most in the gymnasia were Heracles, Hermes, and Eros. While the first stood for physical strength and courage, the second was indicated as a model for young men because of his intelligence and eloquence. As to Eros, he stood for the ideal of physical beauty that had to be pursued through hard training.

Heracles was linked to sports competitions and games also because he was one of the mythical winners at Olympia and Nemea. His youthful tales stressed the care he took in training his body, which he did under the eye of excellent teachers such as Eurytus for the bow and arrow, Castor for hoplite combat, and Amphytrion for chariot racing.

▶ *Lansdowne Heracles,* Roman copy from an original by Scopas from the 4th century BC. Los Angeles, J. Paul Getty Museum.

The Olympia Gymnasium consisted of a large rectangular court surrounded by porticoes and joined to the south by a palaestra with peristyle and rooms that opened on the arcades and were equipped with seats along the walls.

The gymnasium's eastern colonnade was divided by Doric columns into two naves; it was 690 feet long to permit race training over a one-stadium distance and also leave space for the athletes to turn and come back without obstructing those behind them.

Because the building was also designed to lodge the Olympian Games contestants, behind the colonnades were small rooms that have been identified as bedrooms for the athletes.

▲ Olympia Gymnasium, late 3rd–early 2nd century BC.

"The platform was raised over the Pnyx so that one could look out to the sea, but the Thirty Tyrants turned it inland because they knew that the origin of democracy lay in dominating the seas" (Plutarch)

Public Assembly Buildings

Related entries
Political institutions,
theater, Athens Agora,
Olympia

Buildings devoted to the meetings of the governing council and the assembly of citizens, known as *bouleuteria* and *ekklesiasteria* respectively, from the names of these bodies in Athens, existed in all Greek cities. Because the people's assemblies gathered several thousand citizens, for a long time they were held in plazas and, later, in theaters. When specific sites began to be provided for them, they consisted usually of tiers of seats built outdoors or of suitable sites such as the Athens Pnyx, a sloping, terraced hill supported by an embankment and equipped with an orator's platform. Only rarely did architects design covered buildings such as the *ekklesiasterion* of Miletus. Nevertheless, it was important that the area where the *boule* magistrates deliberated be sheltered and that they be able to listen to the speakers.

The first building of this kind was the seat of the administrators of the Olympian shrine: built in the sixth century BC, it was a plain, rectangular hall with the entrance on the short side and an apse on the opposite one. After that, a new type of architecture was inaugurated with the building of the old Athenian *bouleuterion* at the beginning of the fifth century BC: its main features were a square or rectangular plan with a sloping roof, tiers of seats on three sides, an entry hallway on the fourth and a central pit for the speakers. This plan was adopted particularly by the cities of Asia Minor in the Hellenistic age.

▼ Athens, view
of the Pnyx.

The location of the Olympia bouleuterion inside the sacred shrine enclosure is an anomaly, since these structures were usually located in the agoras.

The long, rectangular hall where the council met was accessible from the short side; the tiers of seats where the councilmen sat were lined against the wall and were probably made of wood.

On the opposite side from the entrance was the apsidal area, used as an archive for storing official documents and the written rules of each sports competition.

The members of the Olympian committee met in the bouleuterion to organize the games and choose the juries; they also verified that the athletes met the entry qualifications which required that they be of Greek origin, not slaves, physically able to compete, and at least seventeen years of age.

In the early part of the fifth century BC another hall was added similar to the first. In the center between the two halls an altar to Zeus Horkios, guarantor of oaths, was built. It was there that the athletes took their oath just before the games began.

▲ The Olympia *bouleuterion*, mid–6th century BC.

The seats where the council sat were arranged in straight rows; at first they were made of wood, later of stone, and occupied three sides of the hall. A speaker platform stood in the center.

The old Athens bouleuterion was a square building measuring 75 feet per side, with a four-sided sloping roof supported by rows of columns arranged in a "U" shape.

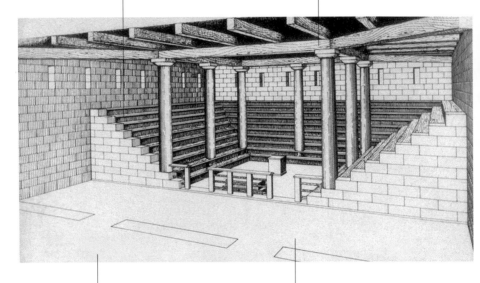

The fourth side of the hall had an entrance vestibule.

Towards the close of the fifth century BC, the old bouleuterion was replaced by a smaller, rectangular edifice measuring 52 x 72 feet and with semi-circular tiers.

▲ Drawing reconstructing the interior of the old Athens *bouleuterion*, early 5th century BC.

The plan of the Priene bouleuterion was an almost perfect square (65.6 x 68.9 feet). Designed on the theater model, it rested on the north side against a natural slope, while the south side opened on a portico with a double colonnade that bordered on the Agora.

Initially, the building was covered by a two-sided sloping roof supported by wooden trusses that rested on two rows of pilasters erected at the top of the steps.

Four narrow stairs on each side of the tiers allowed the participants to easily reach their seats.

The orator's platform has not survived, however the center of the hall is still partially occupied by an altar decorated with festoons and bull protoms.

The tiers of seats, arranged at right angles to each other on three sides, were built entirely of stone. They accommodated about 650 people.

▲ Priene *bouleuterion*, 2nd century BC.

"Solon ordered that those who dined together in the prytaneum *eat barley loaves, and that they add one wheat roll on feast days"* (Atheneus)

Public Buildings and Banquet Halls

In the life of the *polis* there were frequent occasions for communal meals. In addition to the religious festivals that ended with the distribution of the meats from sacrificed animals, in cities such as Sparta it was customary to arrange for *syssitia* which were communal meals that all citizens were required to attend. Furthermore, each city-state had to provide for the material sustenance of the appointed magistrates. In Athens the *prytaneis*—the fifty members of the year-round *boule* that took turns serving for thirty-six consecutive days—lived and ate in public dwellings.

With time, a sizeable crowd of permanent guests of the community was added, such as the envoys from foreign cities, the winners of the Pan-Hellenic Games, the war orphans, and so forth. However, no specific type of architecture existed for the communal meals. Instead of large banquet halls, the preference was for erecting buildings with several dining rooms for a limited number of guests each. In the sanctuary *hestiatoria* that replaced the archaic temporary huts, the dining rooms were often grouped around large courtyards where the processions unfolded. As to state buildings, the banquet halls were located primarily in the *prytaneum*, the "town hall" that contained the sacred hearth of the community, or behind the porticoes that lined the plazas.

▼ Drawing reconstructing the interior of the Athens *tholos*.

The tholos *was a round building with a conical roof supported by six interior columns and covered with rhomboidal tiles, erected around 470 BC on the ruins of the* prytaneum *that dated back to the early sixth century BC, where the sacred fire of Hestia was kept.*

While the bouleuterion *was just a meeting place, the* tholos *was the headquarters of the* prytaneis—*the fifty councilmen who served for the tenth part of a year. There they took their meals and sometimes spent the night in order to be ready for any emergency.*

Although the building was quite large—it had a 59-foot diameter—its circular plan was not very suitable to being furnished with banquet couches for the magistrates and their guests; therefore they probably took their meals sitting on plain benches lined against the wall.

▲ Drawing reconstructing the Athens *Tholos* and *Bouleuterion.*

Table vessels such as this black-painted wine kylix had no standard measure, type, or shape. Here the "demosion" stamp probably referred to the fact that it was part of the crockery used in the tholos for the magistrates' communal meals.

Some of the containers were probably official capacity measures that were kept in the tholos.

Among the artifacts found near the tholos were some ceramic vases stamped with the "demosion" (i.e., "public property") mark.

▲ State-owned ceramics from the Athens *Tholos*, 5th century BC.

The southern stoa of the Athens Agora had a double colonnade behind which were sixteen small, square rooms.

The stoa's dining rooms were probably reserved for the magistrates who lived at the state's expense. An inscription found in the building suggests that at least one of the rooms was reserved for the metronomoi, *the officers who inspected weights and measures.*

The use of these rooms as dining halls is suggested by the fact that the door is not in the center, thus leaving space for one kline to one side. Each room had space for up to seven such dining couches lined against the walls.

▲ South Stoa in the Athenian Agora, 430–420 BC.

The flooring in one of the rooms was typical of banquet halls from the Classical period: around the walls ran a strip of compressed mortar and gravel that made for a more stable floor for the klinai.

293

The Athens Pompeion where the holiday processions were organized stood near the Dipylon's monumental gate, between the Sacred Way and the road leading to the Academy.

In the center of the building was a large, rectangular courtyard surrounded by porticoes.

Already before the building was erected, this site was used by the participants of the Pan-Athenaean procession who gathered here to march toward the Acropolis.

To the north and west of the central peristyle were several square rooms of varying size with about sixty seats for the ritual meals.

▲ Athens Pompeion, late 5th century BC.

The Hestiatorion in the shrine of Hera at Argos is the oldest known example of a building that was erected for the specific purpose of eating the meats of sacrificed animals inside a sanctuary.

The three banquet rooms had space for up to nine couches each; the entrance was to one side, to allow use also of the southern wall.

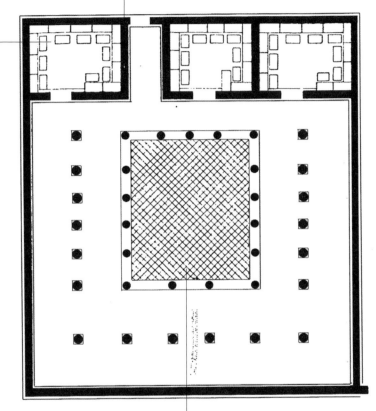

The banquet rooms opened on a large, colonnaded rectangular court where the meat distribution probably took place; most citizens would have eaten standing, without sitting at the banquet proper.

▲ Plan of the Hestiatorion in the shrine of Hera at Argos, 6th century BC (from Settis 2002, *Atlante*).

"Polygnotus painted ... in Athens, the portico known as Stoa Poicile ... for free, while Micon, who also painted part of it, requested payment" (Pliny)

Porticoes

Related entries
Sacrifice, offerings and ex-votos, temples and sacred buildings, public assembly buildings, public banquet halls, Delphi

One type of building that was central to Greek architecture was the *stoa*, a long, rectangular portico set at right angles, with columns, open on one side, sometimes with two or more naves separated by columns, and often with a row of interior rooms. In religious architecture, the first *stoai* were built in the seventh century BC inside the sacred shrine enclosures, to allow the faithful to view the religious ceremonies and shelter them at night. They also served as banquet halls for the sacrificial meals and to display votive offerings. Such was the main function, for example, of the Stoa of the Athenians at Delphi, a portico built along the polygonal wall of the terrace of the Apollonian temple where, as the inscription on the stylobate recites, war trophies and weapons were displayed. The enemy spoils, the sections of ships and the bronze shields admired by Pausanias, were visibly displayed along the inside wall, hanging on tree trunks that rested on a stepped podium. Because the stoa opened on the court where the processions began, its steps were also used as a viewing stand. In non-religious architecture, already in the Archaic age but especially in the fifth and fourth century BC, the porticoes were used to frame the city squares, thus serving as commercial centers, covered markets, meeting venues, the seats of political and administrative offices, and art galleries.

▼ Stoa of the Athenians at Delphi, late 6th to mid–5th century BC.

From the northern and western porticoes of the building, respectively 98 and 78 feet long, one accessed ten small, square rooms, each one set up with seven stone and marble dining tables and stone-slab floors; a strip ran around the floor of the rooms next to the walls, where the eleven banquet couches were placed.

From a narrow passage in the center of the north side one entered another stoa behind the banquet halls; there, the faithful used to leave ex-votos.

The small dining rooms were used for eating the meat from sacrificed animals, but they were probably also used by the "little she-bears," the young girls who spent long stretches of time in the sanctuary in the service of Artemis.

The large U-shaped stoa in the Brauron shrine was located north of the temple of Artemis at the edge of a wide, open space where the ceremonies honoring the goddess were held during the Brauronia festival.

▲ Stoa in the Brauron Artemision, 425–415 BC.

The Stoa of the Kings stood on the western side of the Athens Agora; it is one of the oldest surviving examples of this type of structure erected for public use.

The stoa was only 59 feet long; it originally had a simple rectilinear plan, with eight Doric columns in front and four inside that divided the portico into two naves.

At the end of the fifth century BC, a wing was added on each of the two sides, fronted by three Ionic columns. The building underwent major renovations already in the early part of the third century BC.

The stoa preserved a copy of the entire code of Athenian laws; it also displayed religious laws such as the calendar of official offering ceremonies and of sacrifices to the city's gods.

This stoa was the residence of the archon king, a preeminent city official whose duties included handling religious and legal matters such as trials for the murder of a family member or for ungodliness.

▲ Model reconstructing the Stoa of the Kings in the Athens Agora.

"The health of the inhabitants depends first on the city being in a good situation and position; secondly, they must have good water to drink" (Aristotle, Treatise on Government, Pt. 7, Ch. 11)

Water and Aqueducts

In ancient Greece, water was supplied in large part by wells, because even in cities that were served by aqueducts the places for drawing water were usually few and inconvenient. In the Athenian Agora, more than four hundred wells have been identified, for the most part dug during the fifth and fourth century BC, when the area already had a network of mains and imposing public fountains. The well diggers were organized in a specialized guild and even an Athenian family, the Phereorychoi, took their name from this activity. Still, the more valuable potable water came from natural springs and often cities were founded next to them. In order to collect, store, and draw water easily, at first rudimentary systems were used; later, small buildings were erected at the mouth of springs, called *krenai*, complete with access stairs and paved tanks, and sometimes spouts.

In fifth-century BC Athens, at least one public official was in charge of waterworks and many politicians made private donations for this purpose. When the springs were located far from cities, the water was carried in underground mains, usually clay pipes, sometimes protected by canals lined with stone slabs. One of the earliest aqueducts was built in Athens in about 525 BC to carry to the city the waters from the springs of the Ilissus river.

Related entries
Athens Agora

▼ Attic red-figure cup by Onesimus, *Ephebus Drawing Water from a Well*, 480–470 BC. Rome, Musei Capitolini.

In antiquity, wells were dug entirely
by hand, using only a windlass for
hauling away the earth. They were
usually cylindrical, with a diameter
of about 3.3 feet to allow the digger
enough space to work.

Before the sixth
century BC,
wells were not
lined and the
most common
rims were the
neck and
shoulder of
large ceramic
pithoi. *Starting
in the following
century, lining
clay or stone
cylinders were
used: they were
installed by
burying them
in the well.*

Most of the wells were not
lined, but when they were
going to be used for a long
time, the walls were reinforced
with wood or with rough or
cut stones, into which stairs or
footboards or clay and stone
cylinders could be cut.

Sometimes wells were covered
with roofing to protect them
from dirt and the rims had
holes for ropes or for resting a
wooden pole from which to
hang the water vessels and
store food in a cool place.

▲ Rim of a Geometric age
well, from the Athens Agora.
Athens, Agora Museum.

The fountains not only
distributed water to the private
citizens, but sometimes were
also used for bathing.

Because this
image does not
recall an urban
setting, the
fountain with
Doric columns
and double
sloping roof was
probably that of
the Callirhoe
spring in the
Ilissus valley; at
the time, the
Pisistratidae
brothers had
channeled these
waters to feed
the fountains of
the Agora.

Some young men
have hung their
clothes on trees and
in the shade rub
their bodies with
oil from aryballoi
and alabastra.

Two ephebi scrub themselves
energetically under jets gushing from two
large spouts shaped like lion's heads.

▲ Attic black-figure *hydria* by
the Antimenes Painter, *Ephebi
at the Fountain*, from Vulci,
520–510 BC. Leyden,
Rijksmuseum van Oudheden.

Starting in about 520 BC, vase paintings also included several fountain scenes, painted especially on hydriai, *the large jars used to draw water.*

The popularity of this type of scene is probably linked to the waterworks that were being built by the Pisistratidae who gave Athens several monumental fountains. Until then, the population had been drawing water from wells and cisterns.

The water flowed continuously from spouts shaped like a lion's head or a mounted rider, arranged along the side and back walls. The women placed the hydriai *underneath to fill them with water.*

The fountain was designed as an arcaded structure with four Doric columns in front.

▲ Attic black-figure *hydria* from the "A.D." Painter, *Women at a Fountain House,* from Vulci, ca. 510 BC. London, British Museum.

The branch motifs decorating the space between the figures do not suggest that the fountain was in a wooded area; it was simply a popular filler on vases from that period.

Two large fountains were unearthed at the southeast and southwest corners of the Athens Agora. The southeastern one is probably the famous nine-spout Enneakrounos built by the Pisistratidae that carried the water of the Callirhoe spring by aqueduct to the city.

The fountain was a rectangular structure 59 feet long; it had a solid back wall, a portico facing the Agora with three Doric columns between two antas, and a tiled, double sloping roof.

Along the short sides of the fountain were two tanks about 20 x 10 feet. The western one was used for drawing water with a pan; the other had small masonry posts under the spouts, on which the women placed the hydriai to be filled.

Most probably this is the fountain reproduced in scenes of women drawing water on vases from that period.

▲ Southeastern fountain in the Athens Agora, ca. 525 BC.

In 2000, excavation for the construction of the Athens subway brought to light new sections of the aqueduct's clay pipes.

The aqueduct built by the Pisistratidae was a massive system that carried the waters of the Ilissus river springs on Mount Hymettus down to the city, over an effective distribution network.

The pipes were equipped with inspection holes with removable covers and marked with painted alphabet letters to facilitate their assembly.

Outside the city, the clay pipes ran inside narrow tunnels cut into the rock, at a depth of between 6 and 35 feet, and went four times over the bed of a river.

Some pipes have scratched on them the probable name of the manufacturer: Charon.

▲ Water mains, built under Pisistratus in the Athens Agora, ca. 525 BC.

One of the most famous springs in Greece was the Delphic one at Castalia whose waters, sacred to Apollo, were used for the ritual cleansing of the temple.

In the Archaic age this spring had an architectural façade of marble: the water flowed from an inner basin into a larger one in which the pilgrims took ritual baths before entering the temple.

▲ Delphi, Castalia Spring.

Several other favorite springs were located in Corinth—the Lerna spring was inside the peristyle of the temple to Asclepius; Glauce's spring was fed by four cisterns cut into live rock; the Pirene spring in Corinth's ancient Agora was fed by a large underground cistern and was still in use a century ago.

The walls, floor, and roofing of the stone aqueduct built in Athens in the fourth century BC were made of carefully assembled slabs of limestone.

A hollow cut into the floor slabs suggests that the stone canal was built to protect the clay pipes that carried the water.

Over the years, as the need for water grew, four different clay pipelines were laid inside this canal, at different depths.

▲ Stone aqueduct in the Athens Agora, 4th century BC.

Already in the sixth century BC, a tangled mass of pipelines of all kinds crowded the subsoil under the Agora.

In addition to the clay aqueduct built under the Pisistratidae and the stone one from the fourth century BC with its network that guaranteed water distribution, the area was also crossed by numerous pipes and canals, both in stone and in clay, for rainwater drainage.

The drains from the various buildings flowed into a huge sewer built in the early part of the fifth century BC: starting from the southwest corner of the Agora, it flowed north and emptied into the Eridanus river.

▲ Tangle of pipes under the Athens Agora.

Centers and Monuments

◀ Delos, Terrace of the Lions.

"They say that the water from this spring [Cassotis] flows underground in the most secret place in the temple and that its prophetic power inspires the oracle women" (Pausanias)

Delphi

▶ Roman copy of the
omphalos, the "world's
navel," originally
located in the temple
of Apollo. Delphi,
Archaeological
Museum.

The earliest traces of a cult at Delphi are not the ruins of the sanctuary to Apollo, but those from Marmaria, an area slightly to the east, where small female idols dating to the Mycenaean age were discovered. This would confirm the tradition that has this area originally consecrated to Gaia, the Earth; Apollo made it his seat later by defeating the serpent Python that guarded the cave from which the goddess cast forth vapors that endowed men with the power of divination. The importance of Delphi as a Pan-Hellenic shrine for all the Greeks arose in the sixth century BC when the temple to Apollo was built and the First Sacred War was fought that removed the area from under the dominance of the Phocians in whose territory it was located, and put it under the control of the Delphic Amphictyony, a league formed to protect the sanctuary and headed by Athens.

The Pythian Games, inaugurated in 586 BC, took place every four years, alternating with the Olympian Games; they lasted seven days and included musical and poetic contests in addition to the sports events. Unlike the other cities that hosted the Pan-Hel-

lenic Games, that were thronged with pilgrims only for the festivals, Delphi was visited the year round because the Pythia issued her oracles each month on fixed days, with the exception of the winter months when access to the sanctuary was difficult and even Apollo, it was said, left the temple, returning only on the seventh day of the month of Bysios (February-March), for his birthday.

The temple of Apollo that still stands today is a reconstruction made in 330 BC after either an earthquake, a fire, or a landslide had destroyed the Archaic temple in 373 BC.

A few sculptures that decorated the eastern pediment of the Archaic temple have survived: they were found in a pit where they had been buried after the temple fell. They represent Artemis, Apollo, and Leto on a four-horse chariot at the center of an elaborate composition.

The new temple is dated to the fourth century BC and follows the dimensions of the earlier ones. The Doric peristasis has six columns on the short sides and fifteen on the long ones. Two Doric columns are arranged between the antas of the pronaos and the opisthodomos, while the cell was lined with two rows of eight Ionic columns.

According to recent geological studies, the temple's adyton—its innermost area—was built on the spot where two earth faults meet. There, at a level lower than the floor of the cell, the Pythia issued her prophecies, shrouded in the "intoxicating" vapors that issued from underground.

Some ancient authors wrote that the Archaic temple enclosed the Cassotis spring from which the prophetess drew water before issuing the oracle. The 373 BC earthquake could have stopped the vapors and dried up the spring.

▲ Temple of Apollo and Sacred Way.

Delphi

Legend of the principal
monuments from the Greek age

1. Entrance
2. Bull of Corcyra
3. Monument of the
   Sparta *nauarchoi*
4. Base of the Arcadians
5. Base of Marathon
6. Statues of the Seven
   Against Thebes and
   the Epigones
7. Statues of the Kings
   of Argos
8. Base of the Tarentines
9. Treasury of the Sicyonians
10. Treasury of the Siphnians
11. Base of the Aetolians
12. Treasury of the Athenians
13. *Bouleuterion*
14. Sacred rocks and springs
15. Sphinx of the Naxians
16. Treasury of the Corinthians
17. Portico of the Athenians
18. Temple of Apollo
19. Altar of the temple
    of Apollo
20. Base of the Tarentines
21. Tripod of the Plataeans
22. Sun's chariot
23. Tripod of the Dinomenides
24. Base of the Corcyreans
25. Base of Daochos
26. Location where the
    Charioteer was found
27. Theater
28. *Lesche* of the Cnidians

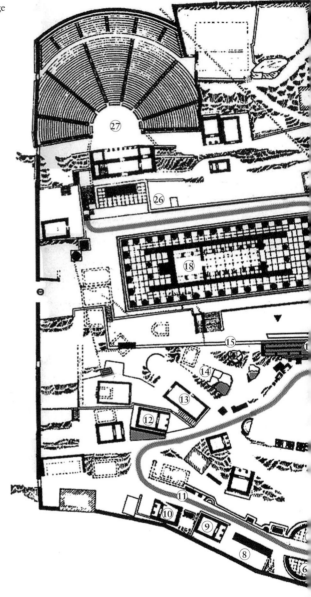

▶ Plan of the sanctuary of
Apollo at Delphi (from
Torelli, Mavrojannis 1997).

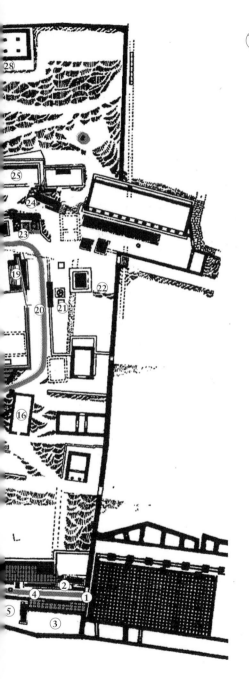

N

0   m   50

The Dioscuri return from the raid carrying two javelins on the left shoulder and two in the right hand.

Each character leads three oxen, the first one is seen frontally.

The short capes open as they march, revealing the tunics cinched at the waist by wide belts.

In the foundations of the Sicyonian Treasury—a small temple with two Doric columns between the façade's antas, built around 500 BC—archaeologists found fragments of twelve metopes dating to the first half of the sixth century BC that had decorated an earlier structure dedicated by the inhabitants of Sicyon.

These are among the most ancient metopes of Greece proper: they do not depict unitary subjects, but mythical episodes unrelated to each other, such as the rape of Europa, the ship Argo, the raid of the oxen by the Dioscuri, and the hunt for the Calydonian boar.

▲ Metope reused in the foundation of the Sicyonian Treasury, *Raid of the Oxen*, early 6th century BC. Delphi, Archaeological Museum.

The goddess Leto places her hands on the shoulders of her daughter Artemis who in turn strokes her brother Apollo's chin who faces her.

According to Pausanias who saw the temple in the second century AD, the Siphnian treasury was erected by order of Apollo himself who had demanded that the city annually pay to Delphi one tenth of its earnings from the gold mines.

The small temple was built entirely of marble; instead of columns, two caryatids supported the architrave and the pediment of the façade, decorated with a Nike-shaped acroterium at the center and two sphinxes at each corner.

The Ionic frieze on the western side of the temple depicted the judgment of Paris; to the north was a battle with the Giants and to the south either the abduction of the daughters of Leucippus or the nuptial race of Pelops and Hippodamia.

The eastern frieze, of which this scene is a part, depicted the assembly of the gods witnessing the Trojan war from Mount Olympus. To the left were the gods favorable to the Trojans; Zeus was in the center, and to the right were the gods who took the Greeks' side.

The composition was enriched with bold colors such as red, light blue, green, ocher, and gold; the names of the characters were written in red on the blue background.

▲ Eastern frieze of the Siphnian Treasury, *Assembly of the Gods*, ca. 525 BC. Delphi, Archaeological Museum.

The Athenian Treasury was rebuilt in 1904 by reassembling the original pieces in their original place. It is the most notable structure of the sanctuary because of its architectural completeness and because it was located in a place visible to all the pilgrims, in the exact spot where the Sacred Way turned towards the temple of Apollo.

The pediments were decorated with battle scenes of perhaps Heracles or Theseus.

In a Doric order and in antis style (meaning that there are two columns between the façade's antas), this small temple was made of Parian marble and decorated with six metopes on the short sides and nine on the long ones.

The metopes on each side have a unitary theme: the battle of the Amazons to the east, the adventures of Theseus, who was the Attic national hero, to the south, the struggle between Heracles and Geryon to the west, and other Herculean labors to the north.

The Archaic style of the metopes seems to conflict with the text of Pausanias who recounts that the treasury was built with the gains from the spoils of the battle of Marathon in 490 BC, but perhaps the traditional style was intentional, in keeping with its votive character.

▲ Athenian Treasury, 490–480 BC.

Circular buildings are very rare in Greek architecture; with the exception of theatrical structures, the Greeks preferred straight lines.

The tholos *was located in the sanctuary of Athena Pronaia on the Marmaria terrace; it had a diameter of about 43 feet and was surrounded by twenty Doric columns topped by a triglyphic frieze and by metopes carved with combat scenes.*

The cell's interior was decorated with nine half-columns resting against the walls on high socles of black stone, the same stone as the flooring.

▲ *Tholos* of Marmaria, 380–370 BC.

The function of the tholos, *of which there is no mention in the ancient sources, is still uncertain: it could have been a temple, a donation center, a structure to house celebratory statues or the* heroon *of Phylacos, the warrior mentioned by Herodotus who had transformed himself into a giant to defend Delphi from the Persian invasion.*

A circular donation temple had already been erected in Delphi in the early part of the sixth century BC; *however only some fragments survive that were reused in the later Sicyon Treasury.*

"Each [work] was immediately ancient on account of its beauty. Today, after so much time, it is recent, new, and flourishing. An everlasting youth springs from the works of Pericles" (Plutarch)

Athens Acropolis

Location
Attica

Chronology
Late 7th–early 6th century BC: First monumental temple with pediment decorated with scenes of lions killing calves
570–560 BC: A larger temple in tufa with pediments decorated with mythological scenes
Ca. 525 BC: Hekatompedon with marble pediments
490 BC: A vote is taken to build a new temple that was never built
447–432 BC: Parthenon
437–432 BC: Propylaea
After 430 BC: Small temple of Athena Nike
420–406 BC: Erechtheum

Related entries
Solon, Pericles, Phidias, Athena, Heracles, sacred temples and buildings

▶ Detail from the western frieze of the Parthenon, still on site, behind the columns of the peristasis.

In the Mycenaean age, the Acropolis was the fortified political and military seat of the city's king. The place was consecrated to Athena in the eighth century BC when the first, plain temple was erected to house the wooden statue of the goddess. Starting in the sixth century BC, Solon first and Pisistratus later added temples to the citadel, and marble statues offered as ex-votos began to appear. After the Marathon victory in 490 BC, a decree was issued to build, next to the structures dedicated to Athena Polias (the city's protector), a large temple dedicated to the goddess in her incarnation as warrior, Pallas. The construction was never completed because in 480 BC the Persian army invaded the city, whose inhabitants had fled, sacked it, and set it on fire.

In memory of the barbarism to which they had been subjected, the Athenians decided not to rebuild the destroyed temples but to bury the desecrated ruins in a religious ceremony, using the rubble to level the land and prepare the area for a completely new plan. This layer of debris, which the archaeologists refer to as the "Persian landfill," is a very important chronological reference point for the study of Archaic art, because it allows us to date the materials it contains to a period before 480 BC. All

the Acropolis buildings that we admire today were built after that date, thanks to Pericles' determination and Phidias's genius: in less than fifty years, they rebuilt the sanctuary of the goddess over the ruins.

At the center of this battle of the Giants is Athena who impetuously advances to the right bearing one of the snakes that decorate her aegis, here rendered as a short peltate leather mantelet.

The Hekatompedon (one hundred feet), so-called because of its length, which is typical of many Archaic temples, stood between the Parthenon and the Erechtheum, and its foundations are still in place; it had a Doric order and a cell divided in a front and a rear side, that housed the treasure of Athena or perhaps was dedicated to another divinity.

The temple was built in limestone, with part of the cornices, the tiles covering the roof, and the pediments made of marble.

Only the tip of a foot is left of the enemy, probably Enceladus, who is battling with Athena.

At the side of Athena and Enceladus stood Zeus and another god fighting the two opponents, while the lower registers on each side contained the figures of two fallen giants.

▲ Eastern pediment of the Hekatompedon, *Battle of the Giants*, ca. 525 BC. Athens, Acropolis Museum.

Because the temples that stood on the Acropolis before 480 BC were wiped out by the Persian destruction, the only surviving fragments are those buried in the Persian landfill and they belong to at least nine different buildings.

The ancient temple of Athena erected under the Pisistratidae when the Pan-Hellenic festival was reorganized, probably stood on the same site where the Parthenon would later be built.

From unearthed fragments, we learn that the temple was in the Doric style, made of limestone with some parts of marble such as the metopes, and an acroterium in the shape of a winged Gorgon at the top of the western pediment.

On the left side the theme of the labors of Heracles continued. The surviving part of the sculpture shows the hero grappling with the scaly body of Triton.

▲ Ancient temple of Athena, eastern pediment known as "the bluebeards," 570–566 BC. Athens, Acropolis Museum.

The eastern pediment, known as "the bluebeards" on account of the vivid red and blue colors of the triple-bodied monster, had in the center the traditional motif of lions about to devour a bull.

To the right of the central group is Heracles battling Nereus whose triple body is represented almost in the round down to the waist, with the lower part coiling around itself in the corner of the pediment, thus adjusting to the gradually narrower space.

The choice of representing battles between the two sea monsters and the hero who embodied the aristocratic ideals of courage and challenge was perhaps born of a desire to intentionally exalt the sea adventures on which Athens was embarking under Pisistratus.

Only a few fragments of the western pediment survive, but we know that it did not continue the theme of the central pediment, but rather depicted the heraldic motif of two crouching lions with a snake on each side.

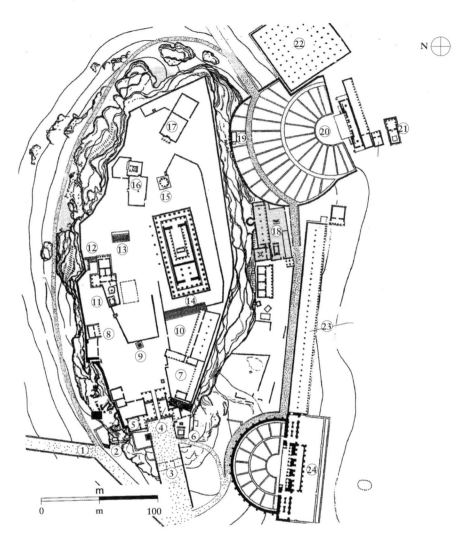

Legend

1. Road leading to the Agora
2. Klepsydra Fountain
3. Beule Gate
4. Propylaea
5. Picture Gallery
6. Small temple of Athena Nike
7. Sanctuary of Artemis Brauronia
8. Seat of the *arrephoroi*
9. Statue of Athena Promachos
10. Chalkotheke
11. Pandroseion and sacred olive tree
12. Erechtheum
13. Altar of Athena Polias
14. Parthenon
15. Temple of Rome and Augustus
16. Sanctuary of Zeus Polieus
17. Pandion's enclosure
18. Sanctuary of Asclepius
19. Monument of Trasilius and other royal monuments
20. Theater of Dionysus
21. Temple of Dionysus
22. *Odeion* of Pericles
23. Stoa of Eumenes
24. Odeion of Herodes Atticus

Built by the architect Mnesicles between 437 and 432 BC after the Parthenon had already been completed, the Propylaea were the monumental gates to the Acropolis, an architecturally daring structure set on a steep slope with marble roofing resting on long monolithic beams reinforced with iron bars.

The central structure was divided into two wings with separate roofs: the outer one was wider and stood slightly lower than the other roof that looked onto the plain of the Acropolis and was a few steps higher and narrower.

Two side wings with Doric column façades marked a rectangular space that was closed on three sides. The northern wing was called the "picture gallery" because the walls were decorated with hanging paintings.

The central structure was rectangular, its walls marked by six Doric columns with a larger space between the central columns to allow the processions to pass through.

The southern wing had no precise function, but did provide access through a small staircase to the rampart where the small temple of Athena Nike stood.

◄ Map of the Acropolis (from Torelli, Mavrojannis 1997).

▲ Entrance to the Acropolis and the Propylaea.

The shrine of Nike, the personification of Victory that was later assimilated to Athena, stood in very ancient times on the western rampart of the Acropolis; its location was meant to help defend the city from raids, in a spot that many considered weak.

Four Ionic columns decorated both of the building's façades; the architrave was topped by a continuous frieze filled with combat scenes on three sides and with gods and goddesses above the entrance.

The cell had two pilasters between the antas; it consisted of one room where the cult statue of the goddess stood. The sources describe it as a Nike Athena sculpted without wings, in the hope that victory might never desert Athens.

The design for this small temple is the work of the architect Callicrates; it was ready in 448 BC, before the Parthenon was built, but construction was suspended probably until the peace of Nicias of 421 BC that decreed the first truce in the Peloponnesian war.

The digs conducted before World War II, when the temple was disassembled almost completely in order to reinforce the ramparts, unearthed an extremely ancient trove of ex-votos and offerings: in it were also the remains of sacrifices and clay figurines, and the ruins of an earlier Archaic temple.

▲ Small temple of Athena Nike.

Because the small temple to Athena Nike
rose on an open rock rampart, around
410 BC it was enclosed with a white
marble balustrade that did the double
duty of protecting the faithful and
marking the shrine's boundaries.

The balustrade
was decorated
with marble relief
slabs depicting a
procession of
Nikes in different
postures, directed
towards Athena
who is witnessing
a sacrifice.

The Nike
represented here,
dressed in a thin,
pleated chiton
worn under a
wide himation, is
raising her right
knee in order to
reach her foot to
tie the sandal.

▲ Balustrade of the small
temple of Athena Nike,
Nike Ties Her Sandal.
Athens, Acropolis Museum.

The theme of the eastern pediment was the birth of Athena from the head of Zeus, in the presence of the leading Olympian deities; on each side were the sun and the moon on their respective chariots.

The large cell was not separated into naves by two rows of columns according to the traditional layout, but had instead a U-shaped colonnade designed to surround and magnify the colossal statue in ivory and gold of the goddess, built by Phidias.

The external Doric frieze consisted of ninety-two metopes that depicted one unitary theme for each side.

▲ The Parthenon.

Even though the temple had a Doric order, the exterior wall of the cell was crowned by a continuous frieze that reproduced the procession of the Great Pan-Athenaean festival and was more than 525 feet long.

The western pediment depicted the quarrel between Athena and Poseidon for dominance of Attica, in the presence of the mythical Attican heroes: at each end, the personifications of the local rivers geographically framed the scene.

The Parthenon has a Doric order, with seventeen columns on the long sides and eight on the short ones; it also had a double row of columns on the two fronts, a novelty for Doric architecture introduced by Ictinus who was inspired by the great temples of Ionia.

The term Parthenon—the name by which the temple of Athena is universally known—was already in use in the fourth century BC, though at first it only referred to the room behind the cell where the virgins who wove the peplum of the goddess gathered and where cult objects and votive offerings were stored.

Behind the cell and accessible only from an outside entrance on the western side, was the room where Athena's treasure was kept; the structure had a roof supported by four Ionic columns.

Legend

A-C. Chariot of Helios (the Sun)
D. Dionysus
E-F. Demeter and Kore
G. Artemis
H. Poseidon
K-M. Hestia, Dione, Aphrodite (?)
N-O. Selene (or Nyx)
a-c, i-k. Conjectural groups (Ares
and Iris, Hermes and
Amphitrite (?))
d. Hephaestus
e. Hera
f. Zeus
g. Athena

Legend

A. "Ilissus"
B-F. Cecrops and sons
G. Nike
H. Hermes
I-K. Triton (?)
L. Athena
M. Poseidon
N. Iris
O. Amphitrite
P. Woman with two
children, Oreithyia (?)
Q-U. Other Attic heroes

▲ Drawing reconstructing
the eastern and western
pediments of the Parthenon
(from Settis 2002, *Atlante*).

The central part of the temple was joined to the north and south by colonnaded foreparts; the northern portico with six Ionic columns was a sort of canopy that marked the sign left by Poseidon's trident on the rock.

The central body of the temple is a rectangular structure with six Ionic columns in front, facing east, and a back wall decorated with half-columns, in which a number of rectangular windows and a small door opened.

The eastern section of the temple was dedicated to the cult of Athena Polias and there stood the extremely ancient statue of the goddess: so ancient that it was believed it had fallen from heaven. The western section of the temple was dedicated to the cult of Poseidon, who had quarreled with Athena over dominance of Attica.

Through a door in the back wall one accessed the open shrine of the nymph Pandrosus; there also stood the sacred olive tree that Athena had caused to grow during her challenge with Poseidon.

The Erechtheum, built between 420 and 406 BC, has an elaborate layout due to the uneven terrain and the need to house many different cults under one roof.

The southern loggia was supported by six caryatids of young girls wearing the Doric peplum, perhaps the daughters of Cecrops, a mythical king of Attica whose tomb was located under the portico.

▲ The Erechtheum.

"Up to now, I have never feared men who have a specific place in the center of the city where they meet and dupe each other with oaths" (Herodotus)

Athens Agora

Location
Attica

Chronology
Early 6th century BC:
First public buildings
Late 6th–early 5th
century BC: An
explosion of public
buildings (Heliaea, old
bouleuterion, *metroon*,
Stoa of the Kings)
Ca. 460 BC: Public
works construction
resumes (*tholos*,
Stoa Poicile)
430–400 BC: Stoa
of Zeus, South Stoa,
new *bouleuterion*,
monument to
the Eponymous
Heroes, Mint
338–326 BC: Temples
to Zeus, Athena,
and Apollo

Related entries
Political institutions,
justice and the courts,
ostracism, temples and
sacred buildings, public
assembly buildings,
public banquet halls,
porticoes, water and
aqueducts

▶ Boundary stone of
the Athens Agora, with
inscribed: "I am the
Agora boundary," late
6th century BC.

The public square (*agora*) as a place of exchange and a center of political life may be deemed to be a Greek invention. Thanks to the American excavations begun in 1931 and continuing to this day, the Athens Agora is the one we know best in terms of its evolution and its manifold functions. Previously the site of a necropolis, the area was set aside for public use in the second half of the sixth century BC. In the ensuing one hundred years, all the major public buildings were erected next to each other on its western side: the *bouleuterion* where the Council of the Five Hundred met; the *tholos* where the *prytaneis* in charge resided; the shrine of Cybele (*metroon*) where the public archives were kept; the Stoa of the Kings where the laws in force were displayed, and the monument to the Eponymous Heroes, where official notices and legislative proposals were posted.

Once a year, an assembly of all the citizens was held in the center of the square; this assembly also ruled on ostracism. Meanwhile, in the surrounding streets and under the arcades market stands were set up, grouped by type of goods, and the shops became crowded, from the metal workshops that rose around the temple of Hephaestus to the marble workshops clustered at the foot of the Areopagus.

The Agora was also a sacred space: it was crossed by the Pan-Athenaean festival, the procession that climbed to the Acropolis, and there stood some of the most venerated temples; whoever had been found guilty of sacrilege was forbidden from entering the Agora, whose borders were marked with boundary stones.

▲ Model reconstructing the Athens Agora, early 4th century BC.

Legend

1. Temple of Hephaestus
2. Old *bouleuterion*
3. New *bouleuterion*
4. *Tholos*
5. *Strategeion*
6. *Aiakeion*
7. South Stoa

8. Southeast fountain
9. Mint
10. Pan-Athenian Way
11. Tribunal
12. Stoa Poicile
13. Altar of the Twelve Gods
14. Stoa of the Kings

The metopes of this temple narrate the labors of Heracles and the adventures of Theseus (hence the temple was also called Theseion). The columns of the pronaos and the opisthodomos were crowned by an unbroken frieze with combat scenes of Cyclops and Centaurs.

This Doric temple is peripteral (with a single row of columns): it has six columns on the short sides and thirteen on the long ones. It was all in marble and the cell had a three-sided colonnade.

The temple was jointly dedicated to Hephaestus and Athena Ergane, the two patrons of craftsmen and manual laborers. It rose on the Kolonos Agoraios Hill at the west end of the Agora.

Metal-working shops crowded around the temple; on the hill, laborers assembled at dawn waiting for work, for which reason they were called kolonetai.

The temple owes its good condition to the fact that in the seventh century AD it was transformed into a Christian church, thus escaping the stripping of materials that were recycled for new constructions.

▲ Temple of Hephaestus, 450–425 BC.

This monument was built under the Pisistratidae and renovated after the peace of Nicias in 421 BC. It stood near the northwest corner of the Agora, next to the Sacred Way.

The altar was considered the center of the city; the inscriptions on milestones refer to it as the zero point from which the distances between Athens and surrounding points, such as the port of Piraeus or other cities, were calculated.

The floor inside the enclosure was covered with blocks of poros stone.

The balustrade had small pilasters alternating with limestone slabs with relief decorations.

Only a corner of the exterior altar enclosure remains: in front is the inscribed base of a statue dedicated to the Twelve Gods by one Leagros.

▲▶ Drawing reconstructing a view of the Altar of the Twelve Gods, ca. 520 BC, and the altar today.

"A dream forbids me from describing what lies behind the sanctuary wall, in fact the uninitiated are not even allowed to learn about what they cannot see" (Pausanias)

Eleusis

Location
Attica, on the Saronic
Gulf, facing the island
of Salamis

Chronology
15th century BC: First
evidence of a cult
Early 6th century BC:
Construction of the
first Telesterion, with a
rectangular plan, on
the site of an ancient
Mycenaean temple; the
shrine was enclosed by
fortified walls, later
rebuilt and widened by
Cimon, Pericles, and
Lycurgus
525 BC: Reconstruction
of the Telesterion, with
a square plan
445 BC: New
Telesterion design, to
be executed by Ictinus
4th century BC: The
Telesterion is finalized

Related entries
Demeter and
Persephone, mystery
cults

▶ Caryatid of the Small
Propylaea bearing on
her head a mystical
cista, 1st century BC.
Eleusis, Archaeological
Museum.

The current layout of the sanctuary of Eleusis, with the monumental Propylaea and the great access esplanade framed by triumphal arches, is the result of restructuring work done by the Romans, when the site became extremely popular and some emperors even became initiated into the mysteries of Demeter and Persephone. Still, the Eleusinian cult has very ancient roots and already in the seventh century BC Athens had secured political control over the shrine, leaving to the Eleusinians only the privilege of appointing the highest priest from a member of a local clan, the Eumolpidae.

Every year in early October, crowds of Athenians celebrated the Great Mysteries. After the hierophantic priest invited the Greek-speaking faithful with "cleansed hands" to the mysteries, and the candidates had been led to the shore for a purifying bath, the twenty-kilometer procession to the sanctuary began, the sacred objects being carried in baskets. After they reached Eleusis

at night, everyone took part in the chants, prayers, sacrifices, fasting, and sacred performances. The initiation of the new adherents—the mystics—unfolded during the two following nights, in the dark, in the large colonnaded hall of the Telesterion at the center of the sanctuary. After these ceremonies, the festival again became public and ended with a Council of Elders meeting where a summary report of the celebrations was read, together with judgments on any breaches that might have been committed.

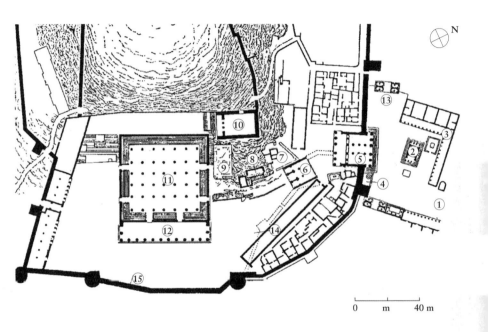

▲ Plan of the sanctuary
of Eleusis (from Torelli,
Mavrojannis 1997)

Legend

1. Sacred Way
2. Temple of Artemis
3. Stoa
4. Callichoros spring
5. Great Propylaea
6. Small Propylaea
7. Plutoneion
8. Exedra

9. Roman-age temple
10. Temple F
11. Telesterion
12. Portico of Philo
13. *Bouleuterion*
14. Granary
15. Walls

The Plutoneion, located at the foot of the
fortress that dominated the sanctuary,
was the cave where, according to the
myth, Hades had climbed back to Earth
from the Infernals to kidnap Persephone.

Around 50 BC Appius Claudius
Pulchrus had the Small Propylaea
built before the Plutoneion with
two caryatids on the façade, thus
marking the entrance to the more
intimate area of the shrine.

▲ Fortress of Eleusis, Plutoneion,
and Small Propylaea.

The Telesterion was the heart of the shrine of Eleusis, where the initiation ceremonies took place. It could not be a traditional temple designed primarily for storing the sacred statue, because it also had to hold a large number of people while maintaining the rituals' secrecy.

The specific needs of this temple were a challenge for many architects, and the structure underwent several reconstructions or extensions between the sixth century BC and the Hellenistic age.

The more ambitious reconstruction of the Telesterion that changed it to the present plan was the work of Pericles who assigned Ictinus, the architect of the Parthenon, to design it.

In the Ictinus plan, the building was designed to hold three thousand faithful. It was conceived as a huge square hall, 164 feet per side, with eight tiers of steps on each of the four sides.

The roof, with a central skylight, had to be supported by only twenty columns set to form two concentric crowns at a distance of 33 feet one from the other, in order to free as much space as possible.

After Pericles died, Ictinus's design was perhaps considered too daring and was partially set aside. The architects who completed the structure in the fourth century BC crowded the interior with 42 columns arrayed in seven rows.

▲ Telesterion.

According to the myth, the Eleusinian girls went to draw water at this well; it was here that an exhausted Demeter collapsed, after wandering long and hard to find her daughter Persephone, and was assisted by the daughters of King Celeus.

The aptly named well of Callichoros, meaning "of the beautiful dances," was one of the sacred Eleusinian sites; its name may derive from the fact that here, on the seventh celebratory day of the Great Mysteries, the initiated broke into ritual dances to celebrate the return of Persephone from Hades.

Although the well with a stone puteal dates to the fifth century BC, it became an object of veneration especially in the Roman age, after Antoninus Pius built the Great Propylaea next to it, as an entrance to the shrine, taking as model the central section of the Propylaea of the Acropolis.

▲ Well at Callichoros.

"In Aegina, going towards Mount Zeus Panhellenios, one finds the shrine of Aphaia: even Pindar wrote an ode for the inhabitants honoring the goddess" (Pausanias)

Aegina

Since prehistoric times, a local deity by the name of Aphaia was worshiped on the island of Aegina; later, this goddess would be assimilated to the Olympian goddess Athena. Here, between 510 and 500 BC, a temple was erected of local gray limestone; its decorations are a milestone in the history of Greek art, for several reasons: the two pediments of the building were sculpted at a distance of about twenty years from each other, allowing us to grasp, better than in any other work of art, the transition from the late Archaic to the Proto-Classical style known as "Severe."

When these sculptures were unearthed in 1811, a lively debate ensued because some of them still carried clear traces of red and blue coloring. The first theory reconstructing the polychromy of the western pediment, based on the still visible colors, was put forward by the art historian Adolf Furtwängler in the early twentieth century. Even though the aggressive nineteenth-century restoration by the sculptor Thorwaldsen had irreparably scraped off the chromatic finishes, recent research conducted with modern techniques, such as reflectography and ultraviolet rays, has allowed us to reconstruct the entire range of colors of these sculptures, showing how blue and red were complemented by green and yellow, in a vivid polychromy that must have been further enhanced by the golden-bronze weapons and ornaments that have been reconstructed from the mounting perforations that are still visible in the marble.

Location
An Aegean island in the Saronic Gulf halfway between Attica and Argolis

Chronology
Mid–7th century BC: First cult building
6th century BC: Second temple of Aphaia
Ca. 510 BC: Last reconstruction of the temple of Aphaia
Ca. 500 BC: Sculptures on the western pediment
Ca. 485 BC: Sculptures on the eastern pediment, perhaps to replace an earlier one damaged in an earthquake

Related entries
Athena, temples and sacred buildings

◀ Temple of Aphaia, detail of the cell wall inside the peristasis.

The Doric temple rose in an isolated area at the eastern tip of the island and was of limited size (95 x 45 feet) with six columns on the short sides and twelve on the longer ones.

The cell was classical, with a pronaos *and an* opisthodomos *with two columns between the* antas.

Because the temple was built entirely of local gray-blue limestone, the columns were given a coat of light-colored stucco to hide the porosity of the material.

▶ Temple of Aphaia.

Although the cell was only about 20 feet wide, thus could accept only a simple trussing, it was divided into three naves by two rows of Doric columns set in two orders, whose significance was probably more decorative than architectural.

341

The western pediment, built around 500 BC, had as theme a number of Greek vs. Trojan combat scenes that were meant to exalt Ajax son of Telamon, the Aeginetan hero who had taken part in the expedition.

Athena stands in the center of the scene, armed with spear and shield.

On each side of the goddess, three warriors repeat the duel with the wounded enemy.

The pose of the warriors changes to adapt to the decreasing size of the pediment: first the standing warriors, then the crouching archers, and at each side the wounded lying on the ground.

▲ Western pediment of the temple of Aphaia. Munich, Glyptothek.

The crouching archer, identifiable as Paris the Trojan prince, was located to the left of Athena and faced the corner of the pediment.

The pointed cap and the shirt that protected the chest were yellow, probably made of leather.

▲▶ Figure of an archer, from the western pediment of the temple of Aphaia, and plaster cast reconstructing the statue's polychromy. Munich, Glyptothek.

The body-fitting suit covering arms and legs was decorated with green, blue, yellow, and red lozenge motifs. We often see similar suits on vase paintings of the same period: they were worn by Persian archers, who were Asiatic like Paris, the son of Priam.

Over her dress Athena wears an aegis consisting of a leather cape bordered with snakes, and she wears a helmet with a tall crest.

The dress colors have faded almost completely; however it was possible to reconstruct the frontal band decorated with a fret design and the peltate motif of the aegis.

▲▶ Athena, from the western pediment of the temple of Aphaia, and plaster cast reconstructing the statue's polychromy. Munich, Glyptothek.

The reconstructed polychromy helps to soften the metallic look that some say is typical of the western pediment statues.

At the center of attention once more is a hero from Aegina: Telamon, father of Ajax.

The crouching archer is Heracles, recognizable by the lion skin he wears on his head. Unlike the statue of Paris on the western pediment, this figure, which was to the right of Athena, does not look towards the corner, but towards the center of the pediment.

The theme of the eastern pediment recalls the first expedition against Troy headed by Heracles, to punish King Laomedon, father of Priam, who had refused to give the hero a just reward for having killed the sea monster that devoured the city's residents.

The few surviving statues do not allow for a positive reconstruction of the pediment; probably here too Athena was in the center; however this time the composition centered around her, since she took a more active part in the combat.

The links between the pediments (the two expeditions, Telamon and Ajax, Athena in the center) suggests that they composed one single figurative plan and that the eastern pediment was executed later, after work had been suspended or because of the need to replace earlier damaged sculptures.

▲ Figure of an archer, from the eastern pediment of the temple of Aphaia. Munich, Glyptothek.

345

"Here is the temple of Zeus at Nemea, worthy of being visited (apart from the fact that the roof has collapsed and no statues are left); around the temple is a cypress grove" (Pausanias)

Nemea

Starting in 573 BC, games were held every two years in Nemea, initially organized by the city of Cleon and later by the nearby city of Argos. Although these were not as important as the four Pan-Hellenic Games, the sanctuary, when it was rebuilt in 330 BC after the destruction wrought by the Peloponnesian war, was one of the best organized for sports competitions. In addition to the temple of Zeus that was possibly designed by Scopas, and the *thesauroi* (treasuries) modeled after small temples, similar to each other and without dedicating inscriptions (in addition to the customary votive use, they may have been used as warehouses or seats of foreign delegations or meeting places), the sacred area was entirely occupied by hospitality structures.

During the games, the athletes were boarded in a large two-story inn (the *xenon*) that had apartments with several rooms equipped with a hearth for cooking. The local priests and the judges were lodged in houses that were the sanctuary's property, as the stamps "property of Zeus" found on crockery excavated at the site seem to indicate. A nearby public bath with a pool and large tubs guaranteed hygienic conditions. The sports structures were located at some distance from the sanctuary and included the stadium with tiers of steps for the spectators, start line mechanisms, and boxes reserved

for the judges, in addition to the dressing rooms that were connected by a vaulted underpass through which the athletes reached the track without mixing with the throng of spectators.

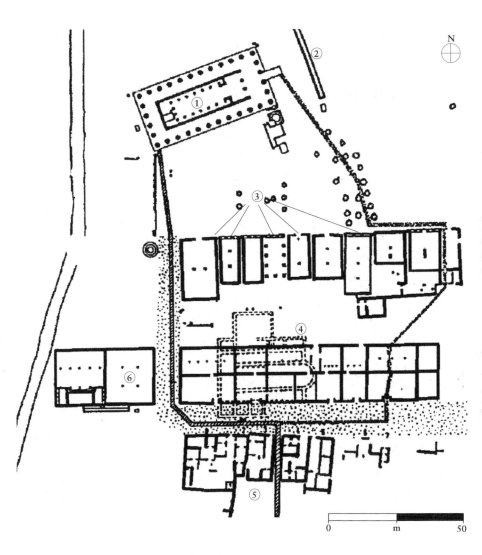

N

▲ Plan of the sanctuary
of Zeus (from Torelli,
Mavrojannis 1997).

Legend

1. Temple of Zeus
2. Altar of Zeus
3. Treasuries

4. *Xenon*
5. Housing for the *hellanodikai*
6. Public baths

0   m   50

The stadium of Nemea had an access tunnel for the athletes that ensured them a grand entrance, at the same time saving their concentration since they did not have to wade through the throng of spectators.

Underpasses such as these were also a fixture of other stadiums of the early Hellenistic age, such as the one at Epidaurus, and even the ancient Olympia stadium had one built in those years.

The tunnel, excavated under one of the embankments on the side of the track, was 115 feet long and was covered by a stone vault.

The tunnel walls still bear the graffiti scratched by the athletes in praise of their own beauty and prowess or that of their friends, or to propitiate their victory or remember past ones.

In one of the inscriptions one Teletas exclaims: "I win!" He has the same name as the Sicyon athlete who won in the "youth" boxing category at Olympia in 340 BC, and who dedicated to the shrine a statue fabricated by Silanion.

▲ Access tunnel to the stadium.

"The architect Theodotus received for the entire year a salary of 353 drachmae ... Timotheus was awarded the execution and supply of the models for 900 drachmae" (Inscriptiones Graecae)

Epidaurus

The shrine of Asclepius, located in a valley about six miles from the city, became monumental only starting in the fourth century BC, when it became the seat of sports games and musical and theatrical competitions during the great festivals dedicated to the god. The heart of the shrine, which one accessed through monumental propylaea that were modeled after those designed by Mnesicles for the Athenian Acropolis, was the small but richly decorated temple of the god, with a cell entirely filled with the god's gold and ivory statue sculpted by Thrasymedes of Paros. Facing the temple was the *tholos*, whose use is still uncertain, and around it rose a number of utilitarian structures (porticoes, inns, baths, palaestrae, banquet rooms) used by the patients who spent the night in the sanctuary to be healed, and by the visitors who came to watch the games.

During the construction, the *hieromnamenoi*, the magistrates in charge of managing the sanctuary, periodically drew up reports that they carved in stone, listing the expenses paid, the contracts awarded for the supply of materials, and the compensation paid for each work. From these reports we learn that Theodotus, the architect of the temple, received a small yearly stipend, not unlike that of a laborer, to oversee the works, while the most expensive items were the acroteria fabricated by Timotheus, who also supplied the "models" for the sculptural decoration, perhaps executed by others.

Location
Argolis, on the
Saronic Gulf

Chronology
6th century BC: The
cult of Asclepius is
introduced from
Thessaly
380–375 BC: The
temple of Asclepius
is built
360–330 BC: The
tholos is built
Ca. 350 BC: The
theater is built
End 4th century BC:
the temple of Artemis
and the *abaton*
(dormitory for the
sick) are built

Related entries
Asclepius, divination,
offerings and ex-votos,
medicine, temples and
sacred buildings

◄ Timotheus,
Acroterium from
the western pediment
of the temple of
Asclepius, *Nereid on
Horseback*, ca. 380
BC. Athens,
National
Archaeological
Museum.

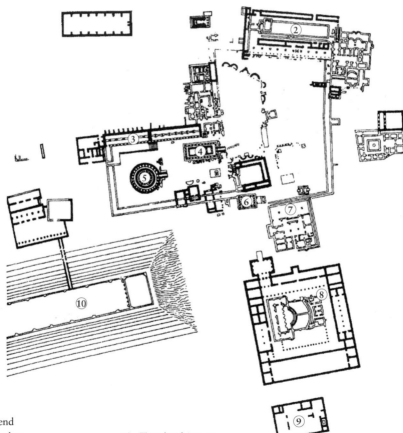

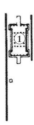

N

Legend

1. Propylaea
2. Stoa
3. Incubation portico
4. Temple of Asclepius
5. *Tholos*
6. Temple of Artemis
7. Palaestra
8. Gymnasium with *odeion*
9. Public baths
10. Stadium

From the sanctuary reports, we have evidence that the tholos was built by Polyclitus the Younger between 360 and 330 BC.

On the circular basement built on an artificial rise behind the temple of Asclepius, stood a colonnade with twenty-six Doric columns of poros stone, crowned by a triglyphic frieze and by metopes decorated with large flowers in relief.

The conical roof was covered with marble tiles and completed with a gutter decorated with a leaf motif that alternated lion's head spouts and palmette-shaped antefixes.

The central hall of the building rested on three concentric rings of stone blocks that could be reached from the cell floor; one could walk through these passages that communicated with each other.

The purpose of the labyrinth under the cell is still controversial: one theory is that the underground corridors were used to keep the snakes sacred to Asclepius.

◄ Plan of the sanctuary of Asclepius (from Torelli, Mavrojannis 1997).

▲ Ruins of the *tholos*.

Epidaurus

Inside the tholos were
fourteen Corinthian columns
detached from the wall that
punctuated a circular corridor
that one could walk through.

Both the ceilings of the exterior
peristyle and those of the interior
ambulatory had marble coffers from
which flowers in deep relief stood out.

The cell floor had a refined
design of curved lozenges in
alternating colors of black
stone and white marble,
arranged in concentric rings.

Because the tholos is mentioned frequently
in the sources as a thymele—a place where
sacrifices were held—the cult use of the
building is beyond question. But, just like
the Delphic tholos of the same period, it
could also have been a heroon, that is, a
funerary monument dedicated to Asclepius
or to another locally worshiped hero.

▲ Detail of the coffered ceiling
of the *tholos*. Epidaurus,
Archaeological Museum.

▶ Bronze statuettes of horse
and rider, from Olympia, late
8th century BC. Olympia,
Archaeological Museum.

"There are many more things still to see among the Greeks, and many marvelous ones to hear; still, none are more divine than the Eleusinian rites and the Olympian Games" (Pausanias)

Olympia

The Olympia site has been systematically searched by German archaeologists since 1875. Already used in the second millennium BC, the shrine was first of regional importance, as documented by the remains of a few plain monuments and the many votive offerings of terracotta and bronze. Starting in the eighth century BC, when the games were first organized to commemorate the chariot race between Pelops, who aspired to marry Hippodamia, and Oenomaus, the local king and the girl's father, its fame spread to all of Greece and monumental structures began to be built there. At the end of the seventh century BC the temple of Hera was built; in the following century the *prytaneum* and the *thesauroi* (where the cities kept their votive offerings) were added, and at the beginning of the fifth century BC the temple of Zeus was erected.

In later centuries, the sanctuary continued to expand with new construction, memorial monuments, and statues of athletes and divinities. Still, for a long time it had no buildings suitable for hosting both athletes and spectators, so that the discomforts associated with watching the games at Olympia became proverbial. The shrine continued to be very popular until the fourth century AD when a decree of Emperor Theodosius I forbade all pagan cults, thus putting an end to the Olympian Games. The area was abandoned, and the decay was compounded by the destruction wrought by earthquakes, the flooding of the Alpheus and the Cladeus rivers, and the landslides of Cronus Hill that covered the rubble with a layer of earth several feet thick.

Location
Elis, on a plain below Cronus Hill, bounded by the Alpheus and Cladeus rivers

Chronology
10th century BC: First traces of a cult
776 BC: The Olympiads are instituted
End 7th century BC: Temple of Hera
Mid–6th century BC: *Bouleuterion*
Early 5th century BC: Stadium
470–456 BC: Temple of Zeus
338 BC: Philippeion
330 BC: Leonidaion
394 AD: 293rd and last Olympiad
5th century AD: Phidias's workshop becomes a Christian church

Related entries
Hageladas and Alcamenes, Phidias, Zeus and Hera, sports

353

The temple of Hera was the oldest structure in the sanctuary. There, every four years the Heraean Games were held, which included races for girls divided by age, over a distance that was five-sixths the length of the stadium used by male runners. These were the only games to which women were admitted, since usually they were not even allowed to be spectators.

In the thesauroi, *small buildings in the shape of aedicules, were stored precious votive offerings sent by the Greek cities; they were lined up in a row on a terrace at the foot of Cronus Hill. The names of the dedicating cities were clearly carved on each building.*

The temple of Zeus, designed by Libon of Elis, is a massive peripter, slightly smaller than the Parthenon, built in local limestone and covered with painted plaster, metopes, pediments, and roof tiles of Parian marble and gold-washed bronze acroteriums. The cell housed the colossal ivory and gold statue of Zeus created by Phidias.

The shop, later used as a Christian church, where Phidias created the colossus of Zeus reproduced the exact dimensions of the temple cell where the statue would be displayed. The place had been formerly the site of foundries, where statues for the shrine were fabricated.

The Leonidaion, named after Leonidas of Naxos, the private citizen who paid for it, was a vast residential complex surrounded on all sides by porticoes. Its lodging rooms and dining halls were used by authorities and important figures, and faced an interior colonnaded garden.

▲ Aerial view of the archaeological site of Olympia.

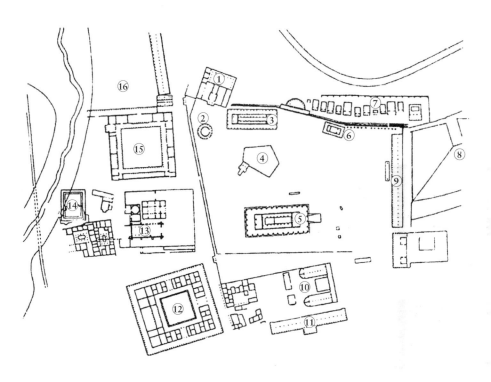

Legend of the principal buildings

1. *Prytaneum*
2. Philippeion
3. Temple of Hera
4. Monument to Pelops
5. Temple of Zeus
6. *Metroon*
7. Terrace of the Treasuries
8. Stadium
9. Echo's Stoa
10. *Bouleuterion*
11. South Stoa
12. Leonidaion
13. Phidias's workshop
14. Roman baths
15. Palaestra
16. Gymnasium

▲ Plan of the sanctuary of Hera
(from "Archeo," 2004).

The eastern pediment depicted the challenge of Oenomaus, king of Olympia, and Pelops, a suitor of Hippodamia, specifically, the scene just before the chariot race.

The western pediment reproduced the battle between the Centaurs and the Lapiths at the wedding of Pirithous and Hippodamia.

The theme of the temple's metopes, decorated only on the two shorter sides, were the twelve labors of Heracles, and this is the first complete representation of all the labors.

Atlas returns victorious from the garden of the Hesperides carrying the stolen apples in his hands while Heracles, helped by Athena, replaces him in supporting the roof of the world.

▲ Metope of the temple of Zeus, *Heracles and Atlas*. Olympia, Archaeological Museum.

The decorations of the temple of Zeus, completed in 456 BC, were for a long time attributed to an unknown "Master of Olympia." Recent studies have led the experts to reconstruct the personalities of the artists who worked on the temple, identifying in Alcamenes the author of the western pediment and in Hageladas of Argos the principal artist who worked on the eastern pediment and the metopes.

The Philippeion, commissioned by Philip of Macedonia to commemorate his victory over the leading Greek cities at Chaeronea in 338 BC, was completed by Alexander the Great.

The circular building is surrounded by eighteen Ionic columns; it had a richly decorated cell with nine Corinthian half-columns resting on high plinths arranged around the walls, and precious coffered ceilings.

In the center of the interior areas, on a semicircular base, Alexander commissioned five gold and ivory statues, the work of Leochares, which portrayed him among his parents and ancestors.

On the occasion of the 2004 Athens Olympics, the Germanic Archaeological Institute completed the restoration of part of the monument using only ancient materials, including some fragments of the architectural decorations that had been held at the Berlin Museum.

▲ Philippeion.

"This temple may stand before all other in the Peloponnesus ... for the beauty of its marble and its harmonious proportions" (Pausanias)

Bassae

Location
Arcadia, near the city of Phigaleia

Chronology
The cult of Apollo flourished in the 5th century BC when the temple was built; it had begun to wane already in the late 4th century BC

Related entries
Apollo, temples and sacred buildings, Delphi, Athens Acropolis

After the plague hit Athens in 429 BC, in which Pericles also succumbed, the surviving Athenians resolved to build a temple dedicated to Apollo Epikourios (the helper), as an ex-voto for having spared them from the disease. The temple was erected in Bassae, a remote area of Arcadia surrounded by mountains, at an altitude of over 3000 feet, and according to Pausanias it was designed by Ictinus who was the architect of the Parthenon. Because marble was difficult to find and ship on location, it was used only for the capitals, the frieze, and parts of the coffered ceiling, and local grey limestone was employed for the rest of the building.

The plan is an original mixture of Archaic motifs and daring innovations that suggest the hand of an architect with a strong personality. One Archaic motif that inspired the design was the elongated shape of the building, perhaps chosen to copy the typical plan of the temple of Apollo at Delphi. On the other hand, the slim proportions of the columns and the wide spaces between them were up to date and directly derived from the Attic architecture of the time—the result was a widening of the exterior hallways. The greatest novelty regarded the cell, decorated with a frieze that ran around the interior walls instead of the outer ones, punctuated by a U-shaped Ionic colonnade with a Corinthian column on the opposite side from the entrance.

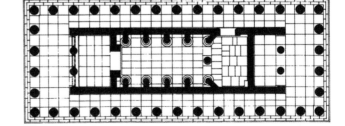

▶ Plan of the temple of Apollo (from Lloyd, Müller, Martin 1972).

The outside of the temple has a quite traditional look, with elongated dimensions (6 x 15 columns) that recall the Archaic style. The cell has a pronaos *and an* opisthodomos *with two columns between each* anta.

The way in which the materials were used suggests a hierarchy of importance between the temple's porticoes: only the coffered ceiling before the pronaos was made of marble, creating a sort of antechamber.

The interior arrangement of the cell was perhaps modified from the original design: it may have included originally a closed back room accessible from the outside through a side door, perhaps linked to the divination rites of the cult of Apollo at Delphi.

Eliminating the back part made the two sides of the cell accessible, and the passage from one to the other was marked with two Ionic half-columns resting on low cross-walls between which was set a Corinthian column.

The use of the Corinthian style, whose capitals were more appropriate to being viewed from different angles, is a totally original solution, the first in Greek architecture. Some scholars attribute it to Ictinus, the Parthenon architect whom even Pausanias cites as the author of this temple.

▲ Temple of Apollo.

Unlike the Parthenon, in this temple to Apollo the uninterrupted Ionic frieze did not run above the architrave or the exterior walls of the cell, but inside, above the purely ornamental Ionic columns lined along the walls.

Achilles has just dealt the mortal blow to Penthesilea.

The Amazon queen collapses on the ground, extending a suppliant hand toward Achilles, while one of her companions assists her.

The theme of this frieze was the battle against the Centaurs on the western side and against the Amazons on the eastern side.

Like the vase iconography on this theme, the central focus of the scene is the meeting of Achilles' and Penthesilea's gaze, alluding to the love that sprang up between them in the exact moment of the Amazon's death.

▲ Eastern frieze of the temple of Apollo, *Achilles and Penthesilea*, late 5th century BC. London, British Museum.

"The city has neither a compact layout, nor sumptuous temples or buildings, but consists of scattered villages, in the fashion of ancient Greece" (Thucydides)

Sparta

Sparta was founded in about 900 BC by joining the four villages of Limnae, Cynosura, Mesoa, and Pitana located at the edge of the plain that stood below the acropolis of Paleokastritsa. This gave the city an "open" feeling heightened by the fact that the Spartans always boasted of not needing any walls, and built one only after their defeat at the hand of the Thebans at Leuctra in 371 BC. Since the sixth century BC, the acropolis was dominated by the temple of Athena, the work of the versatile Spartan architect Gitiadas who inlaid it with bronze sheeting, hence the epithet of Chalkioikos ("of the Brazen House") that was given to the goddess. The architect personally created the cult statue and even wrote a hymn for the consecration ceremony.

Most of the public buildings were located in the district of Mesoa (which means "the middle one") below the acropolis, where the ruins of a vast, circular archaic structure survive, perhaps the circular temple of Zeus and Aphrodite. However the city's center of worship was the shrine of Artemis Orthia in the district of Limnae ("the marshes"), near the Eurotas river. The votive deposits from this shrine, excavated in the early twentieth century, document a cult continuity from the ninth to the fourth century BC, and have produced an enormous number of clay images of the goddess and of ivory and bone carvings, thanks to which Sparta has been identified as the preeminent Greek school of this type of art.

Location
Laconia

Chronology
Ca. 900 BC:
Foundation of the
sanctuary of Artemis
Orthia, a plain outdoor
altar surrounded by
an enclosure.
Early 8th century BC:
A first, small temple is
built of unbaked bricks
laid over a stone socle,
with a central row of
wooden columns.
Ca. 600 BC: The temple
is rebuilt entirely of
stone, with a tile roof
and terracotta
decorations.
6th century BC: The
temple of Athena
Chalkioikos is erected.

Related entries
Lycurgus, Zeus and
Hera, Athena,
Aphrodite and Eros,
Artemis, temples and
sacred buildings.

◀ Marble bust of a
Spartan warrior, from
the Sparta acropolis,
ca. 480 BC. Sparta,
Archaeological
Museum.

Legend

A. Pitana
B. Mesoa
C. Cynosura
D. Limnae
1. Line marking the
Greek walls

2. Roman theater
3. Sanctuary of Athena
Chalkioikos
4. Late-Roman walls
5. Stoa
6. Sanctuary of Artemis Orthia

▲ Map of the excavation of
the ancient city (from "BSA
Annual," XIII, 1906–1907).

The main building of the Spartan acropolis was the temple of Athena Chalkioikos which the British School excavated in the early part of the twentieth century.

Only the perimeter walls and a few other ruins difficult to read remain, however the digs also unearthed some bronze plates that have no reliefs, but could still be part of the bronze lining of the temple that Pausanias had seen in the second century AD.

The identification of the temple was provided primarily by the many ex-votos dedicated to Athena.

▲ View of the excavated acropolis.

The dedication to Athena is inscribed on the helmet crest.

The goddess wears an Attic-type helmet with the cheek protectors raised.

This statuette resembles others found near the temple of Athena Chalkioikos; made locally, it is a miniature reproduction of the Archaic cult statue of the goddess, a work of Gitiadas, that stood inside the cell.

Athena is wearing the traditional Doric peplum that continued to be worn in Sparta even in the Classical age, when it had dropped out of fashion in the rest of Greece.

▶ Bronze statuette from the temple of Athena Chalkioikos, ca. 450 BC. Sparta, Archaeological Museum.

The *few structural remains unearthed in the excavations of the early 1900s in the shrine of Artemis Orthia belong to the Archaic temple dedicated to her, which was restored in the Hellenistic age. Other ruins are the temple altar and the two* leschai, *open porticoes that were often consecrated to a hero, where the Spartans held banquets and symposia.*

Among the votive artifacts found in the shrine are many steles dedicated by the boys who spent there a period of initiation into adulthood by serving the goddess. The initiation ended with the painful scourging rite, which the ephebi *had to undergo to prove their courage.*

The unearthed clay masks and musical instruments were used in ritual dances honoring Artemis, which perhaps mimed the horrors and humiliations that the youths had to bear in order to become worthy citizens.

▲ Ruins of the temple of Artemis Orthia.

"Yet you, oh Phoebus, more than by any other place are pleased in your heart by Delos, / where the Ionians wearing long tunics gather to honor you" (Hymn to Apollo)

Sanctuary of Apollo at Delos

The island of Delos in the center of the Cycladic Archipelago, midway between continental Greece and Ionia, was an important religious and commercial center from time immemorial. At first, the importance of the shrine extended only to the Ionians. The earliest monumental structures, dating to the end of the seventh century BC, were built by the residents of the nearby island of Naxos, who embellished the Sacred Way with the famous marble lions and built the first temple to Apollo, an imposing fabric called the *oikos* of the Naxians, before which stood the colossal statue of the god. In the sixth century BC Athens, desiring to secure hegemony over the Aegean, commissioned a second temple of *poros* stone (*porinos naos*) to replaced the existing one.

Athens began to control the shrine directly starting in 478 BC when the island became the seat of the league of Greek cities organized to fight the Persians; the *porinos naos* was used to store the treasure of the league members and the cult of Apollo was moved to the new temple of the Delians. After the horrid Peloponnesian war, the Athenian shrine administrators decreed that the island undergo purification, removing all the tombs and forbidding anyone from giving birth or dying on the island. This was followed by the erection of a temple (the "Athenian temple") and the inauguration of new, sumptuous festivals. From then on, Athenian sovereignty over the sanctuary continued uninterrupted until Macedonian rule.

▶ Terrace of the Lions.

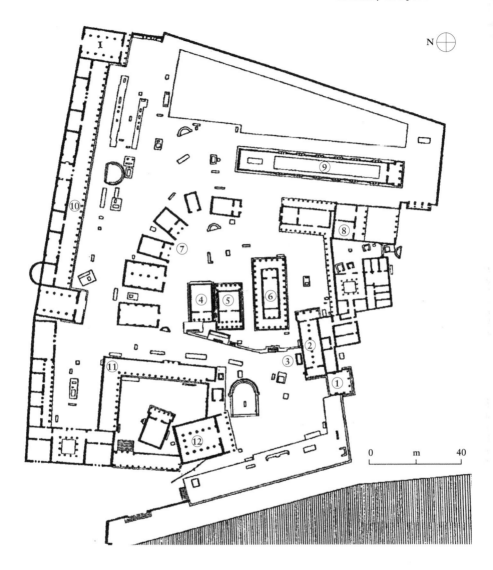

▲ Map of the sanctuary
of Apollo (from Settis
2002, *Atlante*).

Legend of the principal buildings

1. Propylaea
2. *Oikos* of the Naxians
3. Colossus of the Naxians
4. *Porinos naos*
5. Temple to Apollo of
   the Athenians
6. Temple to Apollo of

the Delians
7. Treasuries
8. *Prytaneum*
9. Monument of the bulls
10. Portico of Antigon
11. Stoa of the Naxians
12. Temple of Artemis

In the first version built around the middle of the seventh century BC, the oikos erected by the Naxians was a long, rectangular structure subdivided into three naves by two rows of wooden columns; the entrance was in the center of the long north side.

At the end of the seventh century BC, the structure was rebuilt with granite stone, the entrance was moved to the short west side, and to the cell, preceded by a vestibule with two columns between the antas, was added a single row of Doric columns along its length.

In the early part of the sixth century BC the entrance was moved to the eastern side where a vestibule was added with four columns in front, and the eastern side of the cell was given a marble floor.

▲ *Oikos* of the Naxians.

The colossal statue of Apollo, which represented the god as a kouros with a wide belt and a bronze bow in his left hand, was five times the size of a man and originally stood against the northern side of the oikos *built by the city of Naxos.*

During the pirate raids that scourged the island since antiquity, several attempts were made to remove the colossus by cutting it in half to make transportation easier.

The base of the statue still stands in its original place, with a verse still inscribed on its western side ("I am made of the same marble, both statue and base"), and the dedication of the citizens of Naxos added in 417 BC when the statue was lifted after it had been damaged by a bronze votive palm tree that fell over it.

However, the weight was still excessive for loading it on a ship, therefore the torso and the pelvis were left where they had been carried, in the western corner of the shrine of Artemis.

▲ Torso of the colossus of Apollo offered by the city of Naxos.

This statue, about 35 inches high, originally had outspread wings as if the figure were alighting.

A base was found near the spot where this statue was unearthed, with an inscription to Artemis signed by Mikkiades, Melas, and Archermos.

Because the sources refer to a sculptor from Chios by the name of Archermos, son of Mikkiades, as the inventor of the winged Nike statuary type, scholars have suggested that he might the author of this statue, which he dedicated to the shrine.

According to some scholars, this statue could also have been an acroterium, perhaps part of *the* porinos naos, *the second temple of Apollo, commissioned by Athens after 550* BC.

The identification of this female figure with a Nike, however, is uncertain, because in the Archaic age Artemis also was often represented with wings.

▲ Marble statue, *Flying Nike*, from Delos, ca. 550 BC. Athens, National Archaeological Museum.

The temple of Apollo known as "temple of the Athenians" was a structure still built upon the original plan which, some say, was designed by Callicrates, the architect of the Erechtheum.

The rectangular, very wide cell was separated into two sections by a wall punctuated by three doors.

The temple lacked a pronaos and an opisthodomos; six Doric columns graced the front and the back.

The frontal hall faced west and had four pilasters between the antas.

Coinciding with the erection of this temple, in 425 BC the Delian festival was instituted: celebrated in the summer every five years, it hosted poetic, athletic, and horse-racing competitions.

▲ Basement of the Apollo temple of the Athenians.

References

◀Attic red-figure amphora by the
Cleophrades Painter (detail),
Dionysus and Maenads, from
Vulci, 500–490 BC. Munich,
Antikensammlung.

Map of Ancient Greece

Legend

1. Athens
2. Eleusis
3. Thebes
4. Delphi
5. Corinth
6. Mycenae
7. Epidaurus
8. Sparta
9. Messene
10. Olympia

A. Thrace
B. Macedonia
C. Epirus
D. Thessaly
E. Aetolia – Phocis
F. Euboea
G. Boeotia
H. Attica
I. Achaea
L. Corinthia
M. Argolis
N. Arcadia
O. Elis
P. Messenia
Q. Laconia
R. Delos

Museums

Athens, National Archaeological Museum

Created between 1866 and 1899 to preserve the ancient artifacts found in all the principal archaeological sites of Greece, it is today the most important Greek Art museum in the world. The section devoted to sculpture includes a splendid collection of funerary and votive *kouroi* from Attica, Classical and Hellenistic reliefs, the sculptures from the temples of Hera at Argos, of Asclepius at Epidaurus, and of Athena Alea at Tegea. Among the bronzes are several small votive artifacts from shrines and some large statues such as the *Poseidon* from Cape Artemisium. The minor arts section includes a very rich collection of vases, mostly of the Attic type, especially from the Geometric and Classical ages, and a goldsmithery collection. The museum was recently reorganized in time for the 2004 Olympics, including a renovation of the building and the restoration of about eight thousand finds and one thousand statues.

Athens, Acropolis Museum

Built between 1865 and 1873 and expanded in the nineteen-fifties, the museum houses only the stone sculptures recovered from the Acropolis excavations; the ceramic and bronze pieces were sent from the very beginning to the National Archaeological Museum and the inscriptions to the Epigraphic Museum. In addition to housing the most extensive collection in the world of Archaic and Severe Archaic Greek sculptures recovered from the "Persian landfill," this museum preserves the Parthenon friezes that were not taken out of Greece and sculptures from the Erechtheum and from the temple of Athena Nike. A new, expanded building is under construction, which will also receive in the near future the Parthenon marbles that Lord Elgin had brought to London and which are still at the British Museum. A preview of the new arrangement, including some statues, was on display for the 2004 Athens Olympics.

Athens, Agora Museum

The museum is housed in the Stoa of Attalos originally built by the king of Pergamum in the second century BC and fully reconstructed by the American Archaeological School between 1953 and 1957. It contains the finds from excavations of the Agora and surrounding area, organized by historical period, from the Mycenaean age to Byzantium and later, thus documenting the uninterrupted use of the site. The exceptional nature of the museum is given especially by the finds that illustrate the workings of Athenian democracy in the Classical age, such as the over 1200 *ostraka*, the tablets used to draw by lots the judges who would be in charge of the tribunals, and the urns used as ballot boxes. The display also includes sculptures from the temples of Hephaestus and Ares, about sixty marble portraits, numerous public inscriptions and ceramic finds from the Neolithic age to Turkish rule, found in the wells and cisterns in the area.

Athens, Ceramicus Museum

Located in the Kerameikos archaeological area—the most important necropolis of ancient Athens—the collection was reorganized at the time of the 2004 Athens Olympics. It includes Archaic sculptures, Classical funerary steles, grave furnishings, and a vase collection that is especially important for the history of Attic ceramic art, from the Proto-Geometric to the black-figure style. At present the focus of the collection on display is the most recent exceptional discovery: an Archaic *kouros* found by the Germanic Archaeological Mission in 2003 and attributed to the Dipylon Master.

Olympia, Archaeological Museum

This museum houses the finds from the excavation of the sanctuary of Zeus. It includes a vast collection of Geometric-age and Oriental-style bronze statuettes, a number of mostly votive terracotta pieces ranging from the Neolithic to the Classical periods, and a section devoted to large-size sculpture which includes, in addition to the pediments and the metopes of the temple of Zeus, masterpieces such as the *Hermes with the Child Dionysus* by Praxiteles and the *Paionios Nike*. This museum also was refurbished, including, especially, the educational materials, on the occasion of the 2004 Olympic Games and special attention was given to athletic implements.

Delphi, Archaeological Museum

The first display of this museum was organized in 1903, when it was inaugurated with the intention of collecting the finds from the sanctuary and illustrating its activity over the centuries. In 1974, a new hall displaying the ivory and gold heads buried under the Sacred Way was inaugurated. In preparation for the 2004 Athens Olympics the building was expanded and updated, and the collection reorganized by displaying pieces that had never before been shown to the public. The fourth-century BC sculptures from the temple of Apollo were exhibited for the first time side by side with those from the Archaic temple, and an entire hall was devoted to the *Charioteer*, together with a life-size reconstruction of his *quadriga*.

London, British Museum
The extremely rich Greek Art collection at the British Museum, which runs from Cycladic art to Hellenism, was assembled primarily in the nineteenth century, first through bequests and acquisitions from private collections, and later as a result of excavation missions organized by the Museum. Between 1814 and 1816 the Museum acquired a large number of Classical pieces including the marble frieze from the temple of Apollo in Bassae and the famous "Elgin marbles" purchased by an act of Parliament in 1816 which include, in addition to the Parthenon sculptures (about half of the frieze, fifteen metopes, seventeen pediment sculptures and several architectural fragments), also sculptures from the Erechtheum and from the temple of Athena Nike. In the first part of the nineteenth century, the museum also received a collection of bronzes purchased by R. Payne Knight and many Greek vases that had been part of the Princess of Canino's collection. After the 1850s, the majority of the acquisitions came from English excavations in Greece and Turkey such as those led by Charles Fellows in Lycia, by Evans in Cnossus, and by Hogarth in Ephesus, and the excavations led by the British School of Athens at the shrine of Artemis Orthia in Sparta. After the damages inflicted by the two world wars, the museum was rebuilt and the galleries reorganized in the form they have today.

Paris, Musée du Louvre
The Greek and Roman Antiquities section at the Louvre, organized in 1800, is one of the earliest. The first Roman copies of Greek originals came to the museum by emptying the halls of the Palace of Versailles, and many more were added from Napoleon's plundering of the museums of Western Europe. New, important works were added by purchasing private collections such as, in 1818, the *Ergastinai* from the Parthenon frieze and in 1821 the *Venus of Milo* offered by the Marquis de la Rivière, the French ambassador to Turkey. To this collection of sculptures were added 2600 Greek and Etruscan vases and several bronze items. During the nineteenth century, more art was added as a result of discoveries by French archaeological missions, such as the *Nike of Samothrace*, found by Champoiseau in 1863, some architectural fragments from Olympia donated by the Greek government as a result of Dubois and Blouet's digs, and the terracottas from the Myrina excavations. Some prestigious works such as the *Rampin Head* and the *Lady of Auxerre* were purchased between the end of the nineteenth and the beginning of the twentieth century. The extensive renovation plans begun in 1981 with the Grand Louvre project did not substantially alter the arrangement of the antiquities collections, except for separating more clearly the areas where the original Greek sculptures are displayed, and the displays of the Roman copies.

Berlin, Antikensammlung
Since 1995 the archeological collections of the city of Berlin which had been divided between East and West by the post–World War II events, have been reunited in two prestigious buildings. The first, the Altes Museum, houses displays arranged by themes of sculptures, terracottas, bronzes, vases, and goldsmithery found in royal palaces, to which new twentieth-century acquisitions were added, such as some finds resulting from archaeological missions at Olympia, Dodona, Pergamum, Samos, Miletus, Priene, and Didyma, and a number of terracottas from Athens, Tanagra, and Corinth. The Pergamum Museum, whose nucleus is an altar frieze brought to light by Humann from 1878 to 1886, also houses some important sculptures dating from the Archaic to the Hellenistic period, as well as Roman copies of celebrated Greek originals.

Vienna, Kunsthistorisches Museum
The kernel of the Museum's archaeological collection, inaugurated in 1891, are the sculptures and inscriptions that had been scattered in the imperial Hapsburgs palaces, to which were added the purchases of many new isolated objects and of ancient private collections. The Austrian archaeological expeditions in the latter part of the nineteenth century to Samothrace and Ephesus unearthed new sculptures and architectural fragments, especially from the Hellenistic age, while the acquisition in 1940 of the archaeological collections previously held by the Austrian Museum completed their collection of ancient vases.

Munich, Glyptothek
The Munich Museum was built between 1816 and 1830 to house the antiquities collections assembled by Ludwig of Bavaria during his travels at the turn of the century and, in particular, the seventeen statues from pediments, excavated at the temple of Aphaia on Aegina, purchased in 1812 and restored by the sculptor Thorwaldsen. Though the museum was destroyed in 1943,

most of the sculptures it held, including masterpieces such as the *Munich Kouros* and the *Apollo of Tenea*, and the funerary stele of Mnesarete, were not damaged and were again put on display after the museum was rebuilt.

Munich, Antikensammlung
After the serious damage wrought by World War II, the museum was rebuilt and inaugurated in 1967. The collection of Attic vases dating from the sixth to the fourth century BC is notable, including many that bear the artist's signature such as some of the most important works by painters such as Exekias, Euphronius, Cleophrades, Euthymides, and Andocides.

Copenhagen, Ny Carlsberg Glypotek
This sculpture museum houses the leading collection of ancient art in Northern Europe. It was assembled by the beer magnate Charles Jacobsen who in 1882 put on display his private collection intending it to be a typical example of ancient sculpture. The original collection, built by purchasing the Rayet collection in Paris that includes the famous small head from the Athens Acropolis, was gradually enriched with new additions of marble originals dating from the seventh to the second century BC, some important Roman copies, and a collection of painted vases.

Naples, Museo Archeologico Nazionale
The vast Greek Art collections of the Naples National Archaeological Museum include, in addition to vase art, celebrated Roman copies found in the Neapolitan area or that belonged to the Farnese collection or came from monuments and exca-

vations in Rome, plus some original bronzes from the Pompeii and Herculaneum digs.

Vatican City, Musei Capitolini
The museum collects some Romanage copies of Greek original sculptures that are fundamental for the study of Greek art, such as the *Sosandra* by Calamides, the *Amazons* by Cresilas and Polyclitus, the *Diadoumenos* by Polyclitus, the *Pothos* by Scopas, the *Kassel Apollo* and many others.

Rome, Museo Nazionale Romano (Palazzo Altemps and Palazzo Massimo)
Among the ancient statuary masterpieces collected by the Roman nobility through the centuries are some original Greek statues and many Roman copies of exceptional importance.

New York, Metropolitan Museum of Art
Since it opened in 1870, the Museum has included Classical Art in its collection, except for ancient coins that were considered the province of the Numismatic Society. The first great collection of Greek vases was acquired in 1890 and since the turn of the century this division had been constantly expanding, especially thanks to purchases on the antiquarian market. In the field of Greek sculpture, the Museum houses some important Attic originals, especially Archaic and Classical funerary monuments and many Roman copies such as the *Diadoumenos* and the *Lansdowne Amazon*. The rich bronze collection extends from the Geometric age to Hellenism and is supplemented by a large collection of terracottas of all the major Greek workshops from all periods.

Ca. 1200 BC: Invasion by populations from the North and destruction of Mycenaean settlements.

1050–900 BC: Proto-Geometric ceramics.

11th–9th century BC: Greek migration to Anatolia.

9th–8th century BC: Decline of the monarchic regimes and rise of aristocracy. Birth of the city-state.

900–700 BC: Geometric ceramics.

8th–6th century BC: Second Greek colonization of the Black Sea, southern Italy and Sicily, southern France and Spain.

700–600 BC: Proto-Attic orientalizing ceramics.

776 BC: First Pan-Hellenic Games in Olympia.

754 BC: Initial date of the Spartan List of Ephors.

8th–7th century BC: Beginning of Sparta's expansionism and conquest of Messenia.

End 8th–end 7th century BC: Proto-Attic ceramics.

657 BC: Cypselus becomes tyrant of Corinth.

650 BC: Megara, Sicyon and other cities fall under tyrannical rule.

630 BC: Cylon tries to become tyrant of Athens.

600–525 BC: Black-figure ceramics.

594–593 BC: Solon's archonship and legislative reform.

580 BC: End of tyranny in Corinth and establishment of a moderate government.

561 BC: First attempt by Pisistratus to become tyrant of Athens.

Ca. 550 BC: Sparta forms a military league in the Peloponnesus under its hegemony.

546–528 BC: Pisistratus becomes tyrant of Athens.

530–425 BC: Red-figure ceramics.

528–510 BC: Hippias succeeds Pisistratus.

Ca. 525 BC: Draco legislates in Athens.

514 BC: Hipparcus, Hippias's brother, is murdered by Harmodius and Aristogiton.

510 BC: Under the Alcmaeonid leadership and supported by Sparta, the Athenian nobility in exile expels Hippias.

508–507 BC: Cleisthenes' archonship and constitutional reform.

499–498 BC: The Greek cities of Asia Minor rebel against Persian rule. Athenians and Eretrians come to their aid and set fire to Sardis.

493–492 BC: Themistocles' archonship.

490 BC: Persian expedition into Greece. The Persians land in Euboea and destroy Eretria; then land in Attica but are repelled into the sea at the battle of Marathon by the Athenians led by Miltiades.

486 BC: Xerxes becomes king of Persia.

480 BC: Second Persian expedition into Greece. Athens and Sparta ally against the enemy. The Spartans are defeated at Thermopylae and the Persians sack Athens and set it on fire, however Themistocles' fleet defeats them at Salamis.

479 BC: The Persians are finally defeated at Plataea and Cape Mycale and withdraw.

478–477 BC: The Delian-Attic league is established with seat in Delos, uniting under Athens's hegemony the Greek cities of the Asiatic coast and the Aegean.

471 BC: Themistocles is ostracized and power is transferred to Cimon son of Miltiades, who continues to fight the Persians.

469 BC: Cimon defeats the Persians in the battle of Eurymedon.

469–468 BC: Athens suppresses the uprisings of Naxos and Thasos against its supremacy in the Delian-Attic league.

464 BC: Earthquake in Sparta. The Helots rebel; the citadel of Ithome is under siege.

462 BC: Ephialtes' constitutional reform in Athens.

461 BC: Cimon is ostracized and Ephialtes is murdered in Athens. Power goes to Pericles.

449 BC: Peace of Callias between Athens and Persia.

446 BC: Athens and Sparta sign a thirty-year peace.

431 BC: Sparta can no longer bear Athens's supremacy; the Peloponnesian war begins.

430–429 BC: The Spartans invade Attica destroying the territory; the population seeks shelter inside fortified Athens and its ports. A terrible epidemic ensues, to which Pericles also succumbs.

429–421 BC: The war continues with alternating fortunes. In Athens the parties of Nicias, who wants to end the conflict, and Cleon, who is determined to continue, are opposed. When Cleon and the Spartan commander Brasidas are killed in the battle of Amphipolis, in both cities the parties of peace prevail.

421 BC: Peace of Nicias and fifty-year defensive alliance between Athens and Sparta.

415 BC: Under Alcibiades' command, the Athenian fleet leaves for an expedition to Sicily to counteract Syracuse's growing power and extend Greek domination to the West.

414 BC: The expedition to Sicily causes a resumption of the Athenian-Spartan conflict.

413 BC: The Athenians are soundly defeated in Sicily, while the Spartans occupy Decelea, north of Athens.

412 BC: Almost all the cities allied with Athens rebel. Sparta reaches an agreement with Persia.

411 BC: Oligarchic coup d'état in Athens: the Four Hundred, under

Theramenes' leadership, take over and are partial to Sparta. The Samos fleet remains faithful to democracy.

411–410 BC: Athens defeats Sparta in the naval battles of Cynossema, Abydos, and Cyzicus.

410 BC: Democracy is restored to Athens.

408 BC: Alcibiades returns to Athens and is appointed *strategos*.

407 BC: The Spartans under Lysander defeat the Athenians in the naval battle of Notion. Alcibiades retires to Thrace.

406 BC: Athenian naval victory at the Arginusae islands. Athens rejects peace proposals.

405 BC: Sparta destroys the Athenian fleet at Aegospotami and lays siege to Athens.

404 BC: Athens surrenders. The city's walls are destroyed and the oligarchic regime of the Thirty Tyrants, arranged by Sparta, begins.

403 BC: The Thirty Tyrants regime is overturned by Thrasybulus.

399 BC: Trial and death of Socrates.

396 BC: Expedition by the Spartan king Agesilaus to aid the Greek Ionian cities.

395–386 BC: War of Corinth. Athens, Thebes, Argos, and Corinth ally themselves with Persia against Sparta.

386 BC: "Peace of the King" or "of Antalcidas." The principle of the Greek city-states' autonomy is established, but also Persia's domination of the cities of Asia Minor.

379 BC: Pelopidas and Epaminondas free Thebes from Spartan occupation, restore democracy, and establish a Boeotian league.

378–377 BC: Athens rebuilds the Attic maritime league, guaranteeing full autonomy to the member city-states.

374 BC: Athens and Sparta sign a

Glossary

peace treaty.

373 BC: Thebes destroys Plataea, a city allied with Athens.

371 BC: Thebes defeats Sparta at Leuctra.

371–362 BC: Hegemony of Thebes that repeatedly invades Messenia.

362 BC: Battle of Mantinea and death of Epaminondas. General peace in Greece with the exception of Sparta.

359 BC: Philip II ascends the throne in Macedonia.

357–355 BC: Social war (some allies of the second maritime league battle against Athens).

356–346 BC: Third Holy War: conflict between the Phocians, supported by Sparta and Athens, and the Boeotians who are allied with the Thessalians, for control of the sanctuary of Delphi and hegemony over central Greece. Philip II takes advantage of the situation to intervene in Greek affairs, supporting Thessaly and ensuring his control over Thessaly and Boeotia.

348 BC: Philip destroys Olinthus and annexes the cities of Chalcidice to Macedonia.

346 BC: "Peace of Philocrates" between Philip and Athens. Philip defeats the Phocians and becomes a member of the Delphic Amphictyony.

344 BC: Philip annexes Thessaly.

342 BC: Philip conquers Thrace

338–337 BC: Demosthenes drives Athens and the other democratic cities to war against Philip. The battle of Chaeronea gives the victory to Philip. Creation of a Pan-Hellenic league to fight Persia.

336 BC: Shortly after the war against Persia breaks out, Philip is murdered and his son Alexander succeeds him.

Acroterium: a geometric or figured ornamental element in stone or terracotta, positioned on the apex and at the corners of a pediment.

Adyton: the innermost, most inaccessible part of a temple.

Agora: a marketplace or public square in a Greek city.

Alabastron: a small, elongated, and tapered jar chiefly used for perfume and unguents.

Andron: a formal area in a Greek house reserved for men and symposia.

Aryballos: a small, spherical jar with a narrow neck, used chiefly for fragrant ointments.

Boule: a government council.

Bouleuterion: a building used for council (*boule*) meetings.

Cell: the enclosed chamber in a temple where the cult statue was housed.

Coroplastic: a terracotta sculpture.

Krater: a wide-mouthed jar of many shapes, for mixing water and wine at a banquet.

Crepidoma: platform (usually three-leveled) on which a temple rises.

Chryselephantine: overlaid with gold and ivory.

Dinos: a large round vase with a wide mouth, usually set on a stand; also used as a krater.

Ekklesia: assembly of citizens.

Epinetron: a semi-circular pottery knee-piece used in wool weaving.

Heroon: a building for hero worship or to worship a person heroicized after death.

Hydria: a water jug with three handles, a vertical one used when pouring, and two horizontal ones for lifting it.

Kalathos: basket or basket-shaped vase.

Kalpis: two-handled rounded vase with a narrow neck, used as container for liquids, ash urn, or ballot urn.

Kantharos: a deep drinking cup with two high vertical handles used at banquets.

Kline: a wood, metal, or masonry couch used for sleeping or for reclining at a banquet.

Koilon: a section of a theater with tiers of seats for spectators (Latin: *cavea*).

Kore: a maiden.

Kotyle: deep two-handled cup.

Kouros: a young man.

Kyathos: a vase with a very high vertical handle used to draw wine from kraters and mix it in the drinkers' cups.

Kylix: a wide, low, two-handled cup used for drinking at banquets.

Lebete: a two-handled, rounded vase on a tall platform with a long neck, use for various purposes: the *gamikos* and the *loutrophoros* were used to carry water for the nuptial bath.

Lekythos: a single-handled, elongated vase with a narrow neck used to store fragrant oils and ointments. The larger-sized ones had a funerary use.

Leonte: the Nemean lion's skin that Heracles wore.

Lesche: a public building, often with a portico, used as meeting place.

Louterion: a ceramic, marble, or stone basin, usually on a support, used for bathing.

Loutrophoros: a two-handled vase on a tall platform with a long neck used to carry water for the nuptial bath.

Metope: a rectangular or square slab set between two triglyphs in the Doric order.

Naos: sometimes used as a synonym for temple, it usually refers to the temple cell.

Oikos: home.

Oinochoe: a single-handle jug with sometimes a thee-lobed spout, used at banquets to pour wine drawn from the kraters.

Opisthodomos: the area behind a temple cell, symmetrical with the pronaos.

Orchestra: the section in a theater between the seats and the stage, where the chorus stood.

Ostrakon: a pottery shard with a scratched inscription.

Parodoi: side entrances to the theater; they separated the stage from the seating area.

Pelike: a two-handled, widemouthed, rounded vase used as a bucket and as a container for liquids.

Peripter: a temple colonnaded on four sides.

Peristasis: a colonnade around a temple.

Pinax: a painted or relief-decorated wood or ceramic tablet.

Pyx: a box with cover in terracotta or other materials, used to store jewels and other, mostly feminine, objects.

Pithos: a large vase for food storage.

Polis: city.

Pronaos: the section just before the temple cell.

Propylaeum: a monumental access to a sanctuary.

Prytaneum: a building where the city's sacred hearth was kept and where the *prytaneis*—the magistrates who held power for the tenth part of a year—resided while in office.

Psykter: vase used to cool the wine at banquets: it was placed inside kraters filled with ice or cold water.

Skyphos: two-handled glass or jug.

Stamnos: wide-mouthed, rounded vase with a short neck and two horizontal handles used as a wine jar.

Stylobate: a temple basement on which the columns rest.

Stoa: a portico.

Thalamos: a nuptial bedroom, the central room in the women's quarters in a Greek house.

Thesauros: a small, temple-shaped building found in sanctuaries, where each city kept the votive gifts for the deity. A treasury.

Tholos: a round building.

Triglyph: a fluted architectural element; in the Doric order it frequently alternates with metopes.

Index

Bibliography

The bibliography on Ancient Greece is so vast that even drawing up a summary of it is a challenge. In the following list, we tried to suggest some classic works, some recent publications, and some fundamental works of a general nature where one can find vast bibliographies on specific subjects.

General works with extensive bibliographies
Bianchi Bandinelli R. (ed.), *Storia e civiltà dei greci*, Milan 1979.
Settis S. (ed.), *I greci. Storia, cultura, arte e società*, Turin 1996–2002.

Cities
Ampolo C., *La città antica. Guida storica e critica*, Rome-Bari 1980.
Brulé P., *La cité grècque à l'époque classique*, Rennes 1995.
Greco E. (ed.), *La città greca antica. Istituzioni, società e forme urbane*, Rome 1999.
Greco E., Torelli M., *Storia dell'urbanistica. Il mondo greco*, Rome-Bari 1983.
Hoepfner W., Schwandner E.L., *Haus und Stadt im klassischen Griechenland*, Munich 1994.
Hoepfner W., Zimmer G., *Die griechische Polis. Architektur und Politik*, Tübingen 1993.
Martin R., *Recherches sur l'agora grècque*, Paris 1951.
Martin R., *L'Urbanisme dans la Grèce Antique*, Paris 1956.
McDonald W., *The Political Meeting Places of the Greeks*, Baltimore 1943.
Morachiello P., *La città greca*, Rome-Bari 2003.
Murray O., *La città greca*, Turin 1993.
Pesando F., *La casa dei greci*, Milan 1989.
Polignac de F., *La nascita della città greca. Culti, spazio e società tra l'VIII e il VII secolo a.C.*, Milan 1991.

Snodgrass A.M., *Archaeology and the Rise of the Greek State*, Cambridge 1977.

Specialized economic, social and religious subjects

Alcock S.E., Osborne R. (eds.), *Placing the Gods. Sanctuaries and Sacred Space in Ancient Greece*, New York 1994.

Austin M., Vidal Naquet P., *Economie e società nella Grecia antica*, Turin 1982.

Bottini A., *Archeologia della salvezza. L'escatologia greca nelle testimonianze archeologiche*, Milan 1992.

Bottini A., *Il rito segreto. Misteri in Grecia e a Roma*, Milan 2005.

Burkert W., *Antichi culti misterici*, Rome-Bari 1989.

Ciancio Rossetto P., Pisani Sartorio (eds.), *Teatri greci e romani. Alle origini del linguaggio rappresentato. Censimento analitico*, Rome 1994.

Detienne M., *I giardini di Adone*, Turin 1975.

Detienne M., *La cucina del sacrificio in terra greca*, Turin 1982.

Durand J.L., *Sacrifice et labour en Grèce ancienne*, Paris-Rome 1986.

Finley M., *Economia e società nel mondo antico*, Rome-Bari 1984.

Fischer N.R.E., *Slavery in Ancient Greece*, London 1993.

Garlan Y., *Les esclaves en Grèce ancienne*, Paris 1982.

Garlan Y., *Guerra e società nel mondo antico*, Bologna 1985.

Gnoli G., Vernant J.P. (eds.), *La mort, les morts dans les sociétés anciennes*, Cambridge 1982.

Gschnitzer F., *Storia sociale dell'antica Grecia*, Bologna 1988.

Harris H.A., *Sport in Greece and Rome*, London 1972.

Kerenyi K., *Gli dei e gli eroi della Grecia*, Milan 2001.

Kurtz D.C., Boardman J., *Greek Burial Customs*, London 1971.

Lissarague F., *L'immaginario del simposio greco*, Rome-Bari 1989.

Marrou H.I. *Storia dell'educazione nell'antichità*, Rome 1966.

Meier C.H.R, Veine P., *L'identità del cittadino e la democrazia in Grecia*, Bologna 1989.

Morris I., *Burial and Ancient Society: The Rise of the Greek City State*, Cambridge 1988.

Mossè C.L, *Le istituzioni politiche della Grecia nell'età classica*, Florence 1961.

Mossè C.L, *La vita quotidiana delle donne nella Grecia antica*, Milan 1988.

Mossè C.L, *Le citoyen dans la Grèce antique*, Paris 1993.

Musti D., *L'economia in Grecia*, Rome-Bari 1981.

Schachter A., *Le sanctuaire grec*, Geneva 1992.

Schmitt Pantel P. (ed.), *Storia delle donne in Occidente. L'antichità*, Rome-Bari 1994.

Schmitt Pantel P., *La cité au banquet. Histoire des repas publics dans les cités grècques*, Rome 1997.

Sfameni Gasparro G., *Misteri e teologie. Per la storia dei culti mistici e misterici nel mondo antico*, Cosenza 2003.

Vernant J.P., *Mito e società nell'antica Grecia*, Turin 1981.

Vernant J.P., *L'uomo greco*, Rome-Bari 1999.

Vidal Naquet P., *Il cacciatore nero*, Rome 1988.

Yalouris N., Christopoulos G.A. (eds.), *The Olympian Games in Ancient Greece*, Athens 2003.

Art history

Arias P.E., *Mille anni di ceramica greca*, Florence 1960.

Arias P.E., *L'arte della Grecia*, Turin 1967.

Becatti G., *L'arte dell'età classica*, Florence 1971.

Boardman J., *Greek Sculpture: The Archaic Period*, London 1978.

Boardman J., *Vasi ateniesi a figure nere*, Milan 1990.

Boardman J., *Vasi ateniesi a figure rosse*, Milan 1992.

Boardman J., *Storia dei vasi greci*, Rome 2004.

Boardman J., Finn D., *The Parthenon and Its Sculptures*, London 1985.

Charbonneaux J., Martin R., Villard F., *La Grecia arcaica, La Grecia classica, La Grecia ellenistica*, Milan 1969-1972.

Fuchs W., *Storia della scultura greca*, Milan 1982.

Giuliano A., *Arte greca*, Milan 1986–1987.

Giuliano A., *Storia dell'arte greca*, Rome 1989.

Gramiccia A. (ed.), *I colori del bianco. Policromia nella scultura antica*, Rome-Vatican City 2004.

Griffiths Pedley J., *Arte e archeologia greca*, Rome 2005.

Gruben B., *I templi greci*, Milan 1989.

La Rocca E., *L'esperimento della perfezione. Arte e società nell'Atene di Pericle*, Rome 1988.

Lippolis E., *Gli eroi di Olimpia. Lo sport nella società greca e magnogreca*, Taranto 1992.

Martin R., *Architettura greca*, Milan 1980.

Martini W., *Die archaische Plastik der Griechen*, Darmstadt 1990.

Moreno P., *I bronzi di Riace, il maestro di Olimpia e i Sette a Tebe*, Milan 1998.

Richter G., *L'arte greca*, Turin 1969.

Rolley C., *Les bronzes grecs*, Fribourg 1983.

Scheibler I., *Il vaso in Grecia. Produzione, commercio e uso degli antichi vasi in terracotta*, Milan 2004.

Snodgrass A.M., *Armi ed armature dei Greci*, Rome 1991.

Photo Credits

AKG-Images, Berlin, pp. 29, 31, 51, 52, 130; 79, 256, 291 (Peter Connolly); 24 (Werner Forman); 351 (Rainer Hackenberg); 23, 61, 66 left, 197, 318, 330, 334, 356, 361, 365 (John Hios); 74 (Nimatallah); 57 (Pirozzi)
Antikenmuseum der Universität, Leipzig, p. 80 left
Antikensammlung, Munich, pp. 18, 20, 127, 192, 223, 228
Archaeological Receipts Fund, TAP Service, Athens, pp. 32, 68, 73, 76, 99, 122, 133, 152, 180, 183, 242, 243, 325
Archeological World, Misgav, pp. 160, 244, 247, 250, 294, 337
Archivio Alinari, Florence, pp. 2, 326-327
Archivio Mondadori Electa, Milan, pp. 40; / Giuseppe Schiavinotto, 46; Mondadori Electa by permission of the Ministero per i beni e le attività culturali, 25, 26, 43, 62, 78, 104, 106, 126, 128, 143, 149, 196, 260
Archivio PUBBLI AER FOTO, Varese, p. 354
Athenian Agora Excavations, pp. 21, 22, 45, 64, 66 right, 72, 111, 163, 164, 184, 234, 235, 263, 286, 288, 290, 292, 293, 298, 300, 303, 304, 306, 307, 333
Badisches Landesmuseum, Karlsruhe, pp. 142, 224
© Bianchetti / Leemage, p. 93
Bridgeman Art Library, London, pp. 13, 81, 92, 108, 112, 116, 124, 144, 202, 207, 220, 353
Collezione Banca Intesa, Vicenza, p. 226
Comune di Roma, Soprintendenza ai Beni Culturali, pp. 38, 42, 51, 299
Corbis / Contrasto, pp. 47, 100, 154, 316, 339, 342, 359
© Eric and David Hosking / Corbis, p. 94
The Hermitage, Saint Petersburg, p. 168

Foto Musei Vaticani, pp. 44, 170
Heritage Image Partnership, pp. 17, 36, 69, 70, 71, 146, 177 top, 179, 208, 215, 343, 345
Index, Florence, pp. 53, 76 left, 77 right, 95, 186, 285, 311, 329, 363 (Alberti); 172, 173, 174, 200 (Cantarelli); 181 (Pedrocchi); 229, 368 (Pizzi); 32 (WFA)
Kunsthistorisches Museum, Vienna, p. 124
Le Chateau-Musée, Boulogne, p. 16
© Erich Lessing / Contrasto, pp. 10, 56, 58, 89, 90, 91, 113, 114, 117, 135, 137, 138, 139, 140, 156, 161, 165, 178, 201, 204-205, 254, 266-267, 271, 308, 310, 315, 332, 338, 366, 369
Marie Mauzy, Athens, pp. 11, 55, 75, 141, 253, 280, 282, 319, 320-321, 364
Metropolitan Museum, New York, pp. 19, 96, 131, 187, 190, 218, 231, 248, 261
© Mozzati, pp. 63, 279, 287, 346, 348
Musées Royaux, Brussels, p. 262
Museo della Fondazione culturale Mandralisca, Cefalù, p. 162
Museo del Satiro danzante, Mazara del Vallo, p. 54
Museo Regionale della ceramica, Caltagirone, p. 225
Luciano Pedicini, Archivio dell'arte, Naples, pp. 8, 12, 14, 39, 48
© Photo RMN-© Droits Réservés, p. 198; © Hervé Lewandowski, pp. 60, 80 right, 110, 182, 194, 203, 217, 239; © Les Frères Chuzeville, pp. 82-83, 167, 259
Rijksmuseum van Oudheden, Leiden, p. 301
© Scalagroup, Florence, pp. 34-35, 41, 49,88,98, 101, 102, 103, 105, 109, 121, 123, 136, 145, 150-151, 169, 171, 175, 176, 188, 189, 195, 206, 209, 212, 222, 227, 236, 274, 275, 281, 289, 297
Staatliche Museen, Berlin, pp. 134, 213, 219, 241

The Art Archive / Dagli Orti, pp 230, 249, 265, 269, 270, 272, 273 277, 278, 296, 305, 317, 323, 324 340-341, 357; / Agora Museur Athens / Dagli Orti, 65, 67, 177 232, 233; / Acropolis Museur Athens / Dagli Orti, 85, 86, 147; Archaeological Museum Corfu Dagli Orti, 268; / Archaeologica Museum Delphi / Dagli Orti, 155 314; / Archaeological Museum Ep idauros / Dagli Orti, 352; / Archae ological Museum Piraeus / Dagl Orti, 118-119; / Archaeologica Museum Salonica / Dagli Orti, 7 left; / Archaeological Museum Thebes / Dagli Orti, 166; / Ceram icus Museum, Athens / Dagli Orti 252; / Musée du Louvre, Paris Dagli Orti, 185, 199; / Musec Nazionale Palazzo Altemps, Rom / Dagli Orti, 115; / National Ar chaeological Museum Athens Dagli Orti, 30, 120, 132, 159, 191 214, 238, 245, 246, 264, 276, 349 370; / National Glyptothek Mu nich / Dagli Orti, 344
The British Museum, London, pp 28, 37, 84, 97, 210-211, 216, 221 302, 360
The J. Paul Getty Museum, Lo Angeles, pp. 258, 284

Maps are from "BSA Annual." XI II, 1906–1907; S. Lloyd, H.W Muller, R. Martin, *Architettur mediterranea preromana*, Mila 1972; J. McCamp II, *The Athenia Agora: A Short Guide*, Athen 2003; *Olimpiadi. Viaggio in Greci* monograph, "Archeo," No. 2 May 2004; S. Settis (ed.), *I Grec Storia, Cultura, Arte, Società*, vo IV, *Atlante*, ed. by C. Franzon Turin 2002; M. Torelli, Th Mavrojannis, *Grecia*, Milan 1997

The Publisher has made all reason able efforts to identify the owner of photographic rights and is a their disposal to fulfill all rightfu obligations.